Managing the
Global Commons

Managing the Global Commons

The Economics of Climate Change

William D. Nordhaus

The MIT Press
Cambridge, Massachusetts
London, England

This book was set in Palatino by The Maple-Vail Book Manufacturing Group and was printed and bound in the United States of America.

Library of Congress Cataloging-in-Publication Data

Nordhaus, William D.
  Managing the global commons : the economics of climate change /
  William D. Nordhaus.
      p.   cm.
  Includes bibliographical references and index.
  ISBN 0-262-14055-1
  1. Climatic changes—Economic aspects. 2. Climatic changes—
Mathematical models. 3. Global warming—Economic aspects.
4. Global warming—Mathematical models. I. Title.
QC981.8.C5N66   1994
363.73′87—dc20   94-3992
                                                                    CIP

To Barbara

Contents

Preface

Greenhouse warming poses terrible dilemmas for those who care about both people and the world we inhabit. We do not now know how human activities will affect the thin and incredibly complex life-support system that nurtures our civilization, nor can we reliably judge how potential geophysical changes will affect societies or the world around us. Should we be ultraconservative and tilt toward preserving the natural world at the expense of economic growth and development? Or should we put human betterment before the preservation of natural systems and trust that our ingenuity will find a solution should Nature deal us a nasty hand?

This study attempts to answer these questions in the context of economic analysis—an approach that weighs costs and benefits and constantly seeks the middle ground between excessive zeal and indifference, looking for the balance point between the costs of further investments in conservation or prevention and the benefits in damages avoided. This pilgrimage in cost-benefit balancing is necessarily complex and technical because it requires understanding a number of enormously complicated geophysical, biological, and economic relationships that affect or are affected by global warming.

The present study is the result of almost two decades of research, most of which has been supported directly by the National Science Foundation and indirectly by Yale University and the Cowles Foundation for Research at Yale, and for the last year by the U.S. Environmental Protection Agency. It has benefited from the invisible but substantial contributions of a cadre of colleagues in this field who have contributed to the development of a field of the economics of global environmental issues. Early co-workers in the economics of the greenhouse effect who imparted their wisdom included Jesse Ausubel,

William Clark, William Cline, Howard Gruenspecht, Dale Jorgenson, Geoffrey Heal, William Hogan, Charles Kolstad, Lester Lave, Alan Manne, Robert Mendelsohn, Richard Morgenstern, David Pearce, Howard Raiffa, John Reilly, Richard Richels, Thomas Schelling, John Weyant, the late David Wood, and Gary Yohe. The author is grateful for helpful suggestions from colleagues at Yale, including William Brainard, Richard Levin, and Herbert Scarf, as well as to comments on earlier versions of this work by Edward Barbier, Gantam Barua, Richard Cooper, Peter Diamond, Herbert Giersch, Daniel M. Kammen, Leo Schrattenholzer, and a number of anonymous referees. Scientists in other disciplines have tutored me on innumerable occasions, and I am particularly indebted to Thomas Lee, Thomas Malone, William Nierenberg, John Perry, the late Roger Revelle, Michael Schlesinger, Stephen Schneider, Karl Turekian, Paul Waggoner, and Robert White. Finally, I am enormously grateful to Zili Yang for his dedicated and skillful research assistance. All errors that have survived the interchanges with these colleagues are my sole responsibility.

I   Modeling the Economics of Climate Change

1   Introduction

"God does not play dice with the universe" was Albert Einstein's reaction to quantum mechanics. Yet mankind *is* playing dice with its natural environment through a multitude of interventions—injecting trace atmospheric gases like the greenhouse gases or ozone-depleting chemicals, engineering massive land-use changes such as deforestation, depleting species in their natural habitats even as we create transgenic ones in the laboratory, and accumulating stockpiles of nuclear weapons sufficient to destroy human civilization. As natural or social scientists, we need to understand the sources of these global changes, the potential damage they cause to natural and economic systems, and the most efficient ways of alleviating or removing the dangers. Just as villages in times past decided on the management of their grazing or water resources, so must we today and in the future learn to employ wisely and to protect our common geophysical and biological resources. This task of understanding and controlling interventions on a global scale can be called *managing the global commons.*

The particular issue analyzed in this book is the threat of greenhouse warming, which has received growing attention in recent years. Climatologists and other scientists have warned that the accumulation of carbon dioxide (CO_2) and other greenhouse gases (GHGs) is likely to lead to global warming and other significant climatic changes over the next century. Many scientific bodies, along with a growing chorus of environmental groups and national governments, are calling for severe curbs on the emissions of greenhouse gases, as seen for example in the reports of the Intergovernmental Panel on Climate Change (hereafter, IPCC 1990). The culmination of international efforts to forge new approaches was the Earth Summit in Rio in June 1992, which agreed upon a framework treaty on climate and established a number of working groups to monitor compliance and propose future steps.

Many scientists have expressed deep concern about the threat of global warming and have proposed steps ranging from GHG emissions stabilization to deep cuts in GHG emissions to stabilizing the climate. To date, the calls to arms and treaty negotiations have progressed more or less independently of economic studies of the costs and benefits of measures to slow greenhouse warming. Over the last few years, however, economists have engaged in a major effort to understand both the economic impacts of climate change and the costs of slowing climate change through reduced emissions. The evidence has pointed to the likelihood that greenhouse warming will have at most modest economic impacts in industrial countries over the next century, while programs to impose deep cuts in GHG emissions will exact substantial costs. These studies have led some to conclude that the best course today would be a modest reduction in GHG emissions—perhaps by using a carbon tax.

In earlier studies, I developed a simple cost-benefit framework for determining the optimal "steady-state" control of CO_2 and other greenhouse gases.[1] This earlier study came to a middle-of-the-road conclusion that the threat of greenhouse warming was sufficient to justify modest steps to slow the pace of climate change, but I found that calls for draconian cuts in GHG emissions by 50 percent or more were not warranted by the current scientific and economic evidence on costs and impacts.

The earlier studies had a number of shortcomings, but one of the most significant from an analytical point of view was the inadequate treatment of the dynamics of the economy and the climate. The earlier work examined a "resource steady state," one in which all physical flows are constant (e.g., in which population, emissions, concentrations, and climate change have all stabilized in their steady state) although there might be improvements in real incomes because of resource-saving technological change. It then went on to examine the optimal control strategy in the resource steady state.

A complete analysis of the economics of climate change must recognize the extraordinarily long time lags involved in the reaction of the climate and economy to greenhouse gas emissions. Current scientific estimates indicate that the major GHGs have an atmospheric residence time of over 100 years; moreover, because of the thermal inertia of the oceans, the climate appears to lag perhaps a half century behind the

---

1. The steady-state model appears in abbreviated form in Nordhaus 1991b and in greater detail in Nordhaus 1991c. Also see Nordhaus 1992a, b, 1993.

changes in GHG concentrations; and there are long lags in the introduction of capital stocks and new technologies in human economies in response to changing economic conditions. Dynamics are therefore of the essence, and a study that overlooks the dynamics will produce misleading conclusions for the steps that we should take at the dawn of the age of greenhouse warming.

In order to improve our understanding of the interaction of economy and climate and to design better approaches to economic policy, I have developed a model that links together in a simplified way the major economic and scientific elements involved in designing economic policies to slow global warming. It is called the Dynamic Integrated model of Climate and the Economy (the DICE model). The model itself is relatively small by the standards of both economics and the related natural sciences, but many of the components will be unfamiliar to those outside the disciplines from which the individual ingredients are derived. This new model is an advance over earlier studies because it allows for policies in the transition path that are different from those in the ultimate steady state. It does this through adopting the standard approach of modern optimal economic growth theory and adding to this both a climate sector and a closed-loop interaction between the climate and the economy. It is an integrated model that incorporates both the dynamics of emissions and impacts and the economic costs of policies to curb emissions. The model is sufficiently small as to be transparent (or at least translucent), to allow a range of sensitivity analyses, and to be available for a number of further extensions.

The basic approach of the DICE model is to use a Ramsey model of optimal economic growth with certain adjustments and to calculate the optimal path for both capital accumulation and GHG-emission reductions. The resulting trajectory can be interpreted as either the most efficient path for slowing climate change given initial endowments or the competitive equilibrium among market economies where the externalities are internalized using the appropriate social shadow prices for GHGs.[2]

This book presents the detailed development as well as an extensive analysis of the DICE model and its results. Chapter 2 contains the development of the background equations of the DICE model, as well as

---

2. The "correspondence principle" between optimized systems and competitive economies was first described in Samuelson 1949 and has been analyzed in Gordon et al. 1988 for exhaustible resources.

an explanation of how they are drawn from the relevant discipline and a discussion of their empirical support. Chapters 3 and 4 focus on the uncharted terrain linking the behavior of the economy with the geophysical features of climate change. These chapters derive simplified equations that link emissions, concentrations, climate change, and economic behavior.

Chapter 5 presents the results of the basic DICE model, analyzing the implications of the "best-guess" assumptions about the structure of the DICE model. Chapters 6, 7, and 8 tackle the issue of the uncertainty about climate change. These chapters begin with a sensitivity analysis determining the robustness of the results to alternative assumptions about the major parameters; we also present an analysis of the inherent uncertainty about future economic outcomes and climate change. Finally, the uncertainty chapters investigate the impact of uncertainty on the optimal policy and find that uncertainties imply a more stringent set of GHG controls than is implied by the best-guess case. These chapters allow us to consider how uncertainties about climate change should affect the stringency and timing of our policies.

The need to address the potential issues raised by future climate change is one of the most challenging economic problems of today, and it is daunting for those who take policy analysis seriously. It raises formidable issues of data, modeling, uncertainty, international coordination, and institutional design. In addition, the economic stakes are enormous, involving investments on the order of hundreds of billions of dollars a year to slow or prevent climate change.

The studies presented here suggest that a massive effort to slow climate change today would be premature given current understanding of the damages imposed by greenhouse warming. At the same time, spurred by scientists to remember that the global circulation systems are incredibly complex and poorly understood, we must be ever alert to the possibility that the vast geophysical experiment being undertaken by humanity may trigger catastrophic and irreversible changes in droughts, monsoons, ocean circulation, river flows, and other climate-related systems. Economics does not rule out these outcomes. If scientific evidence indicates that calamitous consequences are likely to accompany global warming, then our economic models will not only signal that a strenuous effort to slow or prevent future climate change is necessary but help devise the scope and timing of policy responses. Our future lies not in the stars, but in our models.

2

The Structure and Derivation of the DICE Model

A Verbal Overview

When considering policies concerning climate change, societies must weigh the costs of taking steps to slow climate change against the potential damages if climate change proceeds unchecked. The DICE model of the economics of climate change developed here balances the costs of emissions controls in energy policies and other areas against the impacts to agriculture, coastlines, and ecosystem values. The issues become particularly difficult because of the long time lags between emissions and impacts and therefore between preventive policies and alleviated damages. Nations must decide whether they will take steps now (in effect, invest in emissions reductions) in order to slow climate change over the coming centuries. Few societal decisions, and no personal ones except those involving Pascal's wager or the afterlife, have comparable time horizons.

A useful way to view decisions involving such long time horizons is with the apparatus of optimal growth theory. This approach was developed by Frank Ramsey in the 1920s (see Ramsey 1928), made rigorous by Tjalling Koopmans and others in the 1960s (see especially Koopmans 1967), and is summarized by Robert Solow in his masterful exposition of economic-growth theory (1970). In the neoclassical growth model, society invests in tangible capital goods, thereby abstaining from consumption today, in order to increase consumption in the future.

The DICE model is the extension of the Ramsey model to environmental policy, with emissions reductions in the extended model playing the role of investment in the mainstream model. Society must take steps today, reducing consumption by devoting resources to reducing GHG emissions, in order to prevent economically harmful climate change and thereby increasing consumption possibilities in the future.

We begin this chapter with a verbal description of the approach taken in the DICE model. The model is an optimal-growth model of the world economy. It is designed to maximize the discounted value of "utility" or satisfaction from consumption subject to a number of economic and geophysical constraints. The decision variables that are available to the economy are consumption, the rate of investment in tangible capital, and the rate of emissions reductions of GHGs. The time path of decisions is designed to maximize the discounted value of utility. The model operates in time steps of 10 years.

The model contains both a traditional economic sector and a novel climate sector. First, begin with the traditional sector of the economy—the economy without any considerations of climate change. The global economy is assumed to produce a composite commodity. It is not necessary that countries actually be identical. Rather, the goods produced must be perfect substitutes and the production functions must be identical except for multiplicative differences in productivity. In plain language, this means that countries can differ in their quantitative attributes, but that there cannot be large differences in the composition of goods or relative productivities. While this is a restrictive assumption, preliminary work with a more complete multicountry model suggests that this assumption has little effect upon the major conclusions.

Our composite economy is endowed with an initial stock of capital and labor and an initial level of technology. All industries behave competitively. Each country maximizes an intertemporal objective function, identical in each region, which is the sum of discounted utilities of per capita consumption times population; the utility function is logarithmic in per capita consumption. Output is produced by a Cobb-Douglas production function in capital, labor, and technology. Population growth and technological change are exogenous, while capital accumulation is determined by optimizing the flow of consumption over time. There is no need for international trade since the outputs of the different countries are perfect substitutes.

The "nontraditional" part of the model contains a number of geophysical relationships that link together the different forces affecting climate change. This part includes an emissions equation, a concentrations equation, a climate-change equation, and a climate-damage relationship. Emissions include all GHG emissions, although they are most easily viewed as CO_2. Uncontrolled emissions are a slowly declining fraction of gross output—a relationship that is consistent with a complex set of assumptions about the underlying production and demand functions. GHG emissions can be controlled by increasing the prices of factors or outputs that are GHG intensive, and we represent the GHG-reduction cost schedule parametrically by drawing upon a number of studies of the cost of GHG reductions.

Atmospheric concentrations of GHGs increase with emissions, with concentrations reduced over an atmospheric residence time of 120 years. Climate change is represented by global mean surface temperature, and the relationship uses the consensus of climate modelers and a lag suggested by recent coupled ocean-atmospheric models. The economic impacts of climate change are assumed to be increasing in the realized temperature increase.

Note that the model can be interpreted either in an optimizing framework or as the outcome of idealized competitive markets. To employ the competitive-markets interpretation, we would need to take the leap of faith that the public goods nature of climate change is somehow overcome in an efficient manner. That is, it assumes that, through some mechanism, countries efficiently internalize in their decision making the *global* costs of their emissions decisions. There is little evidence of such global generosity, but the current approach has the virtue of calculating the equilibrium that would emerge were each country to behave in such a farsighted, efficient, and altruistic fashion.

Derivation of the Equations of the DICE Model

We turn next to a specific list of the equations of the DICE model along with a discussion of their derivation. The relationships are divided into three groups: the objective function, the economic relationships, and the geophysical relationships. For the most part, the economic sectors are conventional in their approach, and the discussion of their derivation is contained in this chapter. The climate sector and the interaction of economy and climate, however, required significant attention as no existing models were appropriate for inclusion in a dynamic macroeconomic model of the kind used here. Therefore, the climate module, the carbon cycle, the cost of emissions reduction, the damages from climate change, and the trend in energy-GHG ratios are presented in greater detail in the next two chapters.

Objective Function

A key question involves the objectives that we seek in the optimization. We assume that the purpose of our policies is to improve the living standards or consumption of humans now and in the future. By consumption we mean a broad concept that includes not only traditional market purchases of goods and services like food and shelter but also nonmarket items such as leisure, cultural amenities, and enjoyment of the environment.

The fundamental assumption we adopt is that policies should be designed to maximize the generalized level of consumption now and in the future. This approach rests on the view that more consumption (again, of the generalized kind just described) is preferred over less, and in addition that increments of consumption become less valuable as consumption levels increase. In technical terms, these assumptions are embodied by maximizing a social welfare function that is the discounted sum of the utility of per capita consumption. This social welfare function is a mathematical representation of three basic value judgments: (1) that higher levels of consumption have higher worth; (2) that there is diminishing marginal valuation of consumption as consumption increases; and (3) that society will undertake investments so as to increase consumption in periods where the marginal utility of consumption is highest. In addition, the approach includes time preference (discussed in detail in this chapter and in chapter 6) that allows for differing the relative emphasis on different generations. The exact objective function, or criterion to be maximized, is

$$\max_{\{c(t)\}} \sum_t U[c(t), L(t)](1+\rho)^{-t}, \tag{2.1}$$

which is the discounted sum of the utilities of consumption, $U[c(t), L(t)]$, summed over the relevant time horizon. Here U is the flow of utility or social well-being, $c(t)$ is the flow of consumption per capita at time t, $L(t)$ is the level of population at time t, and ρ is the pure rate of social time preference. The exact form of the utility function will be described below. The model operates in time steps of 10 years, so all flow variables in the empirical model are flows per decade, while the convention is that stocks are measured at the beginning of the period.

The only parameter in this equation is the pure rate of social time preference, ρ. This parameter is a social choice variable that is implicit in many societal decisions, such as fiscal and monetary policies. In conjunction with other variables, it is closely connected with the market rate of interest (or marginal productivity of capital) and with the savings rate.

A value of ρ of .03 percent per year (or higher) is consistent with historical savings data and interest rates. By contrast, a value for ρ of .01 per year, or even 0, has sometimes been advocated for policies to slow climate change, but these imply both too high a savings rate and too low a rate of return on capital. This preference function, combined with the production function below, leads to savings rates and rates of return on investment that are in the neighborhood of the observed levels in industrial countries.[1]

Economic Constraints

The maximization is subject to a number of constraints. We begin this section with a review of the economic constraints, while presenting the climate-emissions relationships in the next section.

The first equation is the definition of utility, which was described and motivated in the last section. Utility represents the current value of well-being and is assumed equal to the size of population, $L(t)$, times the utility of per capita consumption, $u[c(t)]$. Equation (2.2) is the general case of a power function to represent the form of the utility function

$$U[c(t), L(t)] = L(t)\{[c(t)]^{1-\alpha} - 1\}/(1 - \alpha). \tag{2.2}$$

In this equation, the parameter α is a measure of the social valuation of different levels of consumption, which has several labels. It represents the curvature of the utility function, the elasticity of the marginal utility of consumption or the rate of inequality aversion. Operationally, it measures the extent to which society is willing to reduce the welfare of high-income generations to improve the welfare of low-income generations. In the DICE model, we take (the limit of) $\alpha = 1$, which

1. Cline (1991, 1992a, b) advocates a pure rate of time preference of 0 and a discount rate on goods and services of 1.5 percent per annum. While this approach is philosophically satisfying, it is inconsistent with actual societal decisions on saving and investment. A further discussion of this issue, along with alternative approaches, is contained in chapter 6. Also see Yang 1993.

yields the following logarithmic or Bernoullian utility function:[2]

$$U[c(t), L(t)] = L(t)\{\log[c(t)]\}. \tag{2.2'}$$

Population data are derived from a number of sources. The basic projection method is as follows: Population growth in the initial period is assumed to be equal to the historical rate over the period 1965–87. We then assume that the growth rate declines over time at a geometrically declining rate and then stabilizes. More precisely, let $g_L(t)$ be the growth rate of population in period t and δ_L be the rate of decline in the growth of population. We then have the growth of population in period t as

$$g_L(t) = g_L(t-1) \ (1-\delta_L);$$

$$\delta_L = .195 \text{ per decade};$$

$$g_L(1965) = 2.03 \text{ percent per annum}; \quad L(1965) = 3.369 \text{ billion}. \tag{2.2''}$$

It is easily verified that this assumption leads to a gradual leveling off of population. Its advantage is that the population trajectory can be represented by two parameters and can be easily fit to different projections. For the base case, the initial growth of population in the decade 1960–69 is 2.03 percent per year and the decadal decline in the growth rate is $\delta_L = .195$. This assumption leads to an asymptotic maximum population of 10.6 billion people.

Output $Q(t)$ is given by a standard, constant-returns-to-scale Cobb-Douglas production function in technology, capital and labor, denoted by $A(t)$, $K(t)$, and $L(t)$, respectively. Labor inputs are proportional to population.

$$Q(t) = \Omega(t)A(t)K(t)^\gamma L(t)^{1-\gamma}, \tag{2.3}$$

where γ is the elasticity of output with respect to capital and is taken equal to 0.25. The term $\Omega(t)$ relates to the impact of emissions reductions and climate change on output and will be described in equation (2.13).

The historical output and capital data are gathered from a number of sources for the years 1960, 1965, 1970, 1975, 1980, 1985, and 1990. The basic technique is to collect national data for the major countries or regions and to aggregate them using purchasing-power parity weights. We use the standard Solow identification procedure that

---

2. This formulation subtracts one from power function in the denominator of (2.2) so that the limit of the expression is $L(t)[\log(c(t)]$.

Table 2.1
Projected rate of growth of output per worker (average annual growth rate, percent per annum)

	1975–2000	2000–2025	2025 and Beyond
Mean	2.3	1.6	1.0
Standard deviation	0.7	0.5	0.3
Extreme values	1.2; 3.4	0.9; 2.3	0.5; 1.5

Source: Nordhaus and Yohe 1983.
Note: These represent the average, standard deviation, and extreme values of projected increases from a number of published studies.

allows us to calculate $1 - \gamma$ as the share of labor in national income, which is approximately 0.75 in industrial countries; few reliable data are available for low-income countries.

The variable Ω is assumed to be one during the historical period, and projections for future periods are discussed below. The only unobservable variable is $A(t)$, which can be derived from (2.3) by solving for $A(t)$ as a function of all the other observable variables.

A major uncertainty in the model involves projecting the growth of $A(t)$, or total factor productivity, into the future. For the initial decade, 1965–75, we estimate the average annual growth of global total factor productivity to be 1.41 percent per annum, where this is the average for global output, capital, and population. It is interesting that historical studies find little slowdown in the average growth of global output over the last century or so. By contrast, most modelers project a significant slowdown in the growth of per capita incomes in the future. For example, table 2.1 shows the result of a survey by Nordhaus and Yohe (1983) of long-term projections of per capita income growth.

This study follows the contours of earlier studies in assuming that productivity growth will slow in the coming decades. It uses a modification of earlier approaches similar to that introduced above for population growth in assuming that the productivity-growth slowdown is continuous rather than a step change. More precisely, let $g_A(t)$ be the growth rate of total factor productivity in period t and δ_A be the decline rate in the growth of productivity. Productivity growth in period t is then

$$g_A(t) = g_A(t-1)(1 - \delta_A);$$

$$g_A(1965) = 1.41 \text{ percent per annum;}$$

$$\delta_A = .11 \text{ per decade.} \tag{2.3'}$$

Again, this assumes a leveling off of productivity. As with the representation of population, its advantage is that the productivity growth curve can be represented by two parameters. For the base case, the estimate of the growth of total factor productivity for the period 1961–70 is 1.41 percent per annum. Based on Nordhaus and Yohe (1983) and other studies, we then assume that productivity growth declines by half every six decades, which is consistent with the projections shown above. This gives an estimate of the parameter $\delta_A = .11$.

The next equation shows the disposition of output between consumption, $C(t)$, and gross investment, $I(t)$:

$$Q(t) = C(t) + I(t). \tag{2.4}$$

This represents the accounting identity in a one-sector economy that output can be devoted to either investment in new capital goods or consumption. Data on consumption and investment are from the same sources as described for equation (2.3).

The next equation is the definition of per capita consumption:

$$c(t) = C(t)/L(t). \tag{2.5}$$

Finally, we have the following capital balance equation for the capital stock:

$$K(t) = (1 - \delta_K)K(t-1) + I(t-1), \tag{2.6}$$

where δ_K is the rate of depreciation of the capital stock. In this equation, the depreciation rate of capital is taken to be 0.10 percent per annum, which reflects an average lifetime of capital of 10 years on a declining balance method.

Climate-Emissions-Damage Equations

The next set of constraints is more of a challenge because there are no well-established relationships or empirical studies that can be drawn upon to represent the linkage between economic activity and climate change. These equations comprise the relationships among economic activity, emissions, concentrations, and climate change. As with the economic relationships, it is necessary to keep these equations simple so that the theoretical model is transparent and the optimization model is empirically tractable. The methodology is drawn from macroeconomics, in which economic behavior is represented by equations that capture the behavior of broad aggregates (such as consumers or investors); the challenge in this area is that aggregate relationships are needed for optimization approaches such as the DICE model.

The first equation links GHG emissions to economic activity. In the analysis that follows, we translate each of the GHGs into its CO_2 equivalent. To aggregate the different GHGs, we use a measure of the total warming potential, which is the contribution of a GHG to global warming summed over the indefinite future. Approximately 80 percent of the total warming potential of the major GHGs is due to CO_2, and we therefore devote most of our attention to that gas. The DICE model assumes that CO_2 and the chlorofluorocarbons (CFCs) are controlled (these being the GHGs in the discussion that follows), while the other, less important GHGs are taken to be exogenous in the DICE model.[3]

In modeling GHG emissions, we assume that the ratio of GHG emissions to gross output declines slowly. The uncontrolled ratio of GHG emissions to output is represented by the parameter $\sigma(t)$.

GHG emissions can be reduced through a wide range of policies. We represent the rate of emissions reduction by an "emissions control rate," $\mu(t)$. The control rate μ represents the fractional reduction of emissions relative to uncontrolled emissions. This variable is a central one in the present study; indeed, one of the key questions investigated here is the optimal trajectory of emissions control. The emissions equation is given as

$$E(t) = [1 - \mu(t)]\sigma(t)Q(t) \qquad \sigma(1965) = .519. \tag{2.7}$$

The variable $\mu(t)$ is determined by the optimization. The major empirical issue in equation (2.7) involves the parameter $\sigma(t)$, which is the trend in CO_2-equivalent emissions per unit of gross output in the absence of controls. Consider the rate of growth of σ, which we denote $g_\sigma(t)$; Jesse Ausubel calls this the "rate of decarbonization."[4] Relying

---

3. Aggregation of GHGs poses a frightening series of complexities. To begin with, differing lifetimes mean that the instantaneous radiative impact must be converted into something that is more appropriate for economic decisions; hence, the use of total warming potentials. The aggregation by the IPCC is flawed in that it uses undiscounted integration but truncates after a certain time (say, a century). The more appropriate treatment would be to weight the instantaneous radiative potential by the shadow price of the warming for each period (for a discussion, see Schmalensee 1993). Further complexities arise because some of the associated gases may offset the warming (as in the case of CFCs). Moreover, recent experiments indicate that the climatic impact of the different GHGs may differ markedly (see Wang et al. 1991). The present author believes that given the dominance of CO_2 for future warming, the approach used here will be a reasonably good approximation to a more complete analysis.

4. See Ausubel 1993.

on historical information, we estimate that g_σ has been between -1 and -1.5 percent annually due to both energy efficiency improvements and a transition away from coal.

For the future, we assume that the historial trend continues but that the rate of decarbonization slows pari passu with the declining rate of overall productivity growth. In other words, the rate of carbon-saving technological change is assumed to be proportional to the growth of total factor productivity in equation (2.3'). Hence, we assume that σ initially declines at 1.25 percent annually but that the decline of σ slows at .11 percent per decade. This of course implies that σ eventually levels out at some constant ratio. Hence

$$\sigma(t) = [1 + g_\sigma(t)] \ \sigma(t-1);$$

$$g_\sigma(t) = g_\sigma(t-1)(1-\delta_A);$$

$$g_\sigma(1965) = -1.25 \text{ percent per annum;}$$

$$\delta_A = .11 \text{ per decade.} \tag{2.7'}$$

The next relationship in the economy-climate nexus represents the accumulation of GHGs in the atmosphere. Let $E(t)$ be the emissions of GHGs (in CO_2–equivalent terms). The accumulation and transportation of emissions is assumed to follow this equation:

$$M(t) - 590 = \beta E(t-1) + (1 - \delta_M) \ [M(t-1) - 590],$$

where $\beta = .64$, $\delta_M = .0833$ per decade, and $M(1965)$

$$= 677 \text{ billion tons of carbon equivalent.} \tag{2.8}$$

The equation indicates that the deviation of atmospheric carbon from its equilibrium preindustrial level of 590 GtC will be increased by emissions but is reduced as carbon diffuses into the deep ocean. β is the marginal atmospheric retention ratio and δ_M is the rate of transfer from the rapidly mixing reservoirs to the deep ocean; the deep ocean is assumed to be an infinite sink for carbon. This equation assumes that the fraction β of an emission stays in the atmosphere in the short run. In addition, the GHGs in the short-lived reservoir are transported to a very large reservoir, the deep oceans, at a rate of .0833 per decade. The derivation of this equation is presented in the next chapter. Note that this equation has been derived for CO_2 and is assumed to apply as well to the other GHGs.

The next step concerns the relationship between the accumulation of GHGs and climate change. Climate modelers have developed a wide variety of approaches for estimating the impact of rising GHGs on climatic variables. On the whole, existing models are much too complex to be included in economic models, particularly ones that are used for optimization. Instead, we employ a small structural model that captures the basic relationship between GHG concentrations, radiative forcings, and the dynamics of climate change. In what follows, the climate system is represented by a multilayer system; more precisely, there are three layers—the atmosphere, the mixed or upper layer of the oceans, and the deep oceans. Each of the layers is assumed to be internally well mixed.

Accumulations of GHGs lead to global warming through increasing the warming at the surface by increased radiation. The relationship between GHG accumulations and increased radiative forcing, $F(t)$, is derived from empirical measurements and climate models. We characterize the relationship in terms of the forcings as a function of the CO_2-equivalent of GHG accumulations as follows:

$$F(t) = 4.1\{\log[M(t)/590]/\log(2)\} + O(t), \tag{2.9}$$

where $M(t)$ is the atmospheric concentration of CO_2 (or its equivalent) in billions of tons of carbon and $F(t)$ is the increase of surface warming in watts per square meter (W/m^2), which is the standard measure of radiative forcing. $O(t)$ represents other GHGs (principally CH_4 and N_2O). These other gases represent a small fraction of the total warming potential, their sources are poorly understood, and techniques for preventing their buildup are sketchy today; they are therefore taken as exogenous, with the projections discussed in the next chapter.

The parameterization in (2.9) is not controversial. It relies upon a variety of data on atmospheric concentrations and combines those into a series on radiative forcing using conversions supplied by T. Wigley and used in the IPCC report (1990). The finding is that a doubling of CO_2 equivalent concentrations would lead to an increase in surface warming by 4.1 W/m^2.

The next equation provides the link between radiative forcing and climate change. Higher radiative forcings warm the atmospheric layer, which then warms the upper ocean, gradually warming the deep oceans. The lags in the system are primarily due to the thermal inertia of the different layers. We can write the model as follows:

$$T(t) = T(t-1) + (1/R_1)\ \{F(t) - \lambda T(t-1) - (R_2/\tau_{12})[T(t-1) - T^*(t-1)]\},$$

$$T^*(t) = T^*(t-1) + (1/R_2)\ \{(R_2/\tau_{12})[T(t-1) - T^*(t-1)]\}, \tag{2.10}$$

where $T(t)$ is the increase in the globally and seasonally average temperature in the atmosphere and the upper level of the ocean, $T^*(t)$ is the increase of temperature in the deep oceans, $F(t)$ is the increase in radiative forcing in the atmosphere, and R_1 is the thermal capacity of the upper stratum while R_2 is the thermal capacity of the deep oceans. $\tau_{1\,2}$ is the transfer rate from the upper layer to the lower layer, and λ is a feedback parameter.

Equation (2.10) can be understood in terms of a simple example of the impact of a warming source on a pool of water. Suppose that a heating lamp is turned on (this being the increase in $F(t)$ or radiative forcings). The top part of the pool along with the air at the top are gradually warmed, and the lower part of the pool is also warmed as the heat is diffused to the bottom. The lags in the warming of the surface in this simple example are determined by the size of the pool (that is, by its thermal inertia) and by the rate of mixing of the different levels of the pool. This set of equations will be further analyzed in the next chapter. The parameters that are derived there are shown along with other parameters in table 2.4.

The next link in the chain is the economic impact of climate change on human and natural systems. Estimating the damages from greenhouse warming has proven extremely elusive. For the purpose of this study, it is assumed that there is a relationship between the damage from greenhouse warming and the extent of warming. More specifically, the relationship between global temperature increase and income loss is given by

$$D(t)/Q(t) = \theta_1 T(t)^{\theta_2} = .013\ [T(t)/3]^2 = .00144\ T(t)^2, \tag{2.11}$$

where $D(t)$ is the loss of global output, θ_1 is a parameter representing the scale of damage, and θ_2 is an exponent that represents the nonlinearity in the damage function. The empirical estimate of the parameters of the impact equation will be given in chapter 4. The finding there is that the effect a 3°C rise in average temperature is projected to be a 1.33 percent decline in world output.

The last major link in the chain is the cost of reducing emissions of GHGs. This is the one area that has been extensively studied, and, while not without controversy, the general shape and extent of the cost function have been sketched on a number of occasions. The final form of the equation used in the model is

$$TC(t)/Q(t) = b_1 \, \mu(t)^{b_2} = .0686 \, \mu(t)^{2.887}, \tag{2.12}$$

where $\mu(t)$ is the fractional reduction in GHG emissions and $TC(t)$ is the total cost of the reduction. The coefficients b_1 and b_2 represent the scale and the nonlinearity of the cost function. The empirical estimates of the emissions-reduction cost function will be discussed in chapter 4.

Combining the cost and damage relationships, we have the Ω relationship in the production function as follows:

$$\Omega(t) = (1 - b_1 \, \mu(t)^{b_2})/[1 + \theta_1 T(t)^{\theta_2}]$$

$$= (1 - .0686 \, \mu(t)^{2.887})/[1 + .00144 \, T(t)^2]. \tag{2.13}$$

Equations (2.1) through (2.13) form the mathematical model that is optimized and whose results are described in subsequent chapters. Table 2.2 lists the equations of the DICE model in a single place. The major variables are summarized in table 2.3. The detailed list of parameters is shown in table 2.4. This concludes our overview of the derivation of the equations of the DICE model; the next two chapters tackle the more controversial equations in detail.

Table 2.2
Equations of the DICE model

(2.1) $\max\limits_{\{c(t)\}} \sum\limits_{t} U[c(t), L(t)](1+\rho)^{-t}$

(2.2) $U[c(t), L(t)] = L(t)\{[c(t)]^{1-\alpha} - 1\}/(1-\alpha)$

(2.3) $Q(t) = \Omega(t)A(t)K(t)^{\gamma}L(t)^{1-\gamma}$

(2.4) $Q(t) = C(t) + I(t)$

(2.5) $c(t) = C(t)/L(t)$

(2.6) $K(t) = (1 - \delta_K)K(t-1) + I(t-1)$

(2.7) $E(t) = [1 - \mu(t)]\sigma(t)Q(t)$

(2.8) $M(t) - 590 = \beta E(t-1) + (1 - \delta_M) [M(t-1) - 590]$

(2.9) $F(t) = 4.1\{\log[M(t)/590]/\log(2)\} + O(t)$

(2.10) $T(t) = T(t-1) + (1/R_1) \{F(t) - \lambda T(t-1)$
$\quad - (R_2/\tau_{12})[T(t-1) - T^*(t-1)]\}$
$\quad T^*(t) = T^*(t-1) + (1/R_2) \{(R_2/\tau_{12})[T(t-1) - T^*(t-1)]\}$

(2.11) $D(t) = Q(t)\theta_1 T(t)^{\theta_2}$

(2.12) $TC(t) = Q(t) \, b_1 \, \mu(t)^{b_2}$

(2.13) $\Omega(t) = (1 - b_1 \, \mu(t)^{b_2})/[1 + \theta_1 T(t)^{\theta_2}]$

Table 2.3
Major variables in the DICE model

Exogenous Variables

$A(t)$ = level of technology

$L(t)$ = labor inputs

$L(t)$ = population at time t, also equal to labor inputs

$O(t)$ = forcings of exogenous greenhouse gases

t = time

Parameters

α = elasticity of marginal utility of consumption

b_1, b_2 = parameters of emissions-reduction cost function

β = marginal atmospheric retention ratio of GHGs

γ = elasticity of output with respect to capital

δ_K = rate of depreciation of the capital stock

δ_L = decline rate of population

δ_M = rate of transfer of GHGs from upper to lower reservoir

λ = feedback parameter in climate model

ρ = pure rate of social time preference

R_1 = thermal capacity of the upper layer

R_2 = thermal capacity of deep oceans

$\sigma(t)$ = GHG emissions/output ratio

τ_{12} = transfer rate from upper to lower reservoir

θ_1, θ_2 = parameters of damage function

Endogenous Variables

$C(t)$ = total consumption

$c(t)$ = per capita consumption

$D(t)$ = damage from greenhouse warming

$E(t)$ = emissions of greenhouse gases (CO_2 and CFCs only)

$F(t)$ = radiative forcing from GHGs

$\Omega(t)$ = output scaling factor due to emissions controls and to damages from climate change

$K(t)$ = capital stock

$M(t)$ = mass of greenhouse gases in atmosphere

$Q(t)$ = gross world product

$T(t)$ = atmospheric temperature relative to base period

$T^*(t)$ = deep-ocean temperature relative to base period

$TC(t)$ = total cost of reducing GHG emissions

$u(t)$ = u[c(t)] = utility of per capita consumption

Policy Variables

$I(t)$ = gross investment

$\mu(t)$ = rate of emissions reduction

Table 2.4
Initial values of parameters in the DICE model

$\alpha =$	1	(elasticity of marginal utility with respect to consumption)
$b_1 =$	0.0686	(fraction of output per unit emissions control)
$b_2 =$	2.887	(exponent of control cost)
$\beta =$	0.64	(pure number)
$\gamma =$	0.25	(elasticity of output with respect to capital)
$\delta_A =$	0.011	(per year)
	0.110	(per decade)
$\delta_K =$	0.10	(per year)
	0.65	(per decade)
$\delta_M =$	0.0833	(per decade)
$\delta_L =$	0.020	(per year)
	0.195	(per decade)
$g_L(1965) =$	0.0203	(per year)
	0.224	(per decade)
$g_A(1965) =$	0.0141	(per year)
	0.150	(per decade)
$g_\sigma(1965) =$	-0.0125	(per year)
	-0.1168	(per decade)
$K(1965) =$	16.0	(trillion U.S. dollars, 1989 prices)
$\lambda =$	1.41	(degrees $C/W-m^2$)
$M(1960) =$	677	(billion tons CO_2 equivalent, carbon weight)
$L(1965) =$	3.369	(billion persons)
$\rho =$	0.03	(per year)
$1/R_1 =$	0.226	(degrees $C-m^2$/watt-decades)
$R_2/\tau_{12} =$	0.44	(watts/degrees $C-m^2$)
$Q(1965) =$	8.519	(trillion U.S. dollars, 1989 prices)
$\sigma(1965) =$	0.519	(billion tons CO_2 equivalent per trillion dollars, 1989 prices)
$T(1960) =$	0.2	(degrees C)
$T^*(1960) =$	0.1	(degrees C)
$\theta_1 =$	0.00144	(fraction of output per degrees C squared)
$\theta_2 =$	2	(exponent of damage function)

3 Macrogeophysics: Derivation of the Climate and Carbon-Cycle Equations

Macroeconomists generally rely upon highly simplified representations of economic relationships (such as the much-loved Cobb-Douglas production function), and this approach has proven fruitful in understanding phenomena ranging from business cycles to economic growth. In developing the geophysical aspects of the DICE model, no such macrorelationships could be found: none of the geophysical equations relating to emissions, concentrations, climate change, the costs of emissions reductions, or the impacts of climate change existed in a form that was suitable for optimization models.

It is in the spirit of the methodology of macroeconomics that this and the next chapter propose highly simplified aggregate relationships to include in the DICE model. The use of highly simplified aggregate relationships is motivated on three grounds. First, an understanding of the interaction of economy and climate is advanced if the underlying structure is as simple and transparent as possible; complex systems cannot be easily understood and strange behavior may well arise because of the interaction of complex relationships. Second, because most of the relationships in the DICE model are poorly understood, we will devote considerable attention in later chapters to sensitivity analysis and an analysis of the cost of our ignorance. The larger the model, the more difficult it is to undertake comprehensive sensitivity and uncertainty analyses. Finally, from a computational point of view, the DICE model is already straining at the computational capacity of readily available software packages that can be used on personal computers, and we have set as a goal the construction of a model that can be easily used by other researchers. In modeling, small is genuinely beautiful.

To include more sectors of the economy, more layers of the ocean, more greenhouse gases, more energy resources, more than one region—any of these would reduce transparency, impair the ability to conduct sensitivity analyses, and place the model outside the envelope of current computational feasibility. Apologies are extended to those who feel that their discipline has been violated; along with the apologies goes an invitation to help improve our understanding by providing better parsimonious representations of the crucial geophysical or economic processes.

In the spirit of interdisciplinary macroscience, then, the current chapter analyzes two important physical relationships—the relationship between emissions and concentrations and a climate minimodel. Each of these is a necessary component of the DICE model.

The Carbon Cycle

This section lays out a simple model of the carbon cycle for use in the optimal growth model developed in this study. The first section lays out the model, while the second section provides the statistical estimation and parameter estimates.

The Model

In the most general approach, we assume that GHG accumulation and transportation can be represented as a linear (or more precisely, linearized) box model in which each of the boxes is well mixed. In what follows, we will use the parameters of the carbon cycle to estimate the model because, once CFCs have been phased out, CO_2 is the main area where policies are likely to be concentrated. It should also be noted that because of uncertainty about the *first-order* fluxes, there are major questions about the accuracy of the flows in the model. The essence is as follows. Let

$m_i(t)$ = $M_i(t) - M_i^*$ = deviation of total carbon mass in stratum or box i at time t, $M_i(t)$, from equilibrium preindustrial levels, M_i^*

$\mathbf{m}(t)$ = a column vector of the $m_i(t)$

α_{ij} = the annual transport from box i to box j

$\mathbf{A}$ = $n \times n$ matrix of α's, with the ith element of row j being α_{ij}

$\mathbf{E}(t)$ = column vector of carbon emissions

Notice that the notation in this section uses $\mathbf{m}(t)$ as the deviation of atmospheric concentrations from the preindustrial equilibrium. Elsewhere in this study we examine total stocks, $\mathbf{M}(t)$. We use the notation introduced above to represent more compactly the dynamics and the statistical estimation.

The boxes are 1 = atmosphere, 2 = deep oceans, 3 = mixed layer of the ocean, 4 = long-term biosphere, 5 = short-term biosphere.[1] Note that in the balance of this study, when we use the notation M for the mass of carbon, we are referring to M_1 as the atmospheric carbon. In what follows, we assume that all emissions are into the atmosphere (box 1) and use the notation that $E(t) = E_1(t)$. Hence

$$\mathbf{E}'(t) = [E(t)\ 0\ 0\ \ldots\ 0] = [E_1(t)\ 0\ 0\ \ldots\ 0],$$

where $\mathbf{E}'$ = transpose of $\mathbf{E}$. We can then write our system as

$$\mathbf{m}(t) = \mathbf{A}\mathbf{m}(t-1) + \mathbf{E}(t-1). \tag{3.1}$$

In this treatment, we assume that the short-lived biosphere, the mixed level of the ocean (say, 50 to 100 meters), and the atmosphere are well mixed. (A more complete treatment will change the results only slightly.) The uptake of the short-term and long-term biosphere is omitted from this calculation, and it is assumed that there are no flows between the atmosphere and the deep oceans.

Finally, we assume that the atmosphere contains the fraction β of the mass of carbon in the well-mixed reservoirs (boxes 1 and 3). It is then easily seen that β is the *marginal atmospheric retention ratio*, which is the fraction of an additional unit of emissions that is retained and observed in the atmosphere in the first period. This should be distinguished from the usual definition of the atmospheric retention ratio, the observed ratio of total change in atmospheric M to total emissions (which is the *average atmospheric retention ratio*).

Recall that $m_1 = \beta(m_1 + m_3)$, which gives us

$$m_1(t) = \beta E(t-1) + \alpha^* m_1(t-1) + \beta\alpha_{23} m_2(t-1), \tag{3.2}$$

$$m_2(t) = [(1 - \alpha^*/\beta)] m_1(t-1) + (1 - \alpha_{23}) m_2(t-1), \tag{3.3}$$

where α^* is the transfer coefficient from the combined strata of boxes 1 and 3 and reflects the constraint that $m_1 = \beta(m_1 + m_3)$. Equations (3.2) and (3.3) are the basic equations that we will estimate below.

---

1. This model is a simplification of an analytical approach developed by Machta (1972) and employed in chapter 8 of Nordhaus 1979.

Statistical Estimation

For the purposes of the optimal growth model in the study, it is desirable to find a simple representation of the carbon cycle. This is accomplished by applying the model in (3.2) and (3.3) to observed data on the carbon cycle. Atmospheric concentrations include only CO_2 and are calculated as deviations from a preindustrial baseline, which is taken to be 590 billion metric tons of atmospheric carbon. We treat the deep oceans as an infinite sink, which is probably reasonable for a period of a century or so. However, in conjunction with the assumption of linearity, this approach will underestimate atmospheric concentrations over the longer run. These assumptions imply that $\alpha_{23} = 0$, so we can rewrite (3.2) as

$$m_1(t) = \alpha^* \, m_1(t-1) + \beta E(t-1). \tag{3.4}$$

From carbon-cycle studies, we take α^* to be $1 - 1/\tau^M$, where τ^M is the "e-folding time"[2] or turnover time in years for the deep oceans. There is some controversy about the turnover time, but most estimates range between 100 and 500 years.[3] A simple one-equation representation such as (3.4) can be parameterized by examining the behavior of more complete models. Models developed by Siegenthaler and Oeschger (1987) and Maier-Reimer and Hasselmann (1987) suggest a $\tau^M = 120$ years, with a range of 50 to 200 years (IPCC 1990).[4] This then gives us the equation

$$m_1(t) = [1 - (1/\tau^M)] \, m_1(t-1) + \beta E(t-1). \tag{3.5}$$

---

2. Physical scientists use the concept of e-folding time to describe the delay time in dynamic systems. It is the time for the solution to decay to $1/e = 0.37$ of its original value after a shock. This concept stems from exponential decay. Suppose a process evolves according to $dM(t)/dt = -\delta M(t)$. Starting in equilibrium with $M = 0$, say there is a shock of ϵ to M at $t = 0$, so $M(t) = \epsilon \exp(-\delta t)$. Therefore, when $t = 1/\delta$, $M(t) = M(0)/e = \epsilon/e$. Hence the term e-folding time.

3. The IPCC states that "on average it takes hundreds to about one thousand years for water at the surface to penetrate to well below the mixed layer of the oceans" (1990, 12).

4. The major shortcoming of this approach would arise if the quickly mixing boxes are not in fact in equilibrium in a short time period, if the slowly mixing boxes other than the deep ocean are quantitatively significant, or if there are nonlinearities. It is likely, in particular, that carbon uptake in forests is on a shorter time scale than in the deep oceans, and this could bias the statistical estimates. Moreover, Kasting and Walker (1992) point out that the assumption of linearity may seriously understate the atmospheric retention of carbon. Kasting suggests that a pulse of CO_2 emissions that is three times preindustrial concentrations would have an atmospheric lifetime (e-folding time) between 380 and 700 years rather than the 120 years assumed by the IPCC and used here (personal communication).

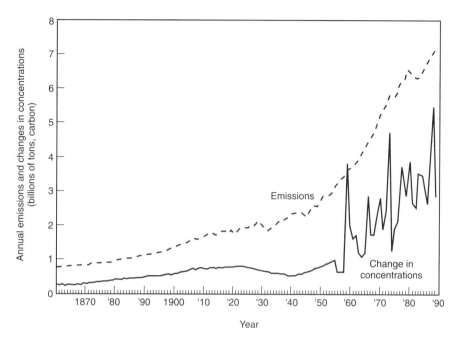

Figure 3.1
CO_2 emissions and changes in atmospheric concentrations of CO_2, 1860–1989
Source: Boden, Kanciruk, and Farrell 1990.

We applied this equation to data on estimated global carbon emissions and concentrations from Boden, Kanciruk, and Farrell (1990) for energy and cement. We augmented the emissions data by adding estimates on deforestation from the U.S. Environmental Protection Agency (hereafter, EPA 1989). Total emissions from the EPA report were 145 billion tons of carbon over the period 1860–1985, whereas the IPCC estimated the total emissions as 115 billion tons of carbon. We therefore adjusted downward the EPA figure for each year by the ratio 115/145. Figure 3.1 shows the constructed series for CO_2 emissions along with the calculated increase in concentrations. It is likely that the emissions data are subject to greater error than are the concentrations data, particularly since direct measurement of the latter began in 1958.

Equation (3.5) is estimated with and without a constant (to allow for the possibility of a missing source of emissions) and with and without first-order autocorrelation of the residuals (to allow for omitted variables). The time period was from 1860 to 1989. The results are shown

Table 3.1
Estimates of carbon-cycle equation

	No Constant			Constant		
	$\tau^M = 200$	$\tau^M = 120$	$\tau^M = 50$	$\tau^M = 200$	$\tau^M = 120**$	$\tau^M = 50$
β	0.56	0.64	0.89	0.61	0.67	0.87
se$(\beta)^+$	(.015)	(.015)	(.015)	(.027)	(.027)	(.027)
SEE*	0.527	0.519	0.514	0.519	0.517	0.514

Sample period: 1860–1989.
*SEE = standard error of equation.
**For $\tau^M = 120$, constant is $-.127$ (.09).
$^+$Standard errors of coefficients are in parentheses.

in table 3.1. The first-order error correction did relatively little because the equation is virtually a first-different specification, so the results with a first-order correction are not included.

As discussed above, there are varying estimates of the effective turnover time of the oceans, and we have taken a preferred estimate of 120 years with alternative values of 50 and 200 years. If a constant term is included (representing errors of measurement of emissions), this yields an estimate of -0.13 (gigatons of carbon per year). The interpretation of the constant term is that emissions are overestimated, although the overestimate is very slight. The equation with a constant term says that there is a missing source of emissions of $-.13$ ($\pm.09$) gigatons of emissions and that $\beta = 0.67$ (± 0.027). If we assume that the constant term is spurious and therefore exclude it, the best guess as to the marginal atmospheric retention ratio is slightly lower with $\beta = 0.64$ (± 0.015).

Figure 3.2 shows the actual and predicted values from the regression for a lifetime of $\tau^M = 120$ years. The prediction is a "dynamic" one; that is, it uses the initial conditions for the concentrations of CO_2 and simulates the equation without correcting for errors along the way. (Equations that use the actual values of the increase in concentrations as the independent variable do much better.) As can be seen, the estimated equation without the constant term tracks the concentrations reasonably well, although the equation tends to overpredict in the period 1940–60. From about 1960 on, the predicted growth is slightly less than the actual, so that by the end of the period the dynamic prediction is close to the mark. In any case, these results are probably well within the errors of measurement of the underlying data.

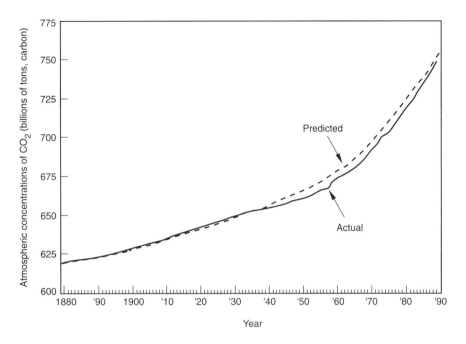

Figure 3.2
Actual and predicted CO_2 concentrations, 1880–1989
Notes: Actual from figure 3.1. Predicted from equation as described in text. Equation
uses atmospheric residence time of 120 years and suppresses constant.

Finally, figure 3.3 shows an estimate of the β parameter using "recursive least squares," which is a technique that estimates the equation
from a given starting point to different endpoints. This estimate uses
the lifetime estimate of $\tau^M = 120$ years and suppresses the constant
term. The equation shows estimates of the parameter for a sample period from 1860 to the date shown on the horizontal axis; in addition,
an error band of plus and minus two standard errors of the coefficient
is shown. The major impression from this figure is that the estimate of
the marginal atmospheric retention ratio (β) has risen as more data
have come in over the last three decades. Estimates through 1960 give
an estimate of 0.55, while those through 1989 give the estimate shown
in table 3.1 of 0.64. The path of the standard errors suggests that the
increase is unlikely to be due to sampling error. Other suspects are
specification error and measurement error. The most likely reason for
the increase is that there is growing saturation in the carbon sinks, so
that the uptake in nonatmospheric sinks is decreasing over time.

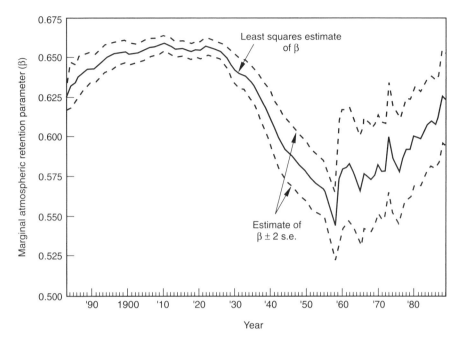

Figure 3.3
Recursive estimates of atmospheric retention parameter
Notes: Equation uses lifetime of 120 years and suppresses constant term. Observation for a given year is the estimated regression coefficient from 1860 through the date shown. The estimated coefficient is shown as a solid line, and coefficient plus and minus two standard errors of the coefficient as dashed lines.

For modeling the carbon cycle, we use the statistical estimate shown in table 3.1. Given the upward drift in the marginal atmospheric retention ratio shown in figure 3.3, we should be mindful of the possibility that the model may underestimate the atmospheric retention.

A Minimodel of Climate Change

Introduction

Climate modelers have developed a wide variety of approaches for estimating the impact of rising GHGs on climatic variables. On the whole, existing models are, unfortunately, much too complex to be included in economic models of the kind employed here. The models typically taken to be the most satisfactory are the large general circulation models (GCMs). These require several hundred hours of super-computer time simply to perform a simulation, and inclusion of these in an optimization model of the kind developed here is infeasible.

Another difficulty of current GCMs is that they have generally been used to estimate the equilibrium impact of a change in CO_2 concentrations upon the level of temperature and other variables. For economic analyses, it is essential to understand the dynamics or transient properties of the response of climate to GHG concentrations. At present, only a handful of models have been used to estimate the transient path, and these have only begun to incorporate the deep oceans into their calculations.

To develop integrated models of climate and the economy, it is necessary to have a relatively small model that links GHG concentrations and the major climatic variables. We have chosen to include only the impact of GHGs on global mean temperature in the analysis that follows. Although this analysis focuses primarily upon globally averaged surface temperature, it is recognized that this variable is not the most important for impacts. Variables like precipitation or water flows —along with extremes of droughts, floods, and freezes—are more important for economic activity than is average temperature alone. Mean temperature is chosen because it is a useful *index* of climate change that tends to be associated with most other important changes. In the language of statistics, temperature is likely to be a "sufficient statistic" for the other variables that have an important impact upon human and natural societies.[5] This point is shown in figure 3.4, which depicts the estimated impact of CO_2 doubling upon both mean temperature and precipitation in a number of models. This diagram shows the high correlation between the predicted temperature and precipitation changes. Because precipitation and other variables are highly correlated with the extent of global temperature change, we can safely employ temperature change as an index or proxy for impacts in global approaches like the DICE model.

The approach taken here begins with a simplified minimodel used to represent the basic dynamics of climate change. We then use larger models to calibrate the major parameters of the minimodel. It must be emphasized, however, that this representation is highly simplified and that a major effort by climatologists and climate modelers will be

---

5. See Savage 1954 for a discussion of sufficient statistics.

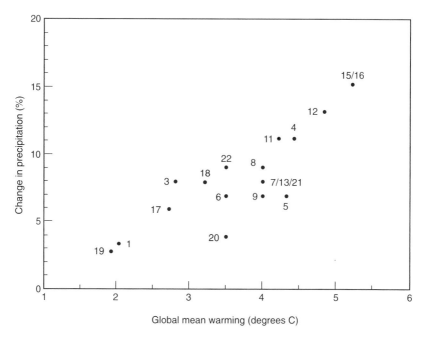

Figure 3.4
Relationship between equilibrium temperature change and precipitation change in models surveyed by IPCC*
Source: IPCC 1990, 138.
*Number next to point refers to IPCC model number.

necessary to develop an adequate and parsimonious representation of the linkage between climate and GHG concentrations.

The Model

We are interested in developing a model that captures accurately the broad aggregates of climate over decadal time scales; this approach differs from the standard GCMs, which operate on the scale of hours or even minutes. For our purpose, it will be useful to develop a globally averaged and highly aggregative model of the climate system.

In what follows, we represent the climate using a multistratum system that includes an atmospheric-land portion and a number of ocean levels. In the simplest approach (which is called the "one-equation model"), the system contains an atmosphere and a single oceanic stratum; in this model, the system is represented by a single variable that is globally averaged surface temperature.

In the more complete approach (which is called the "two-equation model"), the system contains an atmosphere, an upper-ocean stratum, and a lower-ocean stratum. In both cases, the system has an atmosphere that is warmed by solar radiation and is in short-run radiative equilibrium. The atmosphere exchanges energy quickly with the upper oceans, which impose a certain amount of thermal inertia on the system because of their heat capacity. In the two-equation model, the upper stratum of the ocean exchanges water with a lower stratum, representing the deep oceans, and the rate of heat transfer is proportional to the rate of water exchange. This model is a box-advection model, which is simpler to include in economic models than is the mixed box-advection and upwelling-diffusion approach that is widely used in medium- and large-scale models today. The two state variables in the two-equation model are the globally averaged surface temperature and the deep-ocean temperature.

The approach here follows closely the model developed by Schneider and Thompson (1981). For brevity, we describe the two-equation model, and the one-equation model is easily described after the more complete model is discussed. Assume a coupled atmosphere-ocean model in which there are two well-mixed strata—one being the atmosphere and the mixed upper stratum of the oceans, and the second being the deep oceans. Each of the two strata is assumed to be well mixed. The accumulation of GHGs warms the atmosphere, which then mixes with and warms the upper ocean, which in turn heats the deep oceans. The lags in the system are primarily due to the thermal inertia of the two strata.

The modeling of the climate parallels the approach taken for the carbon cycle above. Start with the following variables:

$T_i(t)$ = temperature of stratum i in period t (measured as the difference from the preindustrial period, degrees C)

$\mathbf{T}(t)$ = a column vector of the $T_i(t)$

τ_{ij} = the annual heat transfer from stratum i to stratum j

Γ = $n \times n$ matrix of τ's in which the ith element in row j is τ_{ij}

$F(t)$ = radiative forcing in atmosphere

$\mathbf{F}(t)$ = column vector of radiative forcing such that the transpose is $\mathbf{F}'(t) = [F(t) \; 0 \ldots 0]$

The system can then be written as follows:

$$\mathbf{T}(t) = \Gamma \mathbf{T}(t-1) + \mathbf{F}'(t). \tag{3.6}$$

In the two-equation approach, there are two strata or layers. For simplicity, we designate T (lightfaced) as the temperature of the atmosphere, land, and upper stratum of the ocean and T^* as the temperature of the deep oceans. Schneider and Thompson (1981) use a two-equation model version of (3.6), which, in finite-difference form, gives

$$T(t) = T(t-1) + (1/R_1) \{F(t) - \lambda T(t-1) -$$

$$(R_2/\tau_{12})[T(t-1) - T^*(t-1)]\},$$

$$T^*(t) = T^*(t-1) + (1/R_2) [(R_2/\tau_{12})(T(t-1) - T^*(t-1))]. \tag{3.7}$$

In this approach, R_1 is the thermal capacity of the atmospheric layer and the upper oceans, R_2 is the thermal capacity of the deep oceans, and τ_{12} is the transfer rate from the upper level of the ocean to the deep oceans. A key parameter in all models is λ, or the "feedback parameter." This parameter is a way of representing the equilibrium impact of CO_2 doubling on climate, and I will comment on its significance shortly.

It will be useful to compare the results of the two-equation model with a simpler version (the simpler version is often used to describe the equilibrium behavior of climate systems and was used in the static cost-benefit analysis in Nordhaus 1991c).[6] To obtain a one-equation model, we treat the ocean as a single well-mixed box (although it might be shallower than both strata of the ocean in the two-equation model). This then gives

$$T(t) = T(t-1) + (1/R_1) [F(t) - \lambda T(t-1)]. \tag{3.8}$$

This "one-dimensional" model has been widely used in discussions of the impact of greenhouse forcing. By solving either (3.7) or (3.8) for a constant T, it is easily seen that the long-run or equilibrium impact of a change in radiative forcing is $\Delta T / \Delta F = 1/\lambda$. We use the parameter $T_{2 \times CO_2}$ to represent the equilibrium impact of doubled CO_2 concentrations on global mean surface temperature. Solving (3.7) or (3.8), we see that $T_{2 \times CO_2} = \Delta F_{2 \times CO_2}/\lambda$, where $\Delta F_{2 \times CO_2}$ is the change in radiative forcing induced by a CO_2 doubling. The derivation of $T_{2 \times CO_2}$ is given in numerous sources.

---

6. We discuss in chapter 6 the relative merits of the one-equation and two-equation models.

A more complex variant of this system has been developed for purposes of describing the behavior of large GCMs. For example, a study of Schlesinger and Jiang (1990) developed a seven-layer model and parameterized it using GCM calculations of the Oregon State University model. In principle, that model could be incorporated into the economic model here, although it would not be nearly as flexible or as transparent as the models used in this study. The major advantage of the approach used here is that the two major issues in climate change—the equilibrium temperature-CO_2 sensitivity and the speed of adjustment—can be represented in terms of the parameters λ and $(1/R_1)$.

Calibration to General Circulation Models

The next step is to find the appropriate numerical representation of the simplified climate equations in (3.7) and (3.8). We approach this by calibrating the models to transient runs of three climate models and additionally by estimating the models using historical data. This section describes the calibration to GCMs.

For calibration purposes, we have examined three different models.[7]

ST: The first is the appproch of Schneider and Thompson (1981). This study develops a two-equation model that is identical to equation set (3.7); it has the disadvantage of being highly simplified relative to larger models. To exploit the ST approach, we construct the model explicitly using the parameters developed in the original study.

SMB: The most completely developed model is a coupled atmospheric-ocean model developed by Stouffer, Manabe, and Bryan (1989). This model is a highly disaggregated representation of both the atmosphere and the oceans and provides a transient calculation of the impact of slowly rising CO_2 concentrations.[8]

SJ: A third model, developed in the spirit of the approach used here, is a parametric representation of the Oregon State University model in a small model of the coupled atmospheric and six-layer ocean model by Schlesinger and Jiang (1990). This model uses the larger model to determine the parameters of the smaller model and then uses the smaller model for calculating transient values over longer periods.

---

7. The author is grateful for the wise and generous counsel of Stephen Schneider and Michael Schlesinger in helping understand and apply their models.
8. More recent results include Manabe et al. 1991 and Manabe and Stouffer 1993. The former is an elaboration of the SMB model using the same increase of CO_2 as the experi-

The models in (3.7) and (3.8) can be represented in terms of four parameters: R_1, R_2, τ_{12}, and λ. The first two parameters represent the heat capacity of the atmosphere, land, and upper layer of the ocean (R_1) and of the deep ocean (R_2). The third parameter represents the transfer coefficient between the two strata. The parameter λ is the feedback coefficient that gives the crucial CO_2-temperature equilibrium relationship.

For calibration purposes, we take the feedback parameter (λ) from equilibrium runs of the three models described above (which effectively assumes that there is a unique and stable long-run equilibrium for each radiative forcing). According to scientific studies, a doubling of CO_2 will increase the surface warming by 4.1 watts per meter squared. From this, it can be seen that $4.1/\lambda = T_{2 \times CO_2}$ = the equilibrium impact of CO_2 doubling on global mean surface temperatures. Figure 3.4 shows the value of $T_{2 \times CO_2}$ for a number of models reviewed by the IPCC. The recent report of the U.S. National Academy of Sciences (hereafter, NAS) (1992) concluded that value of $T_{2 \times CO_2}$ lay between 1°C and 5°C. The values of the parameter λ for the different models are shown in table 3.2.

The parameters for the transfer between the upper and lower levels are taken from both empirical studies and empirical estimates of the heat capacities of the different reservoirs, which are easily calculated once the sizes of the reservoirs are determined. The ST model takes the first reservoir to be the atmosphere, land, and upper ocean, which are equivalent to the top 133.5 meters of the oceans. The relevant parameter here is R_1, which is the effective heat capacity of the atmosphere and the upper level of the oceans. The second reservoir is the deep oceans (taken to be 1500 meters of depth); the heat capacity of the deep oceans, R_2, is much larger. Calculations show that for the above assumptions, $R_1 = 13.2$ watt-years/°C $- m^2$ and $R_2 = 223.7$ watt-years/ °C $- m^2$. The major problematical assumption here is the depth of the boundary between the two ocean strata.

---

ment discussed in the text. The estimated global mean temperature profile is very close to the earlier model. The second study examines an additional run that increases atmospheric concentrations of CO_2 to four times preindustrial levels. The striking finding of the 4 × CO_2 run is that the atmosphere-ocean system settles into a second, locally stable equilibrium with a different ocean circulation.

Table 3.2
Parameters for three GCMs for climate minimodel

A. One-equation model (equation 3.8)

Model	λ	$T_{2\times CO_2}$	$c(1) =$ $1/R_1$	$c(3) =$ R_2/T_2	$1/T_2$	e-fold (yrs.)	SEE (°C)
Schneider-Thompson	1.33	3.08	0.026	0	0	29	0.034
Stouffer-Manabe-Bryan	0.98	4.20	0.030	0	0	34	0.011
Schlesinger-Jiang	1.41	2.91	0.024	0	0	30	0.064

B. Two-equation model (equation 3.7)

Model	λ	$T_{2\times CO_2}$	$c(1) =$ $1/R_1$	$c(3) =$ R_2/T_2	$1/T_2$	e-fold (yrs.)	SEE (°C)
Schneider-Thompson	1.33	3.08	0.075	0.44	0.002	13	0.000
Stouffer-Manabe-Bryan	0.98	4.20	0.065	0.44	0.002	25	0.014
Schlesinger-Jiang	1.41	2.91	0.048	0.44	0.002	19	0.050

Source: Parameters calibrated to models as described in text.
Note: Parameters refer to annual data.

On the basis of the calculated heat capacities, we can then calculate $1/R_1 = 1/(13.2 \text{ watt-years}/°C - m^2) = 0.075$ ($°C - m^2/\text{watt-year}$) for the ST model. For the other two models, we estimate the parameter from the equation system in (3.7) and (3.8). The estimated number is likely to differ from the ST model's calculated value because the presence of intermediate layers will give an apparent larger size to the upper stratum than will a two-stratum model.

The remaining parameter, the transfer coefficient, is highly uncertain and cannot be determined with precision from fundamental physics. The transfer coefficient (τ_{12}) refers to the speed at which water transfers between the deep and upper oceans. Schneider and Thompson propose a value of $\tau_{12} = 550$ years based on Broecker and Peng 1982. Other studies use a shorter period. For calibration purposes, we take a slight downward adjustment of the ST value to $\tau_{12} = 500$. By combining this value with the value for R_2, we obtain the last coefficient in the first equation of (3.7), which is $R_2/\tau_{12} = 223.7$ (watt-years/$°C - m^2$)/500 years $= 0.44$ watts/$°C - m^2$.

The final steps to calibrate the models were determined as follows. For the ST model, we programmed the model and calculated the exact path of the temperatures for the different layers. We then estimated the parameters of both equations (3.7) and (3.8) using iterative least squares.[9] Because the temperatures were calculated using the equations in (3.7), the annual equations fit perfectly for the two-equation model. The equation fit less well for the one-equation model because the two layers were forced to behave as one. Table 3.2 shows the estimated parameters of the models for both the one-equation and the two-equation versions. The last column (SEE) shows the standard error of estimate of the equation (in °C). This is not an error relative to actual observation; rather, it represents the error of the approximation in the minimodel relative to the original model. On the whole, the errors are in the hundredths of a °C and therefore represent the larger model calculations quite accurately.

For the SMB model, we began with the calculated temperature path for the model (kindly provided by Dr. Stouffer). This path was for years 5, 15, . . . , 95 of a simulation in which CO_2 concentrations grew at 1 percent per annum compounded. We then fit a polynomial function to the path to obtain interpolated values. Next, we used the program for the ST model to calculate the values of temperature for the lower layer of the oceans. Finally, we estimated the one-equation and two-equation models for the interpolated values for the atmosphere and the estimated values for the lower layer. Again, the values are listed in table 3.2.

In addition, we show in figure 3.5 the original values from the SMB model (shown as filled circles), the interpolated values (TRFOR), and the estimated values for both the one-equation and two-equation models (TRFOREQ1 and TRFOREQ2, respectively). In addition, table 3.3 shows the correlation matrix of the four series. It is apparent that the equations of the minimodel fit the calculations quite well, with the average absolute error being less than 0.1°C.

For the SJ model, we took the same approach as in the SMB model. We took from that study the calculated temperature increases for the atmosphere, upper layer of the ocean, and lower layer of the ocean at 10-year intervals. We then calculated the annual figures using polynomial interpolation. Finally, we estimated the free parameter using ordinary least squares. The estimated values of the parameters are shown in table 3.2.

---

9. By "iterative least squares," we mean the following: The equation set in (3.7) is a recursive set of nonlinear equations and cannot easily be estimated directly, and the lower temperature cannot be directly observed. We therefore estimated each equation using the values from the other equation, and iterated between the equations until the values of the endogenous variables converged. This procedure will underestimate the standard errors but is sufficient for the purposes of this study.

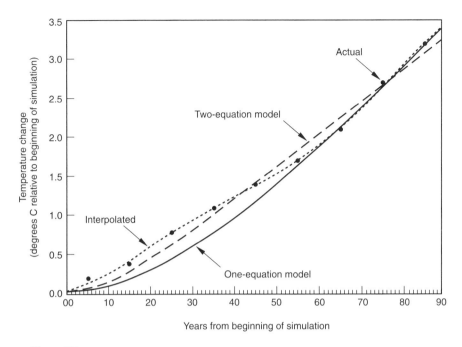

Figure 3.5
Actual, interpolated, and minimodel: Estimates for SMB general circulation climate
model
Source: As described in text.

Table 3.3
Correlations between alternative specification in SMB Model

Variable	TR	TRFOR	TRFOREQ1	TRFOREQ2
TR[a]	1.0000	0.9994	0.9963	0.9947
TRFOR[b]		1.0000	0.9961	0.9951
TRFOREQ1[c]			1.0000	0.9956
TRFOREQ2[d]				1.0000

Notes:
a. TR = Actual model calculation from Stouffer, Manabe, and Bryan 1989.
b. TRFOR = Polynomial interpolation that best fits the TR series.
c. TRFOREQ1 = Ordinary least squares estimate of one-equation model in equation
(3.8) to TRFOR.
d. TRFOREQ2 = Ordinary least squares estimate of two-equation model in equation
(3.7) to TRFOR.

Estimated Values from Historical Data

One of the major tasks of researchers in the area of global climate change is to use historical data to test or validate model calculations. This topic is of independent interest, but in this study we compare model forecasts with the instrumental record to determine whether the models described in the last section fit tolerably well the actual historical record of temperature changes.

In this section, we estimate the equation sets (3.7) and (3.8) using historical data on atmospheric forcing and observed mean atmospheric surface temperatures. The temperature series covered the period 1862–1989 and relied on estimates of Jones, Wigley, and Wright (1990). These data are intended to cover both terrestrial and oceanic stations, although the coverage is sparse for several regions. In addition, we calculated the radiative forcings from the four major GHGs using a variety of data on atmospheric concentrations and combining those into a series on radiative forcing using conversions suggested by T. Wigley and used in the IPCC report (1990).

The estimation technique is the following. For concreteness, we describe the technique for the two-equation model and then explain how it would apply to the one-equation model. We can rewrite the two-equation model as follows:

$$T(t) = T(t-1) + \alpha_1 \{F(t) - \alpha_2 T(t-1) - \alpha_3 [T(t-1) - T^*(t-1)]\},$$

$$T^*(t) = T^*(t-1) + \alpha_4 [T(t-1) - T^*(t-1)], \tag{3.7'}$$

where $\alpha_1 = (1/R_1)$, $\alpha_2 = \lambda$, $\alpha_3 = R_2/\tau_{1\,2}$, and $\alpha_4 = (1/\tau_{1\,2})$. There is insufficient variation in the data to allow us to estimate more than two of the parameters in (3.7'), so we used physical data from the models to calibrate the two least important parameters, α_3 and α_4. On the basis of the last section, these are taken to be $\alpha_3 = 0.44$ and $\alpha_4 = 1/500$. Note that data on the temperature in the deep oceans, T^*, are currently unavailable.

In addition, we assume that there are random terms reflecting either misspecifications of the structure (such as the oscillations due to El Niño) or random external forcings (such as volcanic influences or changes in solar luminosity). We specify these as a random term with a first-order autoregressive error. On the basis of estimating a linear approximation to (3.7'), we obtain an estimate of the autocorrelation coefficient of 0.8, and this is used in the estimation

$$u(t) = 0.8\, u(t-1) + \epsilon(t), \tag{3.9}$$

where $\epsilon(t)$ is assumed to be independently and identically distributed. Note that omission of variables such as volcanic activity, which is statistically independent of anthropogenic GHGs, will not bias the estimates of the parameters and is unlikely to distort the standard errors.

Combining the assumptions, we then obtain the final equation to be estimated:

$$T(t) = T(t-1) + \alpha_1 \{F(t) - \alpha_2 T(t-1) - 0.44 [T(t-1) - T^*(t-1)]\} + u(t),$$

$$T^*(t) = T^*(t-1) + 0.002 [T(t-1) - T^*(t-1)]. \tag{3.10}$$

It is difficult to estimate this equation set directly, so we use a number of procedures to estimate the parameters. The first procedure is to ignore the autoregressive term and estimate the equation by nonlinear least squares. In this procedure, we use two particular values for the temperature sensitivity coefficient and estimate the inertia term (α_1). Table 3.4 shows the results of these estimates. The inertial variable (α_1) does not differ greatly across the different specifications, ranging from 0.014 to 0.020.

Table 3.4
Estimated values for models from historical data

A. One-equation model (equation 3.8)

Assumption	λ	$T_{2\times CO_2}$	$c(1) =$ $1/R_1$	$c(3) =$ R_2/T_2	$1/T_2$	e-fold (yrs.)	SEE (°C)
Low temperature sensitivity	4.00	1.03	0.020 (.0072)	0	0	13	0.121
High temperature sensitivity	1.00	4.10	0.014 (.0105)	0	0	63	0.124

B. Two-equation model (equation 3.7)

Model	λ	$T_{2\times CO_2}$	$c(1) =$ $1/R_1$	$c(3) =$ R_2/T_2	$1/T_2$	e-fold (yrs.)	SEE (°C)
Low temperature sensitivity	4.00	1.03	0.020 (.0072)	0.44	0.002	14	0.121
High temperature sensitivity	1.00	4.10	0.016 (.0099)	0.44	0.002	96	0.123

Source: Data and estimation technique described in text.
Notes: Parameters refer to annual data. Equations were fitted using ordinary or iterative least squares over period 1862–1989. Numbers in parentheses are standard errors of coefficients.

One way of viewing the systems is in terms of their e-folding time. This is the exponential half-life or the length of time for a variable to reach 63 percent of the distance from the original to the equilibrium value. The specifications yield highly different e-folding times primarily because of the differing feedback coefficients.

The inertial parameter (α_1) is not well determined even when the other parameters are specified, particularly when the $T_{2 \times CO_2}$ parameter is at the high end of the range. The data indicate that the time lag of adjustment is longer than that in the GCM models in table 3.2 if $T_{2 \times CO_2}$ is at the high end of the range of values (say 3 or more). For example, using a value of $T_{2 \times CO_2}$ of 4 requires a time-lag coefficient of about two-thirds of the GCM models for the one-equation model and one-third to one-fifth of the GCM models for the two-equation models. Put differently, for a $T_{2 \times CO_2}$ of 4, the e-folding value is around 63 years in the one-equation model for high $T_{2 \times CO_2}$ as compared to values of 29 to 34 years in the GCMs.

The standard errors of the coefficients are given in parentheses under the estimates in table 3.4. In addition, we have shown the standard errors of the equations as SEE. The SEEs are virtually equal for the four estimated equations; it is clear that the likelihood function is extremely flat over four specifications.

To capture the full specification in (3.10), we have provided a likelihood-function estimate of the equation for different combination of parameters. In this set of estimates, we have chosen five different values of the temperature-sensitivity coefficient, $T_{2 \times CO_2}$; these are 1, 2, 3, 4, and 5°C per CO_2 doubling. In addition, we have estimated the likelihood of the equations for four different values of $\alpha_1 = 0.01$, 0.02, 0.05, and 0.10. These represent thermal inertias of from one-half to five times the figures from the theoretical models shown in table 3.4.

Table 3.5 and figure 3.6 show the estimated likelihood of each of the 20 combinations of parameters. These estimates indicate that either the inertia coefficient (α_1) is very low (in the order of 0.01) or the temperature-sensitivity coefficient is at the lower end of the range. A low value of the inertia coefficient indicates that the observed temperature increase is low because the thermal inertia of the system is much higher than any of models indicates. This possibility is shown by the high value of the likelihood for temperature-sensitivity coefficients of 3.1 through 5.0 with $\alpha_1 = 0.01$. The other set of coefficients with high likelihood is for values of $T_{2 \times CO_2}$ of 1 and 2, where almost any of the inertia coefficients are plausible. Conditional on estimates of the inertia pa-

Table 3.5
Likelihood of different parameters: Two-equation model of climate system

Inertia Parameter (α_1)	Temperature-Sensitivity Coefficient $(T_{2 \times CO_2})$					
	5.0	4.0	3.1	2.0	1.0	**Sum**
0.01	0.090	0.102	0.111	0.103	0.050	**0.455**
0.02	0.010	0.024	0.054	0.106	0.072	**0.264**
0.05	0.000	0.001	0.006	0.059	0.087	**0.152**
0.10	0.000	0.000	0.001	0.035	0.092	**0.128**
Sum	**0.100**	**0.126**	**0.172**	**0.303**	**0.300**	**1.000**

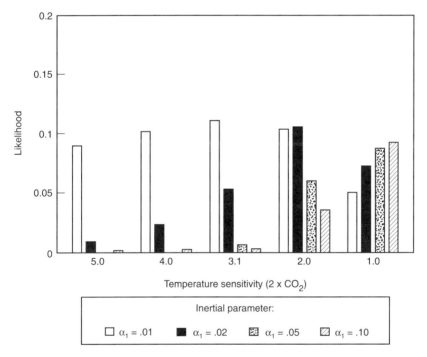

Figure 3.6
Likelihood for different models
(From global temperatures, 1865–1990)
Source: Equation set (3.10) was estimated using data on radiative forcing and observed changes in globally averaged surface temperatures. Likelihood was formed for each of twenty sets of parameters (five temperature-sensitivity coefficients times four inertial coefficients), and these were normalized to sum to unity. Each bar shows the normalized likelihood for the particular parameter combination.

rameter generated by most models (in the order of $\alpha_1 = 0.02$), the best estimate of $T_{2 \times CO_2}$ is 2, although values of 1 and 3 are between one-half and two-thirds as likely. Integrating across the different values of α_1, values of $T_{2 \times CO_2}$ of 1 and 2 have the highest and almost equal likelihood.

Figure 3.7 shows the estimated contribution of historical concentrations of GHGs to temperature changes over the last 100 years according to four of the two-equation models shown in figure 3.8 and table 3.2. The middle two curves are the two combinations of parameters with the highest likelihood ($T_{2 \times CO_2} = 2.0$ and $\alpha_1 = .02$; $T_{2 \times CO_2} = 4.0$ and $\alpha_1 = .01$). These clearly track the historical data tolerably well. The upper path ($T_{2 \times CO_2} = 4.2$ and $\alpha_1 = .02$) is close to the SMB model and has very low likelihood given the historical data. The lower path ($T_{2 \times CO_2} = 1.0$ and $\alpha_1 = .01$) is one that has high inertia and low temperature sensitivity and is also moderately unlikely.

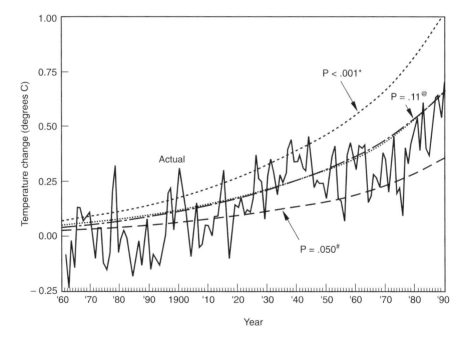

Figure 3.7
Actual and predicted increase in mean global temperature, 1860–1990
Symbols: * = SMB ($T_{2 \times CO_2} = 4.2$; $\alpha_1 = .02$); @ = maximum likelihood combinations ($T_{2 \times CO_2} = 2.0$; $\alpha_1 = .02$) and ($T_{2 \times CO_2} = 4.0$; $\alpha_1 = .01$); # = low-temperature-increase model ($T_{2 \times CO_2} = 1.0$; $\alpha_1 = .01$). P values are likelihoods.

Figure 3.8 shows another way of examining the differences among the alternative models. This shows, for the two-equation model, the results of an increase in CO_2 concentrations of 1 percent per year compounded (doubling in 70 years). The solid circles show the calculations of the SMB model. The three top curves show the transient runs generated by the three models analyzed here using the parameters shown in table 3.2. The lower two curves show the paths generated by the parameters estimated from the historical data (with the high path assuming that $T_{2 \times CO_2} = 4.0$ and the low one assuming that $T_{2 \times CO_2} = 1.0$). This figure shows the predicament that the GCM models appear to predict transient temperature increases well above those consistent with the historical record.

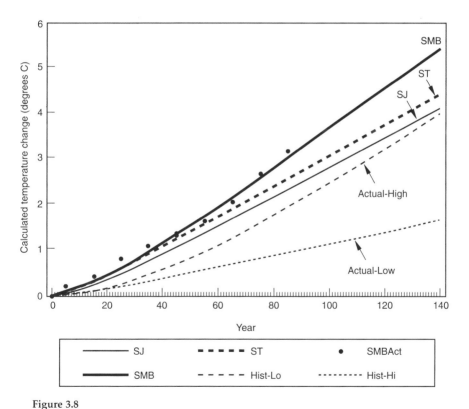

Figure 3.8

Projected temperature rise

Notes: This figure shows the calculated trajectory of climate change for a 1 percent per year compounded increase in CO_2 concentrations. ● indicates that it is a calculation from the full SMB general circulation climate model. All others are for different parameters of the two-equation model in (3.10). The lower two curves show the trajectories consistent with actual historical temperature data.

The Inconsistency of Models and History

We can use the likelihood estimates to evaluate the likelihood of the three models evaluated here in terms of the historical data. We calculate the likelihood of each of the 20 cases as the ratio of its likelihood to the sum of the likelihoods of all 20 cases. The maximum-likelihood case is $p = 0.111$; this corresponds to a temperature sensitivity where $T_{2 \times CO_2} = 3.1$ and $\alpha_1 = .01$. Using the parameters for the one-equation model in table 3.2, the likelihood for the ST model is $p = 0.0312$, for the SMB model $p = 0.0026$, and for the SJ model $p = 0.0470$. By conventional likelihood-ratio tests, none of the models is particularly compelling, but neither can they be definitively ruled out.

On the whole, the historical data have great difficulty distinguishing among the different models. The reason for this is that the strength of the "greenhouse signal" is weak relative to the background noise over the historical period. Moreover, the signal is not strong enough to allow us to estimate both the feedback factor and the time-lag coefficient.

In addition, the statistical estimates for the historical data may be biased if there are slowly moving trend variables that are correlated with the GHG signal. Two such variables have been recently identified: aerosols from combustion and ozone depletion. The forcings for both of these influences are likely to be negatively correlated with the greenhouse forcings, so the temperature-sensitivity estimates may be biased downward. In addition, if there is an underlying trend warming or cooling from natural sources (such as emergence from the "Little Ice Age"), there could be a spurious correlation that would bias upward the coefficient on greenhouse forcings.

The historical data pose a major issue for economic modeling of policies for slowing climate change. If the historical data provide the appropriate parameters, then climate will change much more slowly than the standard models estimate. This is a major uncertainty that will continue to plague policy studies.

Figure 3.9 shows the estimates of the key parameters of the different models and the estimates for the historical data. This figure shows for both the one-equation model and the two-equation model the values of the temperature-doubling coefficient ($T_{2 \times CO_2}$) and the period required for reaching 63 percent of the equilibrium value (the e-folding time). For the DICE model, we employ the parameter pair (Sc2) drawn

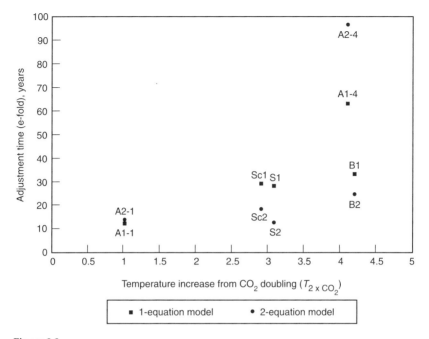

Figure 3.9

Parameters for climate model

Note: Each point shows the parameter pair for a particular model or estimate.

Symbols:

A1-1: History ($T_{2 \times CO_2} = 1$, 1 equation)   A2-1: Same (two equation model)

A1-4: History ($T_{2 \times CO_2} = 4$, 1 equation)   A2-4: Same (two-equation model)

Sc1: SJ model (1 equation)   Sc2: Same (two-equation model)[a]

S1: ST model (1 equation)   S2: Same (two-equation model)

B1: SMB model (1 equation)   B2: Same (two-equation model)

a. Equation used in DICE model.

from the results of the SJ model. The results of this model are in the middle of the pack of most of the GCM results and its value of $T_{2 \times CO_2}$ is at the center of the judgmental figures of recent National Academy Panels as well as the views of the IPCC.[10]

This concludes our excursion into macrogeophysics. The next chapter turns to the linkages between economic activity and emissions and climate change.

---

10. One final transformation is required for the economic model. The time step in the model is 10 years. We therefore took each of the models and simulated it using the one-year parameters shown in table 3.2. We then estimated, using ordinary least squares, the coefficients for the 10-year differences instead of the one-year differences.

4

Geoeconomics: Energy, Emissions, and the Economic Impact of Climate Change

Estimates of the Impact of Climate Change

Background

This chapter continues the detailed derivation of the equations of the DICE model, focusing primarily on the economic linkages. Perhaps the most controversial aspect of an economic analysis of climate change involves the estimates of the impact of climate change. What are the likely economic impacts of projected climate changes over the next century? To begin with, we should recognize that in the long march of economic development, technology has increasingly insulated humans and economic activity from the vagaries of climate. Two centuries ago, work and recreation were dictated by the cycles of daylight, the seasons, and the agricultural growing season.

Today, thanks to modern technology, humans live and thrive in virtually every climate on earth. For the bulk of economic activity, variables like wages, unionization, labor-force skills, and political factors swamp climatic considerations. When a manufacturing firm decides between investing in Hong Kong and Moscow, climate will probably not even be on the list of factors considered. Moreover, the process of economic development and technological change tend progressively to reduce climate sensitivity as the share of agriculture in output and employment declines and as capital-intensive space heating and cooling, enclosed shopping malls, artificial snow, and accurate weather or hurricane forecasting reduce the vulnerability of economic activity to weather.

In thinking about the impact of climate change, we must recognize that the variable focused on in most analyses—globally averaged surface temperature—has little salience for impacts. Rather, variables that accompany or are the result of temperature changes—precipitation, water levels, extremes of droughts or freezes, and thresholds like the freezing point or the level of dikes and levees—will drive the socioeconomic impacts. Mean temperature is chosen because it is a useful *index* of climate change that is highly correlated with or determines the more important variables. Moreover, it must be emphasized that impact studies are in their infancy and that studies of low-income regions are virtually nonexistent.

Existing research uses a wide variety of approaches including time-series analysis, engineering studies, and historical analogs. Climate change is likely to have different effects on different sectors and in different countries. In general, those sectors of the economy that depend heavily on unmanaged ecosystems—that is, are heavily dependent upon naturally occurring rainfall, runoff, or temperature—will be most sensitive to climate change. Agriculture, forestry, outdoor recreation, and coastal activities fall in this category. Countries like Japan or the United States are relatively insulated from climate change while developing countries like India are more vulnerable.

At present, there are few estimates of the impacts, and these generally concentrate on advanced industrial countries. The estimates used here are presented as extremely tentative, order-of-magnitude figures; we expect that these will be improved considerably in the coming years as researchers focus more attention on the impacts of climate change.

Current analyses generally estimate the impact of climate change on a country or region at a particular time; studies typically focus on the impacts of a CO_2 doubling or on a 2.5 or 3°C rise in temperature. This section draws upon impact estimates, but additionally presents a technique for estimating the impact of climate changes over time as a function of the composition of output and of the impacts of climate change by sector. The estimates rely upon studies of impacts by sector for the United States and then apply them to different countries as a function of the projected future industrial compositions.

Impact by Sector: Methods

The basic framework is that damages in each country are a function of the sectoral composition of national output and the extent of climate change. More specifically, assume that output in sector i of country j

Table 4.1
Impact coefficients for different sectors (impact of CO_2 doubling on output by sector)

Sector	GNP Originating (billions of 1981$)	Impact (billions of 1981$)	Impact as Percent of Sector (percent)
Farming[a]	61.0	3.0	4.92
Energy[b]	45.9	1.0	2.18
Coastal activities[c]	76.6	5.3	6.91
Other[d]	2231.5	15.9	0.71
TOTAL	2415.0	24.2	1.00

Notes:
a. This is taken to be proportional to the GNP originating in agriculture.
b. This is taken to be proportional to total energy consumption in value terms.
c. The coastline vulnerability is taken to be the ratio of the coastline to the land area. The impact is assumed to rise with the square root of the coastline vulnerability. The measure of GNP is recreation and real estate.
d. This is proportional to the nonagricultural GNP.

at time t is given by $x_{i\,j}(t)$. For simplicity, we assume that there is no impact of different policies or of climate change on *relative* prices, so impacts can simply be summed across different sectors.

To estimate the total impact of climate change, we assume that the impact of climate change is a function of the change in global mean temperature from preindustrial times, this being $T(t)$. The damage in a particular sector is assumed to take the form

$$d_{i\,j}(t) = \eta_i\, T(t)^2\, Q_{ij}(t), \tag{4.1}$$

where $d_{i\,j}(t)$, is the loss of output in the sector, η_i is a damage coefficient that is specific to a particular sector, and the quadratic term on temperature reflects the assumption, consistent with a few studies, that the damage is quadratic in the temperature increase. For example, if the equation for agriculture is

$$d_{\text{farm, US}}(t) = \eta_{\text{farm}}\, T(t)^2\, Q_{\text{farm, US}}(t) = .01\, T(t)^2\, Q_{\text{farm, US}}(t),$$

this indicates that a rise in global mean temperature of 3°C would lower farm output in the United States by 9 percent.

We have surveyed the estimates of climate damage elsewhere for the United States (see Nordhaus 1991c). From that study, we derive the estimates of the η coefficients shown in table 4.1. The last column in that table shows the estimated damage from a 3°C warming as a percentage of the gross national product (GNP) or gross domestic product (GDP) originating in four sectors. To extend the results for the United States to the rest of the world, we undertake the following adjustments:

1. *Agriculture.* To apply the methodology to future growth, we first project the share of agriculture in each country over the next 100 years. This projection assumes that the share of agriculture is a linear function of the logarithm of per capita GNP. We assume that the coefficient relating the rate of decline of the share of agriculture and the growth of per capita income is two-thirds of the estimated cross-sectional coefficient for the period 1965–87.

2. *Energy.* For energy losses, we assume that the climate-sensitive part of the energy sector is 2 percent of total GNP.

3. *Sea-level rise.* The most difficult calculation involves losses due to sea-level rise. We begin with studies for the United States, which are shown in table 4.1. To apply this technique to other countries requires a detailed investigation of the geography and state of development and infrastructure for each country, a massive task that has not been undertaken for this study.

Instead, we use a very simple correction of coastal activity taking into account the coastline of different countries. We begin with a measure of "coastal vulnerability," f_j, which is the ratio of coastal area to total land area. We define coastal area as that area within 10 kilometers of the coastline. To examine the impact of coastal vulnerability, we estimated a number of regressions between per capita GNP and a number of variables. A representative relationship is

$$\log \left(\begin{matrix} \text{per} \\ \text{capita} \\ \text{GDP} \end{matrix} \right) = \text{constant} + \underset{[0.15]}{0.62} \ \log \left(\begin{matrix} \text{coastal} \\ \text{vulnerability} \end{matrix} \right)$$
$$+ \text{ other variables,}$$

where the standard error of the coefficient is in brackets. This relationship confirms the impression that coastal countries tend to have higher incomes, a relationship that surely goes back at least to Periclean Athens.

For the United States, we calculate that the cost to coastal activities of an equilibrium CO_2 doubling is \$5.3 billion per year at 1981 prices and national income (see Nordhaus 1991c); this represents about 0.2 percent of total output. For other countries, we assume that a country

with the same coastal vulnerability index has the same cost (as a fraction of its GNP) as that of the United States.[1] On the basis of the regression equation above, we assume that the impact is a function of the
square root of the vulnerability index, so that a country with four times
the fraction of its land in coastal zones as the United States will have a
GNP loss twice as large as that of the United States.

4. *Other sectors.* The last category includes all other areas, comprising
the balance of marketed output (manufacturing, services, mining, etc.)
as well as nonmarket impacts (ecosystem effects, gardening, amenities,
etc.). We have only the roughest estimates concerning the impacts outside the market sectors. On the basis of my earlier estimates, I assumed
the total loss in other sectors is three-quarters of 1 percent of national
income, which gives an impact coefficient of .71 percent.[2]

Data and Results for Individual Countries

Data on the various series for 70 countries comprising more than 95
percent of world output and population were obtained from a wide
variety of sources including national statistical offices of major countries, the World Bank, the International Monetary Fund, the OECD,
and the United Nations. In addition, some adjustments were made to
the reported incomes of the former socialist countries to reflect distortions in official or market exchange rates.

  This methodology gives an estimate of the impact of global warming on total output. The lower bound of the impact is .72 percent of
output for landlocked states with no agriculture. For a country with a
great deal of coastal activity and a large part of the economy in agriculture, the loss from a 3°C warming can exceed 4 percent of GNP.

  To obtain a rough estimate of the distribution of impacts of climate
change on different countries, we have calculated the estimated vulnerability of countries as measured by the estimated loss due to a 3°C
warming. We then plot in figure 4.1 the estimated cumulative vulnera-

---

1. An approach that has been used in some studies is to assume that the dollar value of
losses is the same per unit of land threatened. This makes no sense since the contribution
of land to economic activity (and the price of land) varies immensely across different
countries.

2. This estimate is a residual one and is derived from the judgment that the total loss
for the United States is around 1 percent of national output for an equilibrium CO_2
doubling. In the study of Nordhaus 1991c, measured losses were actually one-quarter of
1 percent of national income. The 1 percent estimate is a precautionary guess as to the
magnitude of "surprises" from climate change that are likely to occur in the nonfarm
sectors.

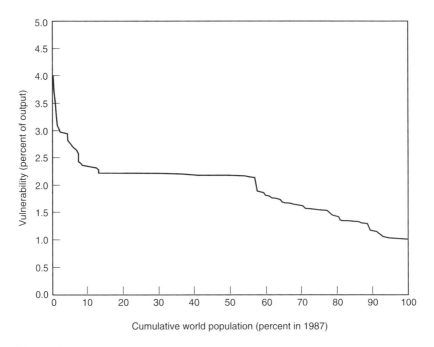

Cumulative world population (percent in 1987)

Figure 4.1
Vulnerability to climate change, 1987
(As function of world population)
Notes: Countries are ranked by their vulnerability to climate change as predicted by
approach in table 4.2. Countries are then rank-ordered and cumulated by 1987 population. Each point therefore shows the fraction of the world's population with vulnerability at or above the given level.

bility to climate change for 1987, where the index of vulnerability or
potential damage from CO_2 doubling is plotted against the percentage
of world population with vulnerabilities at or above that level. Although the United States is estimated to have a vulnerability near 1
percent of national output, the majority of the world's population has
output vulnerability around twice that (primarily because of the large
proportion of the economy devoted to farming in countries with large
populations).[3]

---

3. Nordhaus 1992a shows the same relationship as does figure 4.1 for different periods
and concepts. Examining the estimated cumulative damage function for 2050 shows a
modest shift downward in the curve reflecting the projected decline in the farming sector in most countries. An alternative approach also shown in Nordhaus 1992a is to estimate the impact curve for cumulative output in 1987 and 2050 rather than for cumulative
population. The fraction of the output at risk is less than the fraction of the population
at risk because of the smaller share of farming in high-income countries.

Table 4.2
Impact of CO_2 doubling in different sectors for global economy: Effect of growth and changing industrial composition (percent of global output in year)

Year	TOTAL	Farming	Coastal	Energy	Other	Memo: Share of Farming in Output
1987	1.326	0.306	0.272	0.044	0.704	0.061
2010	1.331	0.292	0.289	0.044	0.706	0.058
2050	1.336	0.271	0.312	0.044	0.709	0.054
2100	1.331	0.259	0.317	0.044	0.711	0.052

Notes: The estimate shows the impact on global output of climate change due to equilibrium CO_2 doubling (with 3°C of warming). The estimates reflect the changing composition of national outputs and the differing vulnerabilities of different sectors and countries as shown in table 4.1.

Overall Losses to World Output

Finally, we estimate the vulnerability of global output to climate change. Total world output losses are derived by taking the weighted average of the losses of the different countries (where the weights are relative GNPs) and by the share of each sector in each year. The total estimates are shown in table 4.2.

Overall, the estimates suggest that the global losses from an equilibrium CO_2 doubling is on the order of 1.33 percent of national output. This estimate depends heavily on the estimates for the United States and the method of extending these estimates to other countries. Both of these are subject to large margins of errors. A more difficult issue is the assumption that a dollar loss in a low-income country is worth the same as a dollar loss in a high-income country. This approach might be based on the compensation principle that if the rich compensate the poor, then a dollar loss is equivalent anywhere. Alternatively, if the costs of control and the damages were both proportionally higher in low-income countries, and if rates of time preference were the same, then with no compensation the optimization would lead to the same outcome.

The result of this calculation is to suggest that, using the United States sectoral impacts, the global losses are likely to be larger than those for the United States. The global impact of a CO_2 doubling is on the order of 1.33 percent of national output at 1987 output weights. The global impact is slightly larger than that for the United States because of the larger share of agriculture outside the United States. The surprising finding is the small size of the resulting differential.

The other major surprise is that the projected shifts in the sectoral and national distributions of output over the next century have a negligible effect upon the estimated impact of climate change on total world output. According to the calculations, the total impact of a CO_2 doubling is within .06 percentage points of 1.33 percent of output for the entire period 1987–2100. The reason for the lack of change in global vulnerability is the following. On the one hand, agriculture's share of output is shrinking in most countries, which leads to a decline in vulnerability. On the other hand, those countries with a large part of their economies devoted to agriculture are growing more rapidly than the industrialized economies, and growth is strongest in countries which appear to have high coastal vulnerability. These two trends appear to offset each other over the next 100 years. It should be noted, again, that, because of infirmities in the underlying estimates of damage, these projections are subject to large margins of error.

On the basis of these calculations, we will use a baseline estimate of the impact on real income of a CO_2 doubling, measured as a 3°C warming, of 1.33 percent of output. In addition, there is evidence that the impact increases sharply as the temperature increases, and we assume that the relationship is quadratic. Therefore, the final relationship between global temperature increase and income loss is

$$d(t) = (.0133/9)\ T(t)^2\ Q(t), \tag{4.2}$$

where $d(t)$ is the loss of global output.

Comparison with Other Estimates

The empirical study on which the DICE model is based can be compared with studies of other researchers. It must be emphasized that impact studies are in their infancy, that studies of impacts in low-income regions are virtually nonexistent, and that estimates for global impacts have scanty empirical support and are generally extrapolations from results for the United States.[4] For comparison purposes, we show the estimates from a number of different studies in table 4.3.

At present there are two comprehensive studies of the economic impacts of climate change by Cline (1992) and Fankhauser (1993). These two studies use largely the same data base as Nordhaus (1991c) and come to largely the same conclusions. Cline includes a larger group of

---

4. See Nordhaus 1993 for a discussion of results in developing countries.

Table 4.3
Comparison of estimates of impact of global warming: Impact on incomes of CO_2 doubling (in billions of 1988 U.S. dollars and percent of total output)

	United States				Global		
	Nordhaus	Cline	Fankhauser	Other	Fankhauser	Other	DICE Model
Heavily affected sectors							
Agriculture	1	15.2	7.4	1.2[b]	39.1	12.0[b]	
Coastal areas	10.7	2.5	2.3				
Energy	0.5	9	0				
Other sectors	38.1						
Wetland and species loss	[a]	7.1	14.8				
Health and amenity	[a]	8.4	30.3				
Other	[a]	11.2	12.1				
Total							
Billions of $	50.3	53.4	66.9				
Percent of output	1.0	1.1	1.3		1.5	1.9[c]	1.33[d]

Sources: Nordhaus 1991c, Cline 1992a, Fankhauser 1993.
Notes:
a. These are included in the total for "other sectors."
b. From Reilly and Hohmann 1993, with full adaptation and CO_2 fertilization.
c. The median response for the 50th percentile of outcomes from a survey of experts (Nordhaus 1994).
d. See table 4.2.

sectors than does Nordhaus. While Cline's discussion encompasses a number of different findings, many of the extensions outside of the marketed sectors are extremely tenuous and his central estimates tend to rely on studies that may lean toward overestimating the impacts. For example, Cline's estimates of the impact of losses from storms assume that storms become more severe whereas both the IPCC and the National Academy studies concluded that the effect of warming on storm intensity is ambiguous.[5] Another example is leisure activities, where he includes losses to skiing but excludes any gains from the much larger warm weather industries such as camping. For agriculture, Cline's central estimate relies on studies that allow for little or no

---

5. See IPCC 1990, 155, and NAS 1992.

adaptation. For the issue of species loss, Cline takes a very costly decision (that of the spotted owl) and uses that as the basis for valuation.

Even with a generally pessimistic cast, Cline's estimates of impacts are only marginally above those used here at the low end (1.1 percent of GNP for a 2.5°C warming in Cline 1992 as opposed to 1 percent of GNP for a 3°C warming in Nordhaus 1991c); and marginally lower than those used here for warming of 5°C and more.

A second study is a survey of different analyses by Fankhauser (1993). This study uses much the same methodology as those of Nordhaus and Cline but relies on additional studies and extends the analysis to the OECD countries and to the world. Fankhauser's results are also close to those used here, finding a 1.3 percent impact of a 3°C warming for the United States and a 1.5 percent impact for the world.

A third study uses a completely different approach but applies only to marketed output in the United States. This approach uses hedonic methods, examining the impact of climate variables cross sectionally on agriculture (in Mendelsohn, Nordhaus, and Shaw 1993, 1994). The results of the hedonic approach are to suggest that the impact of climate change on U.S. GNP (including only marketed sectors) is negligible.

A final estimate, more judgmental in nature, is a survey of experts conducted by the present author. Because estimating the impacts of climate change has proven extremely difficult, the present author has undertaken a survey of experts on the economic impacts of climate change on human and nonhuman systems. For scenario A, which is a 3°C warming in 2090, the "trimmed mean" of the survey is a decline of 2.9 percent of world output, while the median is 1.9 percent of gross world product (GWP). Those who have written on the impacts of global warming ("authors") as well as those who have undertaken empirical studies on the economic impacts ("researchers") have markedly lower estimates of the best guess, 1.6 and 1.8 percent, respectively. For the larger warming scenario of 6°C in 2175, the trimmed mean of experts is for an impact of 6.1 percent of global output, with the median cost of 4.5 percent. These estimates are higher than the numbers used in the DICE model for modest warming but are close to the estimates used here for the larger warming scenario. One major concern of most respondents is that the impact is thought to be considerably higher for low-income countries than for high-income countries.

A difficulty seen in many studies of climate change is that people look for problems and ignore opportunities; it is as if there exists an unconscious impulse to find costs and ignore benefits of climate change. A comparison of two sets of studies is instructive in this respect. Almost two decades ago, a series of studies was undertaken to investigate the impact of flights in the stratosphere on global *cooling*. Studies by d'Arge and others (summarized in National Research Council 1979) found that global cooling of 1°C would impose costs in a number of areas. Of the nine areas of costs identified in the global cooling studies (agriculture, forest products, marine resources, health, locational preferences, fuel demand, housing, public expenditures, and aesthetics), only two were examined in the EPA study (1989) of global warming and *none* were calculated by the EPA to produce benefits. The largest estimated cost in the global cooling studies was the amenity effect of cooling, determined through regional wage differentials. This topic was completely ignored in EPA 1989. One is tempted to say that environmental impact studies can find the cloud behind every silver lining.

A more general problem with most estimates of the impact of global warming is that they do not deal with the extremely long periods involved. Simply put, humans live, move, and die faster than climatic impacts are likely to be noticed. This point can be seen by asking what the effect today would be if one's grandparents or great-grandparents had contemplated a warmer globe. Many of them would have given the prospect a loud hurrah. Can one sensibly talk about health effects when we don't even know what next century's major health problems will be or what the population distribution will look like?

This review of existing analyses reinforces emphatically the point made here repeatedly of the need to study more thoroughly the potential damages from climate change so as to narrow the uncertainties about the impacts of future climate change.

The Costs of Reduction Emissions of Greenhouse Gases

A second central economic relationship is the marginal cost of emissions reduction, which portrays the costs that the economy undertakes to reduce a unit of GHG emissions. A wide variety of approaches is available to slow climate change. Most policy discussion has focused on reducing CO_2 emissions by reducing the consumption of fossil fuels through energy conservation, alternative energy sources (some would even contemplate nuclear power), and other measures. Such policies could be implemented through carbon taxes or tradable emissions permits. Other approaches include reforestation to remove CO_2 from the atmosphere and putting even more stringent controls on CFCs. Another option, definitely not in the environmentally correct package, would be to offset greenhouse warming through climatic engineering, primarily through measures to change the albedo (reflectivity) of the earth. Whatever the approach, economists emphasize the importance of cost-effectiveness—structuring policies to get the maximal reduction in harmful climatic change for a given level of expenditures.

The shape of the cost function for reducing CO_2 emissions has been thoroughly studied by numerous scholars and organizations in many countries. One of the most useful studies is that of John Weyant and his colleagues.[6] This study compares the costs of reducing emissions in a number of different U.S. and world models. Another approach has been a "bottom-up" or engineering approach, represented notably in the report of a U.S. National Academy of Sciences panel.[7]

I have surveyed a number of different models to estimate the costs of controlling CO_2 emissions, and a summary of that survey in shown in figure 4.2; this figure shows the results of the survey in Nordhaus 1991a comparing the costs of reducing CO_2 emissions in nine families of energy models. The relationship shows the marginal cost of controlling CO_2 emissions as a function of the carbon tax (or efficient regulatory equivalent thereof). Clearly, there continues to be much uncertainty and room for analysis in this area.

To motivate the approach followed in the DICE model, we develop a model of the cost of emissions reductions. Assume that there are conventional supply and demand functions for the carbon embodied in goods and services. For simplicity, assume that there are two goods, carbon-based and non-carbon-based output. Further assume that the carbon-based sector can be represented by standard isoelastic demand and supply curves. Then we can write the demand and supply of carbon-based output (measured in terms of the CO_2 emissions) as follows:

---

6. A convenient summary is available in Gaskins and Weyant 1993. The current study differs from most energy models in assuming that the capital stock adjusts quickly (within a 10-year period) to economic shocks. More realistic models assume a technology in which, upon construction, capital is relatively inflexible. Because of the high assumed short-run flexibility, the DICE model will have lower estimates of the short-run cost of reduction of GHGs than will many other models, although the long-run costs will be in line with other estimates.

7. See NAS 1992.

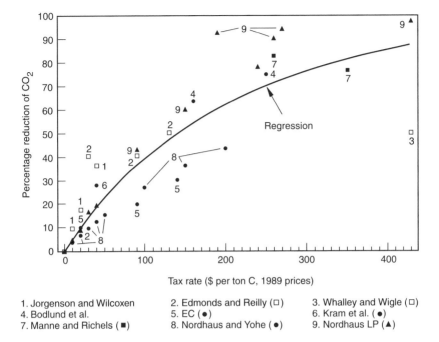

Tax rate ($ per ton C, 1989 prices)

1. Jorgenson and Wilcoxen	2. Edmonds and Reilly (□)	3. Whalley and Wigle (□)
4. Bodlund et al.	5. EC (●)	6. Kram et al. (●)
7. Manne and Richels (■)	8. Nordhaus and Yohe (●)	9. Nordhaus LP (▲)

Figure 4.2

Marginal cost of CO_2 reduction

Notes: Each numerical point or set of points corresponds to a model or family of models. "Regression" is equation fit to different models and used for DICE model cost function. Source: The author of each model is listed below, and the models are described in Nordhaus 1991, figure 2, from which this figure is drawn.

1. Jorgenson and Wilcoxen 1990.
2. Edmonds and Reilly 1983.
3. Whalley and Wigle 1991.
4. Bodlund et al. 1989.
5. EC 1992b.
6. Kram and Okken 1989.
7. Manne and Richels 1990a.
8. Nordhaus and Yohe 1983.
9. Nordhaus 1979.

$$E^d(t) = A(t)\, P(t)^{-\epsilon} \qquad \epsilon > 0, \tag{4.3}$$

$$E^s(t) = B(t)\, P(t)^{\delta} \qquad \delta > 0. \tag{4.4}$$

In these equations, $E^k(t)$ is the quantity supplied ($k=s$) or demanded ($k=d$) of the carbon-based output, which will lead to emissions of CO_2, while $A(t)$ and $B(t)$ are inessential functions of time, income, etc. $P(t)$ is the price of carbon-based output, ϵ is the price elasticity of demand, and δ is the price elasticity of supply.[8]

We are concerned with estimating the impact on GHG emissions of constraints in the form of taxes or regulations. In the model, we impose carbon constraints; this is economically equivalent to levying a carbon tax on the production or consumption of GHGs. This is most easily represented by an ad valorem tax, $\theta(t)$, which is measured as a fraction of the posttax price, $P(t)$. This yields the transformed equations

$$E^d(t) = A(t)\, P(t)^{-\epsilon}, \tag{4.5}$$

$$E^s(t) = B(t)\, [P(t)/(1 + \theta(t))]^{\delta}, \tag{4.6}$$

where $P(t)/(1 + \theta(t))$ is the net or pretax price, and $P(t)$ is the actual market price. The market equilibrium is obtained by solving equations (4.5) and (4.6) for price and quantity. We transform the variables by assuming that lowercase Roman letters represent the natural logarithms of uppercase Roman letters.

$$e^d(t) = a(t) - \epsilon\, p(t), \tag{4.7}$$

$$e^s(t) = b(t) + \delta[p(t) - \ln(1 + \theta(t))], \tag{4.8}$$

which yield equilibrium price and quantity as follows:

$$p(t) = [a(t) - b(t) + \delta \ln(1 + \theta(t))]/(\delta + \epsilon), \tag{4.9}$$

$$e(t) = [\delta a(t) + \epsilon b(t) - \epsilon\delta \ln(1 + \theta(t))]/(\delta + \epsilon). \tag{4.10}$$

Equation (4.10) shows the impact of changing carbon taxes on carbon consumption. For small taxes, $\ln(1 + \theta) \approx \theta$. Taking the derivative of (4.10) for small taxes, we obtain

$$\frac{\partial e(t)}{\partial \theta(t)} = -\frac{\epsilon\delta}{\delta + \epsilon}. \tag{4.11}$$

---

8. Note that the notation in this section is slightly different from that used in the balance of this study.

To determine the welfare effects of taxation, we use the standard formula for local deadweight loss, which gives the deadweight loss for a given tax, $D(\theta)$. This yields

$$D(\theta) = \tfrac{1}{2} \, [E(\theta) - E(0)] \, [P(\theta) - P(0)].$$

For small taxes, this reduces to

$$D(\theta) = \tfrac{1}{2} \, [-\epsilon\delta/(\delta+\epsilon)] \, [\delta/(\delta+\epsilon)]\theta^2 \, P(t) \, E(t)$$

or

$$D(\theta) = -\tfrac{1}{2} \, \epsilon \, [\delta/(\delta+\epsilon)]^2 \, \theta^2 \, P(t) \, E(t). \tag{4.12}$$

This equation shows that the deadweight loss is proportional to total revenue for the carbon-based good (PE) and to the square of the tax rate, and is a complicated function of the supply and demand elasticities.

Finally, we can derive the relationship between the deadweight loss, the carbon tax, and the reduction in emissions as follows. The dollar value of the per unit carbon tax for small taxes is given by $\theta(t)P(t)$. The percentage reduction of carbon usage for small taxes is equal to $-e(t)$. Therefore, we have from (4.11),

$$\frac{\partial e(t)}{\partial[P(t)\theta(t)]} = -\frac{\epsilon\delta}{\delta+\epsilon} = -\gamma, \tag{4.13}$$

where $\gamma = \epsilon\delta/(\epsilon+\delta)$. We can write this in terms of a formula to be estimated as follows:

$$E(\theta) = E(0)(1+\theta)^{-\gamma} \tag{4.14}$$

or

$$\ln[1 - \mu(\theta)] = -\gamma \ln(1+\theta) \tag{4.15}$$

or

$$\mu(\theta) \cong \gamma\theta, \tag{4.16}$$

where $\mu(\theta)$ is the fractional reduction in carbon production or emissions [$= 1 - E(\theta)/E(0)$]. Equation (4.16) states that (for small taxes) the fractional reduction of carbon emissions is proportional to the product of γ (which is a parameter determined by the elasticities of supply and demand) and the ad valorem tax rate on carbon.

Although this derivation was not known at the time, equation (4.15) was used in my survey (see Nordhaus 1991a) and represents a

convenient way to parameterize the marginal cost function for different models. It suggests that the appropriate way to compare models is
in terms of (1) the percentage difference of the carbon emissions from
a baseline (i.e., uncontrolled or untaxed) path, and (2) the percentage
carbon tax. Comparisons that look at the absolute levels of costs across
different models are likely to provide differences simply due to different baseline runs.

In representing the costs of reducing GHGs in optimization models,
it is convenient to work with the total cost function rather than the
marginal cost function. To a first approximation, the equation represented by (4.12) shows the economic costs from reducing carbon emissions. We can then substitute (4.16) into (4.12) to obtain the total cost
of reducing carbon emissions as a function of the reduction:

$$D(\theta) = -\tfrac{1}{2}\, \epsilon^{-1}\, \gamma^2\, \theta^2\, P(t)\, E(t)$$

$$= -\tfrac{1}{2}\, \epsilon^{-1}\, \gamma^2\, (\mu/\gamma)^2\, P(t)\, E(t)$$

$$= -\tfrac{1}{2}\, \epsilon^{-1}\, \mu^2\, P(t)\, E(t). \tag{4.17}$$

This equation states that the cost of reducing carbon emissions or output is inverse in the demand elasticity, quadratic in the reduction, and
proportional to the total expenditures on carbon output.

For flexibility, we estimate (4.17) with free coefficients. For data, we
use the total cost estimates from the survey in Nordhaus 1991a. The
cost function for reducing energy-sector CO_2 emissions was drawn
from the relationship depicted in figure 4.2; this was then combined
with engineering estimates of the cost of reducing CFC emissions
along with the costs of using forests to sequester CO_2. Combining these
three cost functions, we obtain the *cost function for efficiently reducing
greenhouse gases.* Nordhaus 1991c used the exact cost function in the
steady-state model. For the DICE model, however, we have parameterized the cost function by a power function. Estimating the cost function
from Nordhaus 1991a using ordinary least squares yields the following
equation:

$$\ln[D(\mu)/\text{GNP}] = -2.679 + 2.89\, \ln[\mu(\theta)]. \tag{4.18}$$

Figure 4.3 shows the estimated total cost curve for the reduction of
GHGs from the survey in Nordhaus 1991a as the solid line marked
"actual." The dashed line in figure 4.3 shows the parameterization
used in the DICE model. It should be recalled that the concept of GHGs

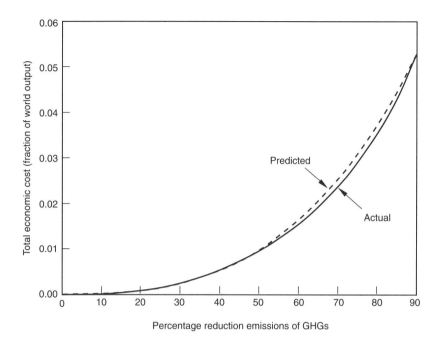

Figure 4.3
Actual and predicted cost function for reducing GHGs
Notes: "Actual" is the estimate of total costs of GHG reduction from Nordhaus 1991a, measured as a percent of world output. "Predicted" is from the parameterized equation in the text.

used in the optimization includes CFCs. The curve fits the data reasonably well. The curve has an exponent greater than 2 because of composition effects. The initial reduction of GHGs is extremely inexpensive because of the low cost of reducing CFC production; after that point, however, the costs become closer to the quadratic form in (4.17). According to equation (4.18), to reduce controllable GHGs (CO_2 and CFCs) by 50 percent would cost approximately 1 percent of global output. Alternatively, a total reduction of GHGs would cost $e^{-2.679}$ times GWP, or 6.86 percent of total output.

Greenhouse Gas Emissions and Energy-Efficiency Improvements

A final issue surrounds the appropriate treatment of alternative greenhouse gases and the trends in the energy-GNP and GHG-GNP ratio. There are no major analytical issues involved here, but the treatment will have a significant impact upon the optimal policy.

Trends in Energy-GNP and CO_2-GNP Ratios

In the aggregative model used here, as well as in other energy models, it is necessary to make a judgment as to the trends in energy use and GHG emissions per unit output. In the DICE model, the trend is represented by the parameter $\sigma(t)$, which is the ratio of uncontrolled CO_2-equivalent emissions to total output.

We begin with an analysis of CO_2 trends and then discuss the role of other greenhouse gases. The current model does not explicitly model the energy sector. For this reason, the trends in energy use per unit output as well as CO_2 emissions per unit output must be taken from other studies as well as from historical data. We begin with a historical review and then look at model projections.

Tables 4.4 and 4.5 show trends in energy-GNP ratios and CO_2 emissions from the use of fossil fuels per unit of GNP for various regions over the period 1929–89. These data have been collated from a wide variety of sources and are of varying comparability and quality. The energy data consist primarily of commercial energy use and exclude firewood and biomass. The data are probably most reliable for the United States and for the OECD region. The data for the former Soviet Union, China, and the rest of the world are dubious for most of the period partially because of unreliable data on energy consumption but much more significantly because of uncertainties about the measurement of output.[9] In addition, the ratios are plotted in figures 4.4 and 4.5.

We have constructed estimates of the rates of growth of these two ratios at the bottom of the tables. The rates of growth are for the entire period as well as for two subperiods. Table 4.4 shows that energy-GNP ratios have been declining steadily in most high-income countries during the last six decades. By contrast, the energy-GNP ratios appear to have increased in the former Soviet Union, China, and the rest of the developing world, but these latter ratios are subject to serious doubt given the uncertainties about the levels and growth rates of output. Overall, energy-GWP ratios appear to have fallen around 1.1 percent

9. Recent estimates of the real output of China and other poor countries suggest that using purchasing-power estimates of exchange rates rather than official exchange rates would lower the energy-GNP and CO_2-GNP ratios by a factor of between three and five. These corrections would bring China back into line with other countries. Even more questionable are the data on per capita GNP for Russia, which was around $100 per year in the 1991–92 period according to official exchange rates.

Table 4.4
Trends in energy-GNP ratios for different regions and subperiods, 1929–89

Energy/GNP in tons of coal equivalent per thousands of 1989 U.S. $ output

	1 USA	2 Japan	3 Rest of OECD	4 Former USSR	5 China	6 Rest of World	7 TOTAL
1929	0.938	0.288	0.626	0.205	0.567	0.359	0.620
1938	0.816	0.342	0.556	0.491	0.619	0.350	0.567
1950	0.762	0.253	0.438	0.539	0.814	0.408	0.552
1960	0.555	0.243	0.283	0.389	0.452	0.209	0.578
1970	0.487	0.312	0.255	0.598	3.182	0.290	0.224
1980	0.566	0.255	0.318	0.754	1.518	0.336	0.260
1989	0.456	0.164	0.310	0.831	1.316	0.460	0.317

Average annual growth rate of energy-GNP ratio, subperiods, %/year

	USA	Japan	Rest of OECD	Former USSR	China	Rest of World	TOTAL
1929–89	−1.195	−0.935	−1.163	2.361	1.414	0.414	−1.113
1929–50	−0.986	−0.618	−1.686	4.718	1.742	0.613	−0.548
1950–89	−1.307	−1.106	−0.880	1.114	1.237	0.308	−1.416

Table 4.5
Trends in CO_2-GNP ratios for different regions and subperiods, 1929–89

CO_2 Emission/GNP in tons of carbon per thousands of 1989 U.S. $ output

	1 USA	2 Japan	3 Rest of OECD	4 Former USSR	5 China	6 Rest of World	7 TOTAL
1929	0.600	0.189	0.428	0.135	0.391	0.237	0.409
1938	0.501	0.223	0.375	0.323	0.429	0.225	0.366
1950	0.446	0.156	0.287	0.358	0.568	0.264	0.343
1960	0.384	0.144	0.251	0.543	3.139	0.262	0.219
1970	0.393	0.180	0.245	0.584	2.100	0.317	0.219
1980	0.323	0.139	0.207	0.617	1.939	0.325	0.241
1989	0.256	0.088	0.164	0.586	1.270	0.333	0.232

Average annual growth rale of CO_2-GNP ratio, subperiods, %/year

	USA	Japan	Rest of OECD	Former USSR	China	Rest of World	TOTAL
1929–89	−1.410	−1.272	−1.581	2.481	1.982	0.566	−0.941
1929–50	−1.408	−0.915	−1.892	4.764	1.791	0.506	−0.832
1950–89	−1.412	−1.464	−1.413	1.272	2.085	0.598	−0.999

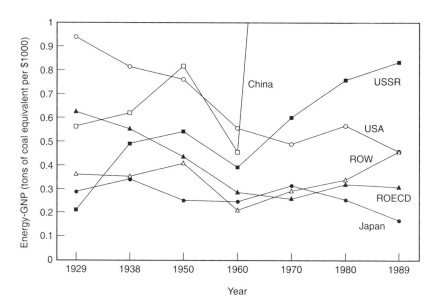

Figure 4.4
Energy-GNP ratios, 1929–89
Source: Table 4.4.

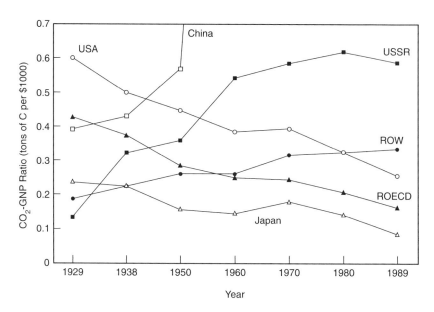

Figure 4.5
CO_2-GNP ratios, 1929–89
Source: Table 4.5.

per annum since 1929, where this is due to technological change, sectoral and country composition, and price changes on energy goods.

This study is primarily concerned with the trends in the CO_2-output ratio, shown in table 4.5. This ratio shows the same general pattern as for the energy-GNP ratio, with declines in the high-income regions and an increase over time in the poorer countries. Overall, the trend shows a decline of around 1 percent per annum in the CO_2-GWP ratio since 1929.

The data for the United States are probably more reliable than for the other regions. The data suggest a more rapid decline in the CO_2-GNP ratio than for the global total—a trend consistent with the apparent increase in CO_2 emissions per unit of output in many socialist and low-income countries. We observe a more rapid decline in the CO_2-GNP ratio for the period after the steep increase of fossil-fuel prices in the mid-1970s.

The appropriate concept for the analysis in the DICE model is the change in the CO_2-GNP ratio that would occur with technological trends, changes in the sectoral composition of output, changes in the fortunes of different regions, and with the market-induced rise in fossil-fuel prices as they are gradually exhausted. This would appear to be consistent with a decline of between 1 and 1.5 percent per annum in the CO_2-GNP ratio, with the smaller number consistent with the data for all countries and the larger number consistent with the longer-term data for the United States and the other high-income countries.

Another place to examine trends in energy and emissions relative to output is in energy models. These models either build in or generate changes in the CO_2-GNP ratio. Table 4.6 shows a sample of estimates from different models. Forecasts for the near term suggest decreases in the CO_2-GNP ratio for global models in the range of 1 to 1.5 percent per annum, although longer-term models suggest somewhat lower figures.

In conclusion, there is clearly no right answer as to the future trend in the CO_2-GNP ratio even in the absence of steps to control GHGs. Much depends upon price trends and the evolution of new technologies. The figure that seems most consistent with both historical trends and with energy models is for a long-term reduction in the CO_2-GNP ratio of 1.25 percent per annum. This might be as high as 1.5 percent per year or as low as 0.5 percent per year. Clearly, as is shown in accompanying figures and tables, there is great uncertainty about the trends.

Table 4.6
Projections of changes in energy efficiency and CO_2-GNP ratios in different studies (rate of change in item per unit GNP; percent per annum)

Study	Coverage	Energy	CO_2
Nordhaus-Yohe[a]	Global		
1975–2025		−1.3	−1.7
2025–2100		−0.3	−0.6
Manne-Richels[b]	US	−0.5	
IEW-1991[c]	World		
1990–2020			
Median forecast		−0.8	−1.4
Low[d]		−1.2	−1.2
High[e]		−1.8	−1.8

Notes:
a. Nordhaus and Yohe 1983, table 2.15.
b. This is change in "autonomous energy efficiency improvement." For a backcast, see Manne and Richels 1990b.
c. Presentation by Leo Schrattenholzer at International Energy Workshop, June 1991. This represents the median and range of forecasts of energy modelers.
d. This represents the 16th percentile of forecasts.
e. This represents the 84th percentile of forecasts.

Modeling of Other Greenhouse Gases

The role of nonenergy CO_2 emissions and non-CO_2 GHGs poses formidable problems for a number of reasons. The major complication is that reliable models for projecting these other GHGs do not exist today.

Fortunately (from a modeling perspective), the role of other greenhouse gases is likely to be relatively minor over the next century. Table 4.7 shows alternative estimates of CO_2-equivalent emissions, using total warming potentials as the weights for converting other GHGs into CO_2. The last column shows data from IPCC 1990 and a conversion of the IPCC data to put them on the same basis as the present study. The estimates of CO_2 emissions used here are slightly higher than those used in the IPCC, whereas the non-CO_2 GHGs use the IPCC figures. Clearly, CO_2 is the most significant contributor. It is likely to be even more important in the coming decades as CFCs are phased out and if, as recent evidence indicates, there are negative radiative offsets to CFC accumulation. Moreover, there appears to have been a decline in the

Table 4.7
Worksheet for different assumptions of greenhouse gas emissions (CO_2 equivalent emissions, billions of tons of carbon per year)

	1985	1990
Earlier study[a]		
CO_2	6.50	
CFCs	0.26	
Others	1.16	
TOTAL	7.92	
This study		
CO_2[b]	6.64	7.36
CFC[c]	0.89	1.09
Others[d]	2.35	2.59
TOTAL	9.89	11.04
IPCC (100-year integration)[e]		
CO_2		7.10
CFCs		1.30
Others		3.24
TOTAL		11.65
IPCC (200-year interpolated)[f]		
CO_2		7.10
CFCs		1.09
Others		2.59
TOTAL		10.78

Notes:
a. From Nordhaus 1991a.
b. As explained in text.
c. 1990 figure from IPCC 200-year integration; 1985 figure reduced by 4 percent per annum.
d. Same as (c), but growth rate is 2 percent per annum.
e. Use 100-year integration period to conform to the assumption of medium (3.0 percent per annum) discounting on GHGs.
f. Use 200-year integration period to conform to the assumption of low (1.0 percent per annum) discounting on GHGs. This reduced CO_2 equivalent by 12 percent for CFCs and 20 percent for other gases.

Table 4.8
Assumptions for endogenous greenhouse gases: Contribution to warming (in watts per meter squared)

A. IPCC assumptions

Year	1 CO_2	2 CFCs	3 TOTAL
1900	0.37	0.00	0.37
1960	0.79	0.02	0.81
1970	0.96	0.07	1.03
1980	1.20	0.16	1.36
1990	1.50	0.29	1.79
2000	1.85	0.37	2.22
2025	2.88	0.52	3.40
2050	4.15	0.67	4.82
2075	5.49	0.76	6.25
2100	6.84	0.76	7.60

B. IPCC assumptions by period used in DICE model[a]

1965	0.88	0.04	0.92
1975	1.08	0.11	1.19
1985	1.35	0.22	1.57
1995	1.68	0.33	2.00
2005	2.06	0.40	2.46
2015	2.47	0.46	2.93
2025	2.88	0.52	3.40
2035	3.39	0.58	3.97
2045	3.90	0.64	4.54
2055	4.42	0.69	5.11
2065	4.95	0.72	5.68
2075	5.49	0.76	6.25
2085	6.03	0.76	6.79
2095	6.57	0.76	7.33
2100	6.84	0.76	7.60

Source: IPCC 1990, 54, 57. [1] is "business as usual." [2] is "accelerated policies." Other CFCs than CFC-11, -12, and -22 are assumed to be .08 from 2000 on.
a. Interpolated from part A of this table.

Table 4.9
Assumptions for exogenous greenhouse gases: Contribution to warming (in watts per meter squared)

A. IPCC assumptions

Year	1 Methane Direct	2 Methane H_2O	3 N_2O	4 TOTAL
1900	0.10	0.03	0.027	0.16
1960	0.24	0.08	0.045	0.37
1970	0.30	0.10	0.054	0.45
1980	0.36	0.12	0.068	0.55
1990	0.42	0.14	0.100	0.66
2000	0.45	0.16	0.120	0.73
2025	0.56	0.19	0.210	0.96
2050	0.65	0.22	0.310	1.18
2075	0.66	0.23	0.400	1.29
2100	0.66	0.23	0.470	1.36

B. Data used in DICE model[a]

1965	0.27	0.09	0.050	0.41
1975	0.33	0.11	0.061	0.50
1985	0.39	0.13	0.084	0.60
1995	0.44	0.15	0.110	0.70
2005	0.47	0.17	0.138	0.78
2015	0.52	0.18	0.174	0.87
2025	0.56	0.19	0.210	0.96
2035	0.60	0.20	0.250	1.05
2045	0.63	0.21	0.290	1.14
2055	0.65	0.22	0.328	1.20
2065	0.66	0.23	0.364	1.25
2075	0.66	0.23	0.400	1.29
2085	0.66	0.23	0.428	1.32
2095	0.66	0.23	0.456	1.35
2105 and beyond	0.66	0.23	0.470	1.36

Source: IPCC 1990, 54, 57. [1] and [2] are "low emissions," while [3] is "business as usual."
a. Interpolated from part A of this table.

growth of concentrations in methane in the last few years, although the reasons are mysterious.

The treatment of nonenergy-CO_2 GHGs is as follows: The costs of reduction of both CO_2 and CFCs were explicitly included in the cost estimates for the reduction of GHGs in section B. Therefore, this component of GHG accumulation is explicitly included in the calculations. In the future, it is assumed that the growth of the uncontrolled nonenergy CO_2 and the uncontrolled CFCs are proportional to that of uncontrolled energy CO_2. This implies that nonenergy CO_2 and CFCs will grow at the same rate as CO_2 in an uncontrolled economy. The controllable part of GHG emissions is confined to CO_2 and CFCs.

The other GHGs are assumed to be exogenous because too little is known today about their sources, sinks, and abatement costs to include them in the economic estimates included in the DICE model. N_2O is of little importance, and we simply add a trend from the IPCC estimates representing the incremental contribution of N_2O to radiative forcing. Methane is a serious problem because we know little about its sources and have no good way of controlling it. Therefore, we simply add to radiative forcing the low projection of the IPCC to obtain the direct and indirect contributions of methane.

Tables 4.8 and 4.9 show the assumptions and estimated forcings of the different greenhouse gases in the IPCC analysis and those used in the DICE model. The exogenous GHGs in this projection are assumed to grow at a rate 1.25 percent per annum slower than real output in the base case, where that rate declines in parallel with the slowdown in the rate of overall technological change.

We have now concluded our discussion of the derivation of the DICE model. In the balance of this study, we discuss the results of the model, alternative approaches to policy, and the implications of uncertainty.

II   Model Results

5 Analysis of Policies to Slow Global Warming

Computational Procedures

Part I outlined the assumptions and structure of the DICE model of the economics of global warming. In this part, we outline the results of the model. We begin by sketching the computational approach taken in estimating the model and then present the results.

One of the difficulties of using mathematical programming (MP) approaches to economic and energy systems has been the complexity of calibrating the models to historical data. Unlike econometric models, MP models are not easily estimated. Moreover, the mapping from the parameters to the likelihood function is highly nonlinear, so even indirect techniques for calculating the "goodness of fit" are not currently available.

In the face of these difficulties, most practitioners calibrate their models to data in an intuitive fashion, selecting parameters on the basis of historical data, stylized facts, or statistical estimates. Generally, the "fitting" consists of a single observation (say one historical time period or the initial conditions). There are few attempts in the literature of MP models in which an attempt is made to match up the results of the models with actual data, and there are no examples that use econometric techniques to estimate MP models.

This study addresses this problem by using an extensive historical period for the first few time periods of the calculation. In the standard runs, we calculate both economic and climatic variables for the three historical periods 1965, 1975, and 1985; for the model, these dates are interpreted as the center points of the decades in which they fall. We can therefore make a rough judgment as to the validity of the model by examining the extent to which the model conforms to the historical data for this three-decade period. It should be emphasized, however, that there are many combinations of parameter values that could explain the historical data, so conformity to historical observation is but a partial validation of the model.

The model is solved using a language and nonlinear programming system known as GAMS (General Algebraic Modeling System). The technique used is a nested two-level algorithm. The inner algorithm is a refinement of the standard primal simplex method for solving linear programming problems first developed by G. Dantzig in the 1940s. The nonlinear constraints and objective function are solved with a reduced gradient and quasi-Newton method along with a projected Lagrangean algorithm attributed to S. M. Robinson. An introductory explanation to this is contained in Brooke, Kendrick, and Meeraus (1988).

The model has been run using the 386 version of the GAMS algorithm on various 386 compatible machines. The canonical runs presented below use a 40-period (400-year) calculation with terminal valuations (marginal values) on GHG concentrations, capital, and atmospheric temperature. These terminal valuations were obtained from a 60-period (600-year) run and are sufficient to stabilize the solution for the first 20 periods (200 years). The canonical 40-period run can be run from scratch in 0.94 minutes on an Intel Pentium-60 processor.

One of the difficulties of modeling dynamic growth processes is the need to truncate the estimation period, as discussed in the last paragraph. To ensure that the runs are not truncated prematurely, we have taken two steps. First, we calculate in a 60-period run the shadow prices at period 40 for carbon, capital, and the atmospheric temperature. We then impose these shadow prices in the 40th period of the 40-period run to ensure that future impacts and costs are not underweighted in the calculations. Second, we then make a number of runs of different lengths to test whether the values of the important variables are sensitive to the length of the period of calculation. By comparing the time-intensive 60-period run with the canonical 40-period run used in the estimates below, we see that there is no change in any of the variables for the first 21 periods (that is, through the calculation period corresponding to 2165). A summary of the comparisons of the runs of different lengths and the impacts upon the important variables is provided in the working paper (Nordhaus 1992a, appendix table A.1). The actual GAMS program is provided in the appendix to this study.

Alternative Approaches to Policy

In the discussion that follows, we analyze seven approaches to climate-change policy. The first is the uncontrolled or "laissez-faire" run in which there are no controls on greenhouse gases. This serves as a base case for comparison with other studies. The second is the "optimal" policy, a scenario in which GHG controls are set so as to maximize the discounted value of the utility of consumption. The third is a scenario in which we wait 10 years to implement policies so that our knowledge might be more secure. The fourth and fifth policies are ones that stabilize emissions—one at the 1990 rate of emissions and the other at 80 percent of the 1990 emissions rate. The sixth proposal is to undertake geoengineering, while the final approach is to curb emissions sufficiently to slow climate change and eventually stabilize climate. We now describe more precisely the policy experiments to which the model is applied.

No Controls ("Baseline")
The first run is one in which there are no policies taken to slow or reverse greenhouse warming. Individuals would adapt to the changing climate, but governments would take no steps to curb GHG emissions or to internalize the greenhouse externality. This policy is one that has been followed for the most part by nations through 1989.

Optimal Policy
The second case solves for the economically efficient or optimal policies to slow climate change. This run maximizes the present value of economic welfare; more precisely, this case maximizes the discounted value of utility subject to the various economic and geophysical constraints and relationships. This policy can be thought of as one in which the nations of the world gather to set the efficient policy for internalizing the greenhouse externality. It is assumed that the policy is efficiently implemented in the decade beginning in 1990, say through uniform carbon taxation with lump-sum recycling of revenues or through auctionable quotas with a perfect enforcement system.

Ten-Year Delay of Optimal Policy
This case is one which delays implementing the optimal policy for 10 years. This policy allows us to calculate the costs and benefits of

delaying implementing policies until our knowledge about the green-house effect is more secure. This approach was advocated by the U.S. government during the Bush administration. In this scenario, we assume that sufficient information is in hand so that the optimal policy is implemented starting in the decade beginning in 2000.

Stabilizing Emissions at 1990 Rates
Most policy proposals deal with intermediate objectives like stabilizing emissions. The first variant is motivated by the proposals put forth by many governments that CO_2 emissions be stabilized at 1990 levels. This policy was rejected by the United States under the Bush administration but was adopted by the Clinton administration in the President's Earth Day Message for 1993. This target is implemented in the DICE model as a stabilization of the radiative equivalent of CFC and CO_2 emissions at 1990 levels, where these are converted to a CO_2-equivalent basis. In quantitative terms, this represents an emissions limitation of 8.045 GtC or billion tons per year of CO_2 equivalent (carbon weight) of CO_2 and CFCs. This policy has no particular scientific or economic merit although it has the virtue of simplicity. Given a growing uncontrolled emissions path, it implies a growing percentage reduction of GHGs in the future.

Twenty Percent Emissions Reduction from 1990 Levels
A more ambitious strategy than emissions stabilization is actually to cut emissions, an approach that has been endorsed by many environmentalists and by "green" governments. A specific target that has been endorsed is a 20 percent cut in emissions. This is interpreted here as a 20 percent cut of the combination of CFC and CO_2 emissions from 1990 levels, where these are converted to a CO_2 equivalent basis. In quantitative terms, this represents an emissions limitation of 6.436 billion tons per year of CO_2 equivalent. Again, this policy has no particular merit, but it is easily understood and can be hammered onto political platforms.

Geoengineering
A radical technological option would be geoengineering, which involves large-scale engineering to offset the warming effect of greenhouse gases. Such options include injecting particles into the atmosphere that would increase the backscattering or reflecting of incoming sunlight; reforesting to increase the biomass in vegetation; or

stimulating absorption of carbon in the oceans. Two particularly interesting proposals include shooting smart mirrors into space with 16-
inch naval rifles or seeding the oceans with iron to accelerate carbon
sequestration.[1] The U.S. National Academy of Sciences survey concludes, "Perhaps one of the surprises of this analysis is the relatively
low costs at which some of the geoengineering options might be implemented."[2] On the basis of the U.S. National Academy of Sciences survey, we treat geoengineering as economically costless.[3] At the same
time, many ecologists have grave reservations about the environmental impacts of the geoengineering options. Nonetheless, because of the
high cost of other mitigation strategies, this scenario is useful as a baseline to determine the overall economic impact of greenhouse warming
and of policies to combat warming.

Climate Stabilization
A final approach is much more ambitious and involves taking steps to
slow and eventually stabilize the increase in global temperature so as
to prevent major ecological impacts. One proposal is to slow the rate
of temperature increase to 0.1°C per decade from 1950. This policy is,
by my calculation, infeasible given the current buildup of GHGs. A
feasible policy is to slow the GHG-induced global temperature increase to 0.2°C per decade after 1985, with an upper limit of a total
increase of 1.5°C from 1900.

Results of the Two Runs

Overall Results

We now summarize the overall results for the seven scenarios
described above. In the results that follow, we show the results
for a subset of the seven runs as figures and show detailed tabular
values for the optimal and uncontrolled runs. Table 5.1 shows the

---

1. The issues of geoengineering are discussed in NAS 1992, chap. 28.
2. NAS 1992, 460.
3. The U.S. National Academy of Sciences report describes a number of options that
provide the theoretical capability of unlimited offsets to the radiative effects of GHGs at
a cost of less than $1 per ton carbon (see NAS 1992, chap. 28). If these prove feasible and
environmentally acceptable, the cost of offsetting all global GHG emissions today would
fall from approximately $1400 billion per year according to the estimates underlying the
DICE model to around $8 billion per year. Given the very small nature of the costs, we
have treated geoengineering as costless.

Table 5.1
Net benefit of alternative policies on discounted consumption

Case	Policy	Discounted Value of Consumption			Impact on Annualized Value of Consumption (billions of $/yr.)
		Base Value (trillions of 1989 U.S.$)	Impact of Program: Difference (billions of $)	Percent Difference	
1	No mitigation	730.90	0	0.00	0
2	Optimum	731.17	271	0.04	11
3	10-year delay	731.14	243	0.03	10
4	Stabilize emissions at 1990 level	723.83	(7,069)	(0.98)	(283)
5	Stabilize emissions at 80 percent of 1990 level	718.38	(12,521)	(1.74)	(501)
6	Geoengineering	736.50	5,601	0.76	224
7	Stabilize climate at maximum of 1.5 degrees C increase	689.92	(40,980)	(5.94)	(1,639)

Notes: The present value of consumption is calculated as the consumption stream from 1990 on discounted to 1990 at the rate of interest on goods and services calculated in the optimal program. Values in parentheses indicate negative values. All values are in 1989 U.S. dollars. Annualized consumption is calculated at rate of interest less rate of growth (equal to .04) times discounted value of consumption.

overall evaluation of the different policies. The first column shows the discounted values of consumption for the seven paths. This is calculated as the present value of consumption after 1990 discounted at the market rate of return on capital (discounted back to 1990 in 1989 prices).

The optimal policy in row 2 has greater value than any policy other than geoengineering; it has a net benefit of $271 billion relative to a no-controls policy. This number is absolutely large, although it is only 0.04 percent of the discounted value of consumption. The cost of delaying the optimal policy by 10 years is estimated to be $28 billion.

The different policies for stabilizing emissions and climate are economically disadvantageous and show different levels of net cost. A policy that stabilizes emissions at 1990 levels has the lowest net cost of the three stabilization scenarios, with net discounted costs (that is, costs in excess of benefits) of slightly over $7 trillion; the more stringent emissions stabilization approach has net discounted costs of $12.5 trillion. The most costly option is stabilizing climate, which has a discounted net cost of $41 trillion.

The sixth row shows the value of the geoengineering option, which is the same as the overall economic impact of climate change. The net benefit from a costless geoengineering option is $5.6 trillion, relative to a policy of no controls.

In general, these numbers are mind numbing in absolute size—largely because we are considering global output over the indefinite future. An alternative measure is in terms of a consumption annuity, shown in the last column of table 5.1. This shows the cost or benefit in terms of an annuity that converts the present value into a stream of net costs or benefits at an annuity rate of 4 percent per annum; this number represents the approximate difference between the real interest rate and the rate of growth of consumption. The annualized consumption streams can be compared to an annual consumption rate of approximately $20,000 billion in period 4 (1990–99).

Table 5.2 shows the levels of output and consumption in the optimal and baseline runs, while table 5.3 shows the differences between the two runs. In general, we report results only through 2100 because the results beyond that date are too conjectural. *However, it is important to note that the calculations take into account economic growth, warming, and damages beyond 2100.* This point is important, for studies by the present

Table 5.2
Values of output and consumption in uncontrolled and optimal runs of DICE model

Decade Centered on Year	World Output*		World Consumption*	
	Uncont	Optimal	Uncont	Optimal
1965 proj	8,520	8,520	6,652	6,652
act	8,519		na	
1975 proj	12,680	12,680	10,017	10,017
act	12,708		na	
1985 proj	17,890	17,890	14,273	14,273
act	17,819		na	
1995 proj	24,073	24,073	19,364	19,363
2005 proj	31,095	31,094	25,182	25,179
2025 proj	46,928	46,931	38,390	38,389
2075 proj	88,213	88,311	73,145	73,217

* In billions of 1989 U.S. dollars.
Symbols: "proj" = projected levels from model; "act" = actual levels; "uncont" = values when no controls are placed on greenhouse gases; "optimal" = values when GHG controls are set to maximize utility of consumption; "na" = not available.

Table 5.3
Impact of optimal program on consumption and on value of objective function in DICE model

Decade Centered on Year	Difference between Uncontrolled and Optimal Paths for	
	Output	Consumption
1995	0	−1
2005	−1	−3
2015	1	0
2025	3	−1
2035	10	3
2045	21	12
2055	39	26
2065	65	45
2075	98	72
2085	139	105
2095	187	145
2105	242	191
Discounted value to 1989 prices		
In billions of U.S. $	a	271[b]
As percent of total discounted global consumption, 1990 on	a	0.037 percent

Notes:
a. Because output double counts returns, the discounted value of output is not calculated.
b. This value is the difference in the attained maximum values of the objective function converted to 1989 prices by using the marginal values of consumption for 1995.

author have been incorrectly criticized by William Cline as "focusing on the impact of a doubling of carbon-dioxide-equivalent rather than very long term warming."[4]

For these calculations, the value of output is "green" gross world output (GGWP). Conceptually, GGWP equals output less the flow of

4. Cline 1992a, 307. Cline misstates the reason for the difference in results of his work from Nordhaus 1991c and the DICE model, arguing that it arises from inclusion of very long-term warming and the nonlinearity of the damage function (Cline 1992, 309). As chapter 6 shows, neither of these is the source of the difference; rather, the high level of abatement in the Cline study comes solely because of the very low discount rate chosen. The critical importance of the discount rate was clearly shown in Nordhaus 1991c, is apparent in the DICE model, and will be fully discussed in chapter 6.

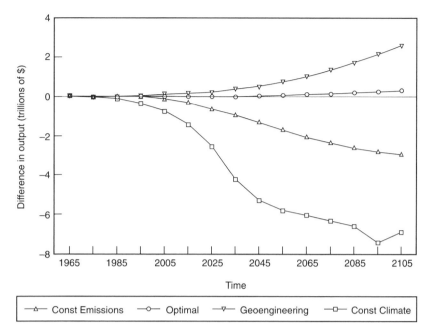

Figure 5.1
Differences in global output
(Difference from no-controls baseline, trillions 1989 U.S. dollars)

damages from climate change less the costs of mitigation. For the best-guess parameter values, there is relatively little difference in output or consumption for the first few decades. Until the middle of the next century, the optimal GHG controls are at modest levels. For the second half of the next century, however, the value of controlling GHGs makes a substantial difference to global output, with net benefits (that is, reduced damages less costs of controls) on the order of $200 billion in 1989 prices.

Figure 5.1 shows graphically the impact of four of the policies. We have omitted the others to reduce the clutter in the figure. One surprise in this calculation is that the difference between a policy of no controls and the optimal policy is relatively small through the next century. This is because of the modest level of warming for the coming decades as well as the low levels of GHG controls in the near term. By the end of the next century, however, the optimal strategy enjoys annual output levels almost $200 billion higher than the uncontrolled path; this is the difference between the damage averted and the costs of controls.

The flow impact, relative to the optimum, is somewhat less than one percent of real output at the maximum.

While the difference between the no-controls and the optimal policies is small, big stakes exist both in the geoengineering option and in the climate-stabilization and emissions-stabilization options. The impact of an inexpensive geoengineering solution would be quite substantial, because it would cut the costs of both climate damage and mitigation. At the other extreme, there is potential for a major waste of resources if the greenhouse policies go too far. The impact on world output of stabilizing greenhouse gases is *net* losses in output of over $3 trillion annually by the end of the next century, while the cost of stabilizing climate is around $7 trillion annually by the end of the next century.

Emissions, Concentrations, and Climate Change

We next show some of the details of the model runs. Figure 5.2 shows the emissions in different scenarios. Recall that our estimates of GHG emissions include only CO_2 and CFCs, and the other GHGs are taken as exogenous for control purposes. Table 5.4 shows the numerical results for the baseline and optimal paths.

The result of the lower emissions on GHG concentrations is shown in figure 5.3 and table 5.4. We calculate that the concentrations of GHGs (CO_2 and CFCs only) will have risen from 745 billion tons of carbon equivalent in 1990 to 1500 billion tons by the end of the twenty-first century in the uncontrolled case. As a result of imposing controls, GHG concentrations at the end of the next century would be reduced by slightly more than 100 billion tons of carbon equivalent, to around 1400 billion tons of carbon equivalent, in 2100. Note that even with emissions stabilized at 80 percent of 1990 levels, the atmospheric concentrations of CO_2-equivalent concentrations continue to rise. The 10-year delay in implementing GHG restraints shows virtually no difference from the optimal path and is not included in the graph. The climate-stabilization approach shows dramatic cuts in emissions; the resulting impact on concentrations is to peak at around 800 GtC in 2025, after which concentrations need to decline.

The effect of alternative policies on the projected global mean temperature is shown in figure 5.4 and table 5.5, where the calculated change in global mean surface temperature (relative to the base period

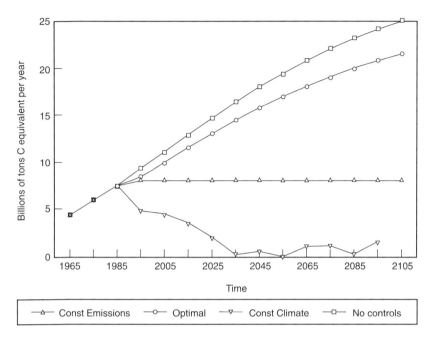

Figure 5.2
Greenhouse-gas emissions
(CO$_2$ and CFCs only)

of 1865) is shown. According to the model used here, global mean temperature has risen 0.6°C from the base period to 1985. In the uncontrolled case, global mean temperature is estimated to rise 3.4°C by the end of the next century, for an average decadal increase of 0.24°C per decade. In the optimal case, the global mean temperature is estimated to rise 3.2°C by the end of the next century, for an average decadal increase of 0.22°C; the optimal path shows a modest decline in the growth rate of global temperatures, with a rise of about 0.2°C less than the uncontrolled path by the end of the next century. The policy that cuts emissions to 80 percent of the 1990 level shows continued growth in temperatures, rising to 2.25°C by the end of the next century. This surprising result shows that even ambitious emissions-reduction policies will slow climate change only modestly.

Many readers have been struck by the very small impact that the optimal policy or even more ambitious policies make upon the concentration and temperature trajectories. The reason for the modest impact is straightforward. According to our estimates, the impact of warming

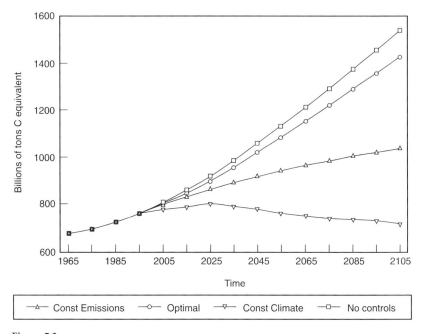

Figure 5.3
Atmospheric GHG concentrations
(CO_2 and CFCs only)

Table 5.4
Values of GHG emissions and concentrations in base and optimal runs of DICE model (billions of tons carbon equivalent)

Decade Centered on Year		GHG Emissions (per year)		GHG Concentrations (end of period)	
		Uncont	Optimal	Uncont	Optimal
1965	proj	4.42	4.42	677	677
	act	na	na	677	677
1975	proj	5.89	5.89	698	698
	act	na	na	na	na
1985	proj	7.53	7.53	727	727
	act	7.53	7.53	na	na
1995	proj	9.28	8.46	764	764
2005	proj	11.07	10.07	809	803
2025	proj	14.62	13.00	921	902
2075	proj	21.96	19.01	1293	1221

Note: Total GHG emissions and concentrations are the CO_2 equivalent of both CO_2 and CFCs converted into the equivalent mass of carbon in CO_2 that would yield the equivalent radiative warming.
Symbols: "proj" = projected levels from model; "act" = actual levels; "uncont" = results of uncontrolled run; "optimal" = results of run with emissions optimized; "na" = not available.

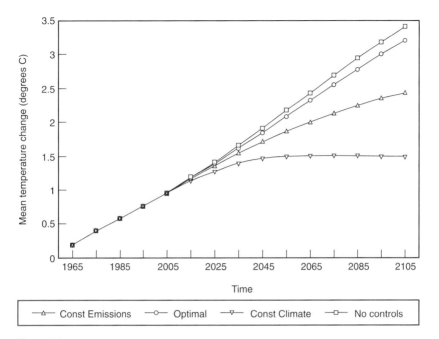

Figure 5.4
Global mean temperature
(Change from 1865)

Table 5.5
Values of global mean surface temperature in uncontrolled and optimal runs of DICE
model (difference from 1865 levels, °C)

Decade Centered on Year	Temperature Increase	
	Optimal	Uncont
1965 proj	0.20	0.20
1975 proj	0.40	0.40
1985 proj	0.58	0.58
act	0.3–0.6*	0.3–0.6*
1995 proj	0.76	0.76
2015 proj	0.96	0.96
2025 proj	1.38	1.40
2075 proj	2.55	2.68
2105 proj	3.20	3.40

*Estimated rise of global mean temperature from the 1865 period according to IPCC
1990 and NAS 1992.
Symbols: "proj" = projected levels from model; "act" = actual levels; "uncont" = results
of uncontrolled run; "optimal" = results of run with emissions optimized.

upon the global economy is relatively small, amounting to around 1.3 percent of global output for a 3°C average warming. The costs of slowing the warming are very small for the first increment of policy and then rise sharply as the degree of emissions restraint increases. The resultant of these two factors is that the optimal degree of slowing global warming is but a small part of the future warming.

Two other factors lead to the small decrease in the extent of warming in the optimal path. First, there is a great deal of momentum of climate change given the existing degree of buildup of GHGs and the lags in the response of the climate to GHG increases. According to the model used here, if GHG concentrations were stabilized at the level expected in the year 2000—an extremely ambitious target requiring a drop in emissions of about 70 percent over the next two decades—global mean temperature would still rise by around 1.6°C above the base level.

The second reason why the reduction in the rate of warming is so slight is the nonlinear relationship between GHG concentrations and warming. According to scientific studies, the relationship between equilibrium warming and CO_2 concentrations is logarithmic. This implies that moving from 300 to 315 ppm of CO_2 increases equilibrium temperature by .215°C while moving from 585 to 600 ppm of CO_2 increases equilibrium temperature by only .111°C. The implication of this nonlinear relationship is that policies that reduce the last few percent increase of CO_2 concentrations have a relatively small impact upon the path of temperature. This result is the opposite of the usual diminishing returns seen almost everywhere in economic systems.

Other Economic Variables

The model outputs in the mathematical programming analysis consist of both physical output (such as energy consumption or GHG emissions) as well as economic values (such as the values of output and consumption). The economic values are generated in unusual form as "present values."[5] In the presentation that follows, however, we have converted all the present-value prices to constant prices that correspond to 1989 U.S. dollars.

---

5. A word of explanation concerning the difference between the variables is useful. The constant-dollar prices are the familiar indexes that show economic values that have been corrected for inflation. They simply take the nominal value of an economic variable and divide it by a price index. The present-value prices use instead the prices discounted back to the present (or first period). For example, assume that the price of a ton of coal

Table 5.6
Savings rate and rate of return in uncontrolled and climate-stabilization runs

Decade Centered on Year	Net Savings Rate (percent of net output)			Rate of Return (percent per year)		
	Optimal	Stab	Diff	Optimal	Stab	Diff
1975 proj	7.6	7.6	0.0	6.5	6.5	0.0
1985 proj	7.1	7.1	0.0	6.2	6.2	0.0
1995 proj	6.4	7.3	−0.9	5.9	6.1	−0.2
2015 proj	5.3	8.5	−3.3	5.4	5.5	−0.1
2025 proj	4.7	10.0	−5.3	5.2	5.1	0.1
2075 proj	2.7	9.8	−7.1	4.4	4.5	−0.1

Note: The savings rate is equal to the ratio of net investment to net output. The rate of return is calculated as the marginal product of capital on an annualized basis.
Symbols: "proj" = projected values from model; "optimal" = value in optimal control run; "stab" = values in run that stabilizes climate; "diff" = difference between the optimal and stabilization scenarios.

Table 5.6 shows for the optimal and the climate-stabilization approaches the values of the net savings rate (net world output less consumption divided by net world product) and the net rate of return on capital (measured as the current-period rate of return on capital net of depreciation). As can be seen in these figures, there are no substantial differences in the rates of return between these two scenarios (or, indeed, among any of the scenarios). However, the model shows a decline in the net return on capital over time. The decline in the net return on capital is important for evaluating different control strategies. Most analyses of environmental issues take the discount rate as constant and exogenous. In fact, the assumption of exogeneity seems satisfied in the case examined here; however, given the assumptions that are built into the model, the discount rate should decline over time as economic and population growth slows.

On the other hand, the net savings rate differs markedly between the optimal and the climate-stabilization scenarios. In this calculation, I measure net savings as the difference between the net world product in the optimal case and consumption in the optimal or climate-stabili-

---

in the year 2015 is $45 and that the appropriate discount rate is 9.5 percent per year. To calculate the present-value price in 1990, we divide the $45 by the present-value factor of 9.5 percent per year compounded over 25 years, which is a factor of 10. This gives the present-value price of $4.50 for the coal. In the presentation here, we will translate the present-value prices into constant-dollar prices.

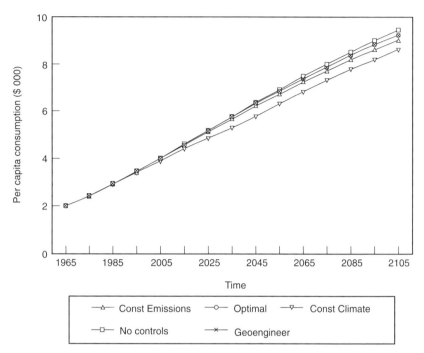

Figure 5.5
Consumption per capita
(1989 U.S. dollars per capita)

zation cases, and the net savings rate is net savings divided by net world output. This calculation is broader than the normal definition of investment to reflect the fact that investment can take place either in physical capital or in "climate" capital in the form of reducing emissions. The striking result of this calculation is to show that *the savings rate in the climate-stabilization case rises sharply over time because of the need to reduce emissions so sharply.*

Figure 5.5 shows the trajectory of real consumption per capita in five of the cases. The noteworthy feature of this figure is that, even though there are differences among the cases studied here, the overall economic growth projected over the coming years swamps the projected impacts of climate change or of the policies to offset climate change. In these scenarios, future generations may be worse off as a result of climate change, but they are still likely to be better off than current generations. In looking at this graph, I was reminded of Tom Schelling's remark a few years ago that the difference between a climate-change and a no-climate-change scenario would be thinner than the line drawn by a number 2 pencil used to draw the curves. Thanks to the improved resolution of computerized graphics, we can now barely spot the difference!

Emissions Controls and Carbon Taxes

Table 5.7 and figure 5.6 show the all-important control rate of greenhouse gases for the different policies. These show the extent to which GHG emissions are reduced below their uncontrolled levels. In the optimal path, the rate of emissions reduction is approximately 10 percent of GHG emissions in the near future, rising to 15 percent late in the next century. The environmental path of a 20 percent cut in emissions from the 1990 level shows steeply rising control rates, with the rate of control reaching 70 percent by the end of the next century, while the climate-stabilization policy has emissions-control rates of near 100 percent after the first third of the next century.

Governments may choose to implement a GHG control strategy by imposing carbon emission taxes; carbon taxes[6] are defined as the tax that would impose an equivalent tax per unit of global warming potential on all emissions of greenhouse gases. These can be calculated in the optimal program as the level of the carbon tax that would lead to the desired control rate. Technically, this is calculated as the derivative of the objective function with respect to an additional unit of carbon emissions, where the objective function is scaled in terms of consumption in 1989 prices.

Table 5.7 and figures 5.7 and 5.8 show the optimal carbon taxes over time in the different runs. The optimal path shows a carbon tax of around $5 per ton carbon (or the equivalent in other GHGs) for the first control period, 1990–99. For reference, a $10 per ton carbon tax will raise coal prices by $7 per ton, about 25 percent at current U.S. coal prices. The carbon tax in the optimal case increases gradually over

---

6. The calculation of the carbon tax is indirect because it is a "dual variable." The model produces calculated dual variables for both consumption and for carbon emissions. The units of these are, respectively, the change in the objective function from a unit change in consumption $(cc.m)$ and the change in the objective function from a unit change in carbon emissions $(ee.m)$. Dividing $ee.m$ by $cc.m$ gives the implicit price of carbon per unit of consumption, which provides a calculation of the carbon tax. For technical reasons, we use capital's shadow price rather than consumption's shadow price. Hence, in terms of GAMS output, the carbon tax is -1000 times "$ee.m/kk.m$," where the minus sign reflects the fact that carbon emissions are a "bad" rather than a "good."

Table 5.7
Level of control and carbon tax equivalent on greenhouse gases in optimal run of
DICE model

Decade Centered on Year	Rate of Control of GHGs* (percent)	Carbon Tax Equivalent (1989 $ per ton C)
1965 proj	0.0	$ 0.00
1975 proj	0.0	0.00
1985 proj	0.0	0.00
1995 proj	8.8	5.29
2005 proj	9.6	6.77
2025 proj	11.1	10.03
2075 proj	13.4	17.75

* As percent of uncontrolled emissions.
Note: Carbon tax is per ton of CO_2 equivalent, carbon weight.
Symbol: "proj" = projected values from model.

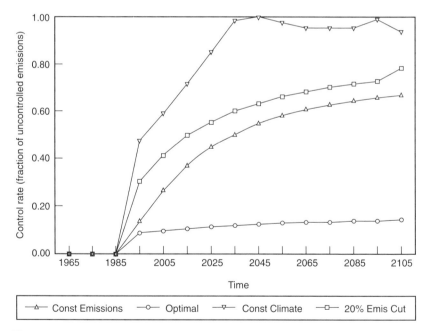

Figure 5.6
GHG control rate
(Reduction in GHG emissions)

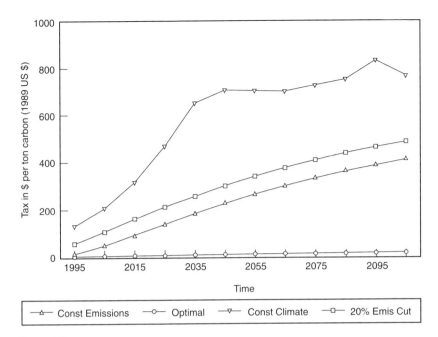

Figure 5.7
Carbon tax rate

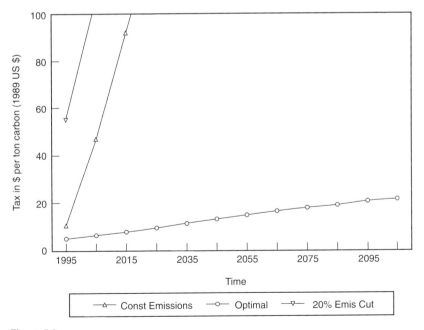

Figure 5.8
Carbon tax rate
(Reduced scale)

time to around $20 per ton carbon by the end of the next century. The rising tax primarily reflects the rising level of global output rather than increasingly stringent control efforts.

The 10-year delay (not shown) has a zero tax in the fourth period, but then is virtually indistinguishable from the optimal policy. The policy of no mitigation obviously has a zero carbon tax. The emissions-stabilization policies have steeply rising carbon taxes, reaching $200 per ton early in the next century and climbing to between $400 and $500 per ton by the end of the next century. The climate-stabilization policy shows even more dramatic carbon taxes, in the range of $600 to $850 per ton after 2025. Clearly, very substantial fiscal or regulatory steps are necessary to bring about stabilizing emissions or climate.

Conclusions

This chapter presents the results for the best-guess case of the DICE model. In this section, we summarize the principal conclusions. The present study has investigated the implications of economic growth on future climate change as well as the impact of different environmental control strategies upon the global economy. This study takes the approach that an efficient strategy for coping with greenhouse warming must weigh the costs and benefits of different policies in an intertemporal framework. Using this approach, the major results and reservations are the following.

This study has examined seven different approaches to GHG control: no controls, economic optimization, geoengineering, stabilization of emissions and climate, and a 10-year delay in undertaking climate-change policies. Among these seven, the rank order from a pure economic point of view given current information is geoengineering, economic optimum, 10-year delay, no controls, stabilizing emissions, cutting emissions by 20 percent, and stabilizing climate. The advantage of geoengineering over other policies is enormous, although this result assumes the existence of an economical and environmentally benign geoengineering option.

It is instructive to compare these results with those from other economic studies. The studies of Manne and Richels (1990a, 1992), Peck and Teisberg (1992), and Kolstad (1993) yield conclusions that are roughly similar to those reported here. All these studies contain explicit or implicit relationships between emissions control rates and carbon taxes; the relationships are broadly similar to those found in this study, although studies with more detailed energy sectors have more complex dynamics than those seen here. The studies by Jorgenson and Wilcoxen (1990, 1991; see especially the 1991 study) show a lower set of carbon taxes needed to reduce GHG emissions than those shown here largely because of the slow growth rate assumed in the Jorgenson-Wilcoxen model.

Several other studies—those by Cline (1992), Peck and Teisberg (1992), Kolstad (1993) as well as earlier studies by Nordhaus (1979, 1991b, c)—also determine the optimal emissions control rates and carbon taxes. With the exception of Cline 1992, all the earlier studies show optimal policies in the general range of those determined here. A study by Hammitt, Lempert, and Schlesinger (1992) traces out alternative control strategies to attain certain temperature constraints; while not determining an optimal path, this study concludes that a "moderate reduction strategy" is less costly than an "aggressive" approach if either the temperature-concentrations sensitivity ($T_{2 \times CO_2}$) is low or if the allowable temperature change is above 3°C. The study by Cline (1992), in contrast, has much higher control rates. The more stringent controls in the Cline study are due to a number of features—primarily, however, because the Cline result is not grounded in explicit intertemporal optimization, makes a number of assumptions that tilt toward stringent controls, and assumes a very low discount rate that raises serious theoretical and empirical questions (a point that is investigated in detail in chapter 6).

It must be emphasized that the present analysis has a number of important qualifications. The most important shortcoming is that the damage function, particularly the response of developing countries and natural ecosystems to climate change, is poorly understood at present; moreover, the potential for rapid or catastrophic climatic change, for which precise mechanisms and probabilities have not been determined, cannot currently be ruled out. Furthermore, the calculations omit other potential market failures, such as ozone depletion, air pollution, and research and development (R&D), which might reinforce the logic behind GHG reduction or carbon taxes. And finally, this study abstracts from issues of uncertainty, in which risk aversion and the possibility of learning may modify the stringency and timing of control strategies. These topics are ones that will be tackled in the chapters that follow.

III

Risk and Uncertainty
in Policy toward
Climate Change

Sensitivity Analysis of the DICE Model

Introduction to the Analysis of Risk and Uncertainty

Efforts to deal with the challenges of climate change must recognize the enormous uncertainties concerning both future climate change and our knowledge of the future—indeed, uncertainties are a critical constraint on determining appropriate policies toward climate change. We have little knowledge of many economic and scientific aspects of climate change. For example, our models of both the economy and ecology rely on imperfectly understood geophysical processes, such as the climatic reaction to changing GHGs or the time scale of the reaction. In addition, projections of future emissions, concentrations, and temperature paths crucially depend on conjectural forces affecting population, productivity growth, and energy efficiency. Moreover, we do not know how fast our uncertainties will narrow or where we would be best advised to apply our research dollars to narrow the uncertainties.

In part III, I will focus on these crucial issues of uncertainty. The purpose will not be to resolve the uncertainties, which is impossible without the passage of time and the accumulation of better natural and social scientific understanding. Rather, the purpose will be to analyze the impact of uncertainty about the underlying parameters and models on the uncertainty about the overall projections of the pace of climate change, on the impact on the economy, and on the optimal policies that we should follow today. Knowing the odds will not allow one to become a sure winner at the gambling table, but it allows one to estimate the distributions of gains and losses and suggest good strategies.

The approach followed here will be an application of the theory of expected utility and subjective probability. This approach was pioneered by J. von Neumann and Oskar Morgenstern (1943), L. J. Savage (1954), R. D. Luce and H. Raiffa (1958), and others. Under this approach, we identify the uncertain features of our system, make an estimate of the probabilities of the uncertain variables (these being "subjective probabilities"), and then treat the systems as if the subjective probabilities were objective betting odds.

The analysis will proceed in three steps. In this chapter, I perform a preliminary analysis of the different uncertainties. At this stage, I will identify the uncertain parameters in the DICE model and estimate the sensitivity of the results to a hypothesized change in each of the variables. Then the second half of the chapter discusses issues that are less easily treated, such as uncertainties about the model specification or the use of optimization models. At the end of this chapter, the reader should have a good sense of which parameters are likely to change the results significantly and which are relatively unimportant to the outcomes.

The next chapter takes up the use of subjective probabilities more rigorously. On the basis of the analysis of this chapter, I identify eight of the most important uncertain variables or parameters. Then, relying on existing studies, I develop subjective probability distributions for each of the important uncertain variables. I then perform a Monte Carlo estimate of the impact of uncertainty on both the climatic and economic outcomes and on the optimal policies. On the basis of these runs we will see that there is indeed great uncertainty about the optimal policy, both from the point of view of the optimal reduction of greenhouse gases and that of the optimal carbon tax rate necessary to induce the optimal reductions.

The final chapter of this part investigates the issues of learning and the value of information. It matters greatly for our policies how much we can reduce the uncertainties and when the uncertainties will be reduced. If the economic and scientific uncertainties will be resolved very soon, we may decide to wait before instituting drastic control policies; if uncertainties will not be resolved quickly, we might be advised to undertake expensive precautionary measures today to prevent catastrophic losses. Chapter 8 on uncertainties addresses the issues of how the unfolding of uncertainty should affect our policies. It also estimates the value of better information: How much should society pay to gain better information about future economic, geophysical, or technological events?

Estimates of the Uncertainty of Future Climate Change Due to Parameters of the Model

Background

One of the major obstacles to an analysis of the uncertainty of future paths is the sheer size of the problem of assessing all of the uncertainties and making numerical estimates of the joint distribution of all the uncertain variables on the endogenous or policy variables of interest. It was decided therefore to analyze this question in two phases: the first phase, which is included in this chapter, is an exploratory or screening stage in which the most important uncertain variables are identified. The second stage, which is undertaken in the next chapter, is the formal analysis in which the estimates of uncertainty are made for the whole model.

The first exploratory phase of the analysis is to identify the important uncertain variables. This phase proceeds by making a "sensitivity test" on each of the variables in the model. This phase is designed to identify the order-of-magnitude impacts of uncertainty for each variable on the system so as to allow the second stage to concentrate the research on the most important variables.

Selection of Parameter Values

The procedure in the exploratory phase was the following: First, we identified each of the exogenous parameters (or, in some cases, variables) in the model. A list of all the parameters in the model is shown in table 6.1. Some parameters were not investigated for technical reasons.[1] For each of the investigated parameters, we make a rough estimate of an uncertainty range—that is, an alternative "high" value for the parameter. In terms of a subjective probability, we identify the high as the 90th percentile of the cumulative subjective probability distribution of that variable while the central value is the 50th percentile. The test highs are sometimes based on a relatively thorough examination of the uncertainties (as in the case of data based on the estimates

---

1. The initial conditions for capital, population, and output were omitted because these are inessential for the numerical results; if the initial conditions for these variables were incorrectly estimated, there would be an automatic offsetting correction in the value of other variables, to wit, the intercept of the production function or the CO_2-output ratio.

Table 6.1
Parameters and initial test values for uncertainty study

Parameter	Definition	Base Value	Test High
α	Elasticity of marginal utility of consumption	1	2
b_1	Intercept of cost function	0.0686	0.133
b_2	Exponent of cost function	2.9	3.5
β	Marginal atmospheric retention rate of CO_2	0.64	0.78
δ_K	Depreciation rate of capital	0.10	0.15
δ_M	Removal rate of atmospheric CO_2	0.0833	0.05
δ_A	Deceleration rate of productivity	-0.11	-0.0407
δ_L	Deceleration rate of population	-0.19	-0.05
F_{exog}	Exogenous GHG forcings (factor)	1.0	1.5
$g_A(1965)$	Growth rate of productivity, 1965	.150	.200
g_A^*	Asymptotic growth rate of productivity	0.000	0.004
$g_L(1965)$	Growth rate of population, 1965	0.223	0.275
g_L^*	Asymptotic growth rate of population	0.000	0.005
$g_\sigma(1965)$	Decline rate of CO_2-output ratio	-1.25	-0.11
λ	Feedback parameter for climate system $(1/T_{2 \times CO_2})$	1.41	0.95
$M(1960)$	Initial concentration of atmospheric CO_2 equivalent	677	743
ρ	Pure rate of time preference	0.03	0.01
$1/R_1$	Climate lag factor	0.226	0.326
R_2/τ_{12}	Exchange time shallow to deep oceans	0.44	0.22
$\sigma(1965)$	Initial CO_2-output ratio	0.519	0.571
$T(1960)$	Initial temperature, atmosphere	0.2	0.3
$T^*(1960)$	Initial temperature, deep oceans	0.10	0.15
θ_1	Intercept of damage function	0.0133	0.0270
θ_2	Exponent of damage function	2	4

from Nordhaus and Yohe 1983) and in some cases are only rough judgments.

Because the derivation of the estimates for the most important uncertainties are provided in the next chapter, only a synopsis of the justification of the parameter estimates in table 6.1 is given at this point. We proceed in order of the list in table 6.1. The high value for the elasticity of the marginal utility of consumption uses an alternative value that is often derived in the economic literature. The intercept and exponent of the cost function as well as the marginal atmospheric retention rate are discussed in the next chapter. The depreciation rate on capital uses a plausible shorter lifetime. The removal rate of GHGs uses an alternative residence time used in the IPCC (1990) report. The deceleration rates of productivity and population are discussed in the next chapter. The amount of exogenous greenhouse forcings (such as methane) is derived from the 1990 IPCC report, which shows approximately that amount of deviation across difference scenarios. The initial growth of population and productivity are plausible alternative estimates of these parameters, while the alternative asymptotic growth rates of population growth and productivity are plausible higher levels than the base case.

The alternative decline rate of the CO_2-output ratio and the climate feedback parameter are derived in the next chapter. The uncertainty about the initial concentration of atmospheric CO_2-equivalent GHGs assumes that the non-CO_2 GHGs are underestimated by a factor of 2. The pure rate of time preference, and the method of changing it in the DICE model, are discussed in the next chapter. The climate lag factor takes an alternative value that comes from different climate models reviewed in part I, while the exchange parameter simply doubles the exchange time. The initial value of the CO_2-output ratio assumes that persistent measurement errors in CO_2 emissions are plus or minus 10 percent and therefore adds 10 percent to the level of initial emissions. The initial conditions for upper and lower temperatures reflect uncertainties about trends in these two values over the last century. The last two parameters reflect the uncertainties about the damage function, an issue that is discussed in depth in the next chapter. It should be emphasized that at this initial stage the purpose is to begin with order-of-magnitude estimates of the uncertainties simply in order to determine the important ones and screen out those that contribute little to the uncertainties about climate policy or future conditions.

The next stage is to form a criterion function by which we can measure the contribution of each variable, taken separately, to the uncertainty of the outcome. For this purpose, we create an index of changes in important policy, economic, and climatic variables (which we call "target variables") that will allow us to determine the extent to which the model runs are sensitive to the uncertain parameter under examination. For this purpose, we define an index, which measures deviation of the target variable in the test high run as compared to the base run. More precisely, we define the *sensitivity index*, I, as the standard deviation of the run from the base path for different time periods as follows:

$$I_i = \sum_t \{([X_i^H(t) - X_i^*(t)] / X_i^*(t))^2\}^{.5}, \tag{6.1}$$

where $X_i^H(t)$ is the test high value of the ith target variable and $X_i^*(t)$ is the base value of the ith target variable. For purposes of calculation of the index, we examine the values of the variables in 1995, 2045, and 2095. The target variables are consumption per capita, the carbon tax, world output, the GHG reduction rate, GHG emissions, GHG concentrations, and the global temperature increase.

Results

The overall results of the exploratory stage are tabulated in tables 6.2 through 6.4. Table 6.2 and figure 6.1 show the overall index of uncer-

Table 6.2
Overall index of uncertainty

Variable	Index*	Definition	Tax × $(1 - \mu)$
δ_L	3.3749	Decline rate of growth of population	1.4986
g_L^*	3.3445	Asymptotic growth rate of population	2.0508
g_A^*	3.2336	Asymptotic growth rate of productivity	0.5081
δ_A	2.0227	Decline rate of growth of productivity	0.2914
$g_A(1965)$	1.9727	Initial growth rate of productivity	0.3043
ρ	1.9016	Pure rate of time preference	2.0300
$g_\sigma(1965)$	1.4344	Exogenous decline in output-CO_2 ratio	0.0958
θ_1	0.8553	Intercept of damage function	0.8705
θ_2	0.8387	Exponent of damage function	0.8501
λ	0.8138	Climate-GHG sensitivity	0.4324
$g_L(1965)$	0.7808	Initial growth rate of population	0.2331
b_2	0.4347	Exponent of mitigation cost function	0.0709
β	0.4153	Rate of atmospheric retention of carbon	0.1964
$1/R_1$	0.3815	Climate lag parameter	0.1740
F_{exog}	0.3814	Factor for exogenous greenhouse gases	0.1030
$M(1960)$	0.3126	Initial stock of atmospheric CO_2	0.0140
R_2/τ_{12}	0.3000	Exchange time shallow to deep oceans	0.1573
$\sigma(1965)$	0.2405	Initial CO_2-output ratio	0.0128
α	0.2362	Rate of relative risk aversion	0.2111
δ_K	0.2358	Depreciation rate of capital stock	0.0347
b_1	0.2345	Intercept of mitigation cost function	0.0382
δ_M	0.2175	Removal rate of CO_2 from atmosphere	0.0780
$T(1960)$	0.0201	Initial temperature upper ocean stratum	0.0007
$T^*(1960)$	0.0171	Initial temperature lower ocean stratum	0.0031

*Weights are inverse to the absolute average deviation of each target variable.

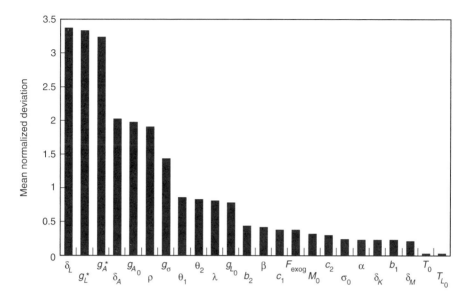

Figure 6.1
Overall uncertainty
(Average for all variables)
Source: Table 6.2. Index is defined in equation (6.1). Some variable labels have been
shortened, and these are in the same order as in table 6.2.

tainty for each parameter. This reflects the average of the normalized
standard deviations[2] of changes summed over the three periods. Values of 1 or more indicate that the model is quite sensitive to this parameter. For example, the most sensitive parameter is δ_L, the decline
in the rate of growth of population; the impact of the test value is to
change the target variables by an average factor of 3.4. Variables that
have a major impact on the outcome are primarily the economic variables (population and productivity growth, time preference, and the
trend in the emissions-output ratio). Some variables are relatively unimportant, including initial values of temperature and the depreciation
rate of capital.

Table 6.3 shows the summary results for each uncertain variable and
each target variable; the key to the variable list is shown in table 6.2.
The entries in table 6.3 show the average normalized mean absolute
error for each target variable—this being $\{([X_i^H(t) - X_i^*(t)]/X_i^*(t))^2\}^{.5}$—
for the three years 1995, 2045, and 2095. For the carbon tax and the

---

2. The normalized standard deviation is calculated so that the contribution of each target variable to the index of uncertainty is equal.

Table 6.3
Rank of uncertainties for model variables

Variable	Tax × $(1-\mu)$	Y	C/L	μ	E	M	T	Tax
δ_L	1.4986	0.8987	0.0326	0.7175	0.6748	0.4663	0.0914	1.8231
g_L^*	2.0508	0.7601	0.0327	0.9536	0.4555	0.3161	0.0635	2.7426
g_A^*	0.5081	0.6361	0.6346	0.2623	0.5513	0.3893	0.0671	0.5926
δ_A	0.2914	0.3953	0.3942	0.1570	0.3572	0.2458	0.0499	0.3281
$g_A(1965)$	0.3043	0.3764	0.3755	0.1632	0.3441	0.2027	0.0759	0.3374
ρ	2.0300	0.0466	0.0148	0.9150	0.0890	0.0460	0.0240	2.4950
$g_\sigma(1965)$	0.0958	0.0045	0.0040	0.2811	0.6369	0.3747	0.1357	0.0698
θ_1	0.8705	0.0085	0.0078	0.4393	0.0622	0.0322	0.0150	0.9891
θ_2	0.8501	0.0017	0.0016	0.4154	0.0664	0.0460	0.0097	1.0303
λ	0.4324	0.0044	0.0041	0.2283	0.0327	0.0171	0.1897	0.4786
$g_L(1965)$	0.2331	0.2140	0.0060	0.1280	0.1939	0.1086	0.0494	0.2551
b_2	0.0709	0.0005	0.0004	0.5517	0.0734	0.0354	0.0186	0.0061
β	0.1964	0.0018	0.0016	0.1084	0.0148	0.0586	0.0786	0.2138
$1/R_1$	0.1740	0.0013	0.0012	0.0956	0.0135	0.0069	0.1020	0.1894
F_{exog}	0.1030	0.0021	0.0020	0.0572	0.0082	0.0040	0.1324	0.1114
$M(1960)$	0.0140	0.0009	0.0009	0.0101	0.0011	0.0285	0.1247	0.0152
R_2/τ_{12}	0.1573	0.0016	0.0014	0.0869	0.0123	0.0064	0.0702	0.1711
$\sigma(1965)$	0.0128	0.0008	0.0007	0.0485	0.0924	0.0480	0.0368	0.0101
α	0.2111	0.0227	0.0094	0.1173	0.0081	0.0039	0.0055	0.2293
δ_K	0.0347	0.0397	0.0488	0.0224	0.0373	0.0191	0.0119	0.0376
b_1	0.0382	0.0002	0.0002	0.2952	0.0401	0.0206	0.0095	0.0038
δ_M	0.0780	0.0011	0.0011	0.0452	0.0058	0.0380	0.0469	0.0841
$T(1960)$	0.0007	0.0000	0.0000	0.0000	0.0001	0.0000	0.0093	0.0007
$T^*(1960)$	0.0031	0.0001	0.0001	0.0000	0.0003	0.0001	0.0070	0.0031

Note: The rank order in this table is the overall ranking shown in table 6.2.

control rate, this figure can be calculated from the data given in table 6.4. For example, the entry for ρ for the control rate μ is .9150. This indicates that the selected change in ρ changed the control rate by an average of 91.5 percent for the three years, a very large change indeed. On the other hand, the test change in the initial emissions-output ratio changed the control rate on average by only 4.9 percent.

The only target variable that is not self-explanatory is the tax revenue variable shown in the second column as "tax × $(1-\mu)$." This variable represents the normalized revenues from a carbon tax measured as the carbon tax times one minus the emissions-control rate; this variable is a good proxy for the combined uncertainties on the control rate and on the social cost of emissions. The data in table 6.3 are sorted in order of uncertainty in table 6.2.

Table 6.4
Impact of test changes for model variables on carbon tax and control rates

	GHG Control Rate			Carbon Tax (1989 $)		
	1995	2045	2095	1995	2045	2095
Base	0.090	0.125	0.143	5.32	13.68	21.03
ρ	0.195	0.252	0.282	23.58	52.58	77.50
b_2	0.148	0.191	0.212	5.29	13.69	21.27
θ_1	0.130	0.180	0.205	10.67	27.23	41.46
δ_L	0.130	0.217	0.282	10.72	38.77	76.10
g_L^*	0.129	0.230	0.370	10.51	43.42	127.79
λ	0.110	0.154	0.176	7.85	20.22	31.18
α	0.108	0.137	0.151	7.48	16.52	22.58
$g_\sigma(1965)$	0.105	0.165	0.194	5.46	13.12	18.05
$g_L(1965)$	0.101	0.142	0.161	6.64	17.35	26.28
β	0.101	0.139	0.156	6.65	16.59	24.79
$1/R_1$	0.099	0.137	0.156	6.34	16.30	24.91
R_2/τ_{12}	0.098	0.136	0.155	6.23	16.04	24.58
$g_A(1965)$	0.098	0.148	0.174	6.28	18.89	30.51
δ_M	0.096	0.131	0.146	5.97	14.81	22.03
F_{exog}	0.096	0.132	0.150	6.02	15.18	22.98
$\sigma(1965)$	0.095	0.131	0.149	5.39	13.66	20.69
δ_A	0.093	0.143	0.185	5.61	17.68	34.43
g_A^*	0.093	0.151	0.221	5.70	19.49	47.97
$M(1960)$	0.092	0.126	0.143	5.53	13.76	21.00
$T(1960)$	0.090	0.125	0.143	5.33	13.68	21.03
$T^*(1960)$	0.090	0.125	0.143	5.35	13.73	21.02
θ_2	0.089	0.178	0.259	5.20	26.80	65.36
δ_K	0.088	0.122	0.140	5.13	13.14	20.25
b_1	0.064	0.088	0.100	5.34	13.66	20.86

Note first that the relative importance of each variable will change depending upon the target variable of interest. Population growth is extremely important for the control rate, the tax rate, and the revenue, but much less important for the level of per capita consumption. The contribution of exogenous non-CO_2 GHGs (F_{exog}) is crucial for the uncertainty about climate but of minor importance for the tax or revenue uncertainties because there is no instrument that affects these emissions.

Table 6.4 then shows the impact of the uncertain variable on two important policy variables—the GHG control rate and the carbon tax rate—for the three time periods. This table is sorted by the GHG control rate in the first period to show the impact of the uncertainty on the optimal policy at the beginning; in a sense, this is the most operational measure of uncertainty in that it shows the implications of the uncertainty for our actions today. There are no major surprises here except perhaps to show the relative importance of the uncertainty about the pure rate of time preference for present policies.

A few comments on the results will wrap up this section; the detailed discussion refers to the detailed results in table 6.3. Output uncertainty not surprisingly depends notably on the uncertainty about productivity and population growth, with little dependence on most of the climate and energy parameters. Per capita consumption depends overwhelmingly on the uncertainty about productivity growth, while parameters of the climate system are relatively unimportant.

Emissions uncertainty depends significantly upon the rates of growth of population and productivity growth and on the rate of exogenous improvement of the CO_2-GNP ratio. Uncertainty about concentrations depends on the rate of exogenous improvement of the CO_2-GNP ratio, population and productivity growth, and on the parameters of the carbon cycle. Climate uncertainty depends on the parameters of the climate model, particularly on the climate parameter λ, as well as on the major scientific and economic variables.

In terms of the policy parameters, the uncertainty about the GHG control rate depends significantly upon the economic variables, such as the rate of time preference and growth of population and productivity. Other important uncertainties arise from population growth, the mitigation-cost function, and some of the climate parameters. The uncertainties that affect the carbon tax resemble closely those for the GHG control rate.

Selection of Variables for Further Analysis

Which are the most important uncertainties? Given there is no unambiguous ranking, some choices need to be made. The three variables each for population and productivity growth do not present genuine independent uncertainties; the uncertainties about the asymptotic growth rates of population or productivity are closely related to the decline rate of these growth rates. We have selected the decline rates of the growth rates for these two variables as the uncertain variable because they best capture the issue of the near-term time path of these variables. For the two parameters of the climate-damage function, we take the intercept, which is easiest to relate to existing studies. Similarly, we substitute the intercept of the mitigation-cost function for its exponent because the former is more easily extracted from model comparisons. With these choices, the top eight uncertain variables from table 6.2 are the following:

δ_L: decline of rate of growth of population

δ_A: decline of rate of growth of productivity

ρ: pure rate of social time preference

g_σ: rate of decline in the GHG-output ratio

θ_1:   intercept of the damage function

λ: climate-GHG sensitivity coefficient

b_1:   intercept of the mitigation-cost function

β: rate of atmospheric retention of CO_2

For interest's sake, the least important parameters in ascending order of irrelevance are

δ_M: removal rate of atmospheric GHGs

T_0:   initial temperature of the atmosphere

TL_0:   initial temperature of the deep oceans

The overall ranking is rich in surprises and puzzles, but these will be left for the interested reader to pursue. To conclude, the rankings shown in the figure and tables will provide the basis for the Monte Carlo runs in the next chapter. Moreover, note that it would take a massive misestimate of the uncertainty to change the rankings in table 6.2 by a significant margin. Assuming that the response to parameter changes is linear, if we have underestimated the uncertainty about the relative atmospheric retention rate of CO_2 by 50 percent, this would only move its rank up by one place. All uncertainties are not created equal.

Impacts of Alternative Specifications

The previous section of this chapter examined the importance of each of the model parameters in affecting climate change, economic impacts, and climate-change policies. In this section, we examine a number of specific alternative assumptions or scenarios to determine the impact of each. The choice of the alternative scenarios comes from two

Table 6.5
Results of alternative specifications

Run	Control Rate, 1995 (percent)	Carbon Tax, 1995 ($/tC, 1989 $)	Annualized Global Impact (billions, 1989 $/year)
Base	8.8	5.24	0
High climate change	11.8	9.09	− 149
Low climate change	3.5	0.91	174
Catastrophic climate change	17.2	18.66	− 269
Costs from rate of climate change	.136	11.86	− 88
One-equation model	9.3	5.87	− 27
High economic growth	8.9	5.69	15578
"Free lunch"	37.1	4.97	54
Tax with wasteful spending	0.3	0.02	− 11
Tax recycled by lowering high DWL taxes	32.0	59.02	137
600 year horizon	8.8	5.24	0
Alternative discount rate			
$\rho = .01$; $\alpha = 2$	12.5	10.11	na
$\rho = .001$; $\alpha = 2.5$	15.8	15.83	na

separate areas. For some, uncertainties about the specification of the model suggest alternative specifications. A second set of alternative specifications has come from the reviewers of the model; ever creative in constructive criticisms, they have provided a treasure trove of alternative approaches to draw upon.

High Climate Sensitivity

One of the major uncertainties is the sensitivity of climate to rising GHGs. For a first alternative, we choose one of the more sensitive models, the Stouffer-Manabe-Bryan (SMB) model analyzed in chapter 3. The SMB model parameters place it at the high end of the range of estimates of temperature-CO_2 sensitivity according to the IPCC (1990) survey. For this model we have used a temperature-CO_2 sensitivity of 4.1°C per CO_2 doubling ($\lambda = .98$) and a shorter lag coefficient representing a mean lag of 34 years ($c_1 = .306$).

The basic results are summarized in table 6.5. This table collates all the results from the sensitivity runs derived in this and the next section. The first column shows the results of the sensitivity test on the GHG control rate; the second column shows the impact upon the carbon tax; and the final column shows the annualized value of the impact upon the objective function in terms of the flow of consumption valued annuitized at a real annuity rate of 4 percent per annum (equal to the real interest rate of 6 percent per annum less the growth rate of 2 percent per annum).

For the case of high climate sensitivity, the initial optimal control rate rises by about one-third and the initial optimal carbon tax rate rises to $9.09 per ton carbon. While there is no substantial change in the conclusions, this run shows that the uncertainty about the climatic impact of GHG emissions is substantial.

Low Climate Sensitivity

Although the approach used in this study adopts the scientific consensus concerning the impact of rising GHGs on climate, the historical temperature data give little statistical support to the models, as was shown in chapter 3. Not all scientists would adopt the conventional view about global warming. For example, Professor Richard Lindzen of M.I.T. states: "I assert that there is no substantive basis for predictions of sizable global warming due to observed increases in minor greenhouse gases such as carbon dioxide, methane, and chlorofluorocarbons. . . . A large number of calculations show that if [atmospheric carbon dioxide doubled], we might expect a warming of from .5 to 1.2 degrees centigrade."[3]

In chapter 3, we presented a statistical estimate of the parameters that are consistent with historical data on temperature changes. These estimates find a temperature-CO_2 sensitivity of 1.0°C per CO_2 doubling ($\lambda = 4.0$), which is consistent with Lindzen's statement, and a longer lag (with a coefficient of $c_1 = .0942$). This run finds a much reduced optimal control rate, as is shown in table 6.5. These show that the initial optimal control rate is considerably lower at 3.5 percent and that the initial optimal carbon tax rate falls to $.91 per ton carbon. For this scenario, there is little rationale for undertaking costly international efforts to control GHGs for purposes of slowing climate change. As in the high climate case, this example shows the importance of improving our understanding of the climate system.

---

3. See Lindzen 1992, 87, 89.

Catastrophic Climate Change

Perhaps the major concern about current analyses of the economics of greenhouse warming is that they may dramatically underestimate the impact of climate change on human societies and natural ecosystems. Although the catastrophic consequences are difficult to foresee, some analysts suggest the possibility of devastating impacts. Some of the potential impacts of climate change are major surges of the West Antarctic ice sheets, leading to a sea-level rise of 20 feet or more; unexpected shifts in ocean currents, such as displacement of the warm current that warms the North Atlantic coastal communities; a runaway greenhouse effect in which warming melts tundras and releases large amounts of additional GHGs like methane; large-scale desertification of the current grain belts of the world; recent evidence of very rapid shifts in temperature and sea levels; or the evolution and migration of lethal pests in new climatic conditions.

Recent studies begin to lend some credibility to concerns about draconian changes in the climate system or major increases in the variability of climate. The Greenland Ice-Core Project (GRIP) has recently shown that, at least for that area, the current climate is extremely stable relative to past climates. Ice cores indicate that very rapid temperature changes have occurred in warm periods (earlier results had found climate instability only associated with transitions between warm and glacial periods). An astonishing preliminary finding in the Greenland core (but not the Antarctic core) was that surface temperatures went through a cycle of about 12°C in a 70-year period.[4] A second set of results comes from recent model runs of a GCM with a coupled ocean-atmospheric model. This study found that if the globe warmed past some threshold, North Atlantic circulation would change regimes and the climate would enter a different, locally stable regime. After a doubling of CO_2, the model returned to the original equilibrium; after a quadrupling of atmospheric CO_2, by contrast, the model climate stayed in the new equilibrium.[5]

It is important to examine these results carefully. They do not prove instability; more important, they do not necessarily indicate that the conditional probability of catastrophic climate change would increase if climate warmed (for the conditional probability of a new ice age is

---

4. See GRIP 1993 and Dansgaard et al. 1993. Further studies have found some inconsistent results, however.
5. See Manabe and Stouffer 1993.

likely to decline in the near future). But if these results are confirmed on a global or even hemispheric scale, and if such instabilities might be triggered by greenhouse warming, then the whole nature of the societal impacts will need to be rethought in a completely different light.

It is difficult to know how to calibrate these catastrophic scenarios, which might be equivalent to the damages from a major war, or from a half century of Communist rule (estimated today to be one-half to three-quarters of per capita output for East Germany). To structure the sensitivity analysis on catastrophic climate change, I assume that as the temperature increase passes 3°C, an irreversible set of geophysical reactions takes place that wreck human civilizations. On the basis of a survey recently completed by the author,[6] some experts believe that there is a nonnegligible probability of a large impact at 3°C warming (see the discussion in the next chapter). We assume that the calamity takes the form of an extreme nonlinearity in the damage function as represented by a power function with a very high exponent. More precisely, the new damage function is $d = .027(T/2.5)^{12}$. This will lead to only modest costs when the temperature increase is up to the threshold, after which the marginal damages increase sharply. If the global temperature increase reaches 3.5 degrees, this costs 60 percent of global output. Obviously, it is crucial for this analysis that policymakers are aware of the threshold.

The impact of the catastrophic threshold is surprising. The impact on greenhouse policy is relatively modest in the early period, with the control rate being 17 percent in the decade of the 1990s with a carbon tax of $19. However, both the tax and the control rate rise sharply in coming decades to keep society away from the threshold. The reason for the modest controls in the early periods is because of the high productivity of capital, which implies that investment to slow climate change should be postponed in favor of investment in conventional capital until the fateful threshold is relatively close.

Costs of the Climate Change

One of the concerns with the DICE model is that it represents the costs of climate change in terms of the change instead of the *rate* of change of major climatic variables. In a survey undertaken to determine the

---

6. Nordhaus 1994.

views of experts on the impacts of climate change, virtually every person viewed more rapid change as significantly more costly than slow change; indeed, for many, when climate change is sufficiently slow, it is seen as having no appreciable economic impact.[7]

To determine the effects upon policy of this alternative view of impacts, I have respecified the damages in terms of the rate of change. According to the survey of experts, a temperature increase of 0.3°C per decade for the next two centuries would have an average impact of 1.9 percent of output over the period, while a rate of warming that is twice as great would have an impact of 5.5 percent of output averaged over the next century. We therefore made a run in which all the costs of climate change are a function of the rate of change rather than the level of climate change.[8] The result is shown in table 6.5. Incorporating the estimated costs of climate change as well as of the level effects results in a markedly higher level of control and a higher optimal carbon tax.

One-Equation Climate Model

The DICE model is constructed using a relatively sophisticated climate model, relying on the work of Schneider and Thompson. The model is the two-equation version that represents a three-layer, one-dimensional dynamic reaction of global temperature to radiative changes. The climate model is more elaborate than the other geophysical sectors partly because of the intrinsic importance and interest in this sector and partly to reflect the greater scope of models available in this area.

As was discussed in chapter 3, we investigated an alternative and simpler representation of the climate-GHG link in what we called the one-equation model. This approach was actually employed in the earlier model in Nordhaus 1991c. The one-equation model calibrates the response of climate in the different general circulation models to the equation shown in (3.8) above and yields

$$T(t) = T(t-1) + 0.17[F(t) - \lambda T(t-1)],$$

where $\lambda = 1.41$ for the SJ model. This equation does not fit appreciably worse than that of the two-equation model used in the base runs. On the whole, the model with the one-equation climate system (called DICE-131) approximates the standard model with the two-equation

---

7. Nordhaus 1994.
8. More precisely, the damage function is assumed to be $D(t) = X(t)0.084[\Delta T(t)]^{1.534}$.

system (called DICE-123) reasonably well in the short run and fits exactly in equilibrium; only in the medium run do the one-equation and two-equation models differ appreciably.

In a first set of runs, the two models were compared with the control rates constrained to be zero to test for the change in the baseline system. There is little difference between DICE-123 and DICE-131 for several decades, although the one-equation model tends to project a slightly higher temperature increase. The difference between the increase in average temperature in the two models is 0.5 percent in 2025, 8 percent in 2075, and 12 percent in 2105.

In terms of current policy, the one-equation model leads to marginally higher control rates and carbon taxes, as is shown in table 6.5. The control rate rises from 8.8 to 9.3 percent in the first period, the carbon tax rate rises from $5.24 to $5.87, and there is a small loss in annualized income. From this experiment, it would appear that the one-equation model is a reasonably succinct representation of the climate system for dynamic cost-benefit analyses of the kind undertaken here.

High Economic Growth

An alternative assumption is to inquire whether good economic news is bad environmental news. Many analysts believe that the major culprit in causing ecological damage is the process of economic growth. In this scenario, we ask about the impact of continuation of economic growth at the pace that occurred in the 1965–90 period. In the base case, we assume a slow decline in economic growth (with a halving of the rate of productivity growth every 70 years); for the high-growth case, we assume instead that there is no decline in productivity growth.

The impact on economic activity is, of course, spectacular. In the base case, we assume that per capita consumption plateaus at around $12,000. In the high-growth case, by contrast, per capita consumption grows to $451,000 in 25 decades. Good news for people, some would say, but bad news for Planet Earth and nonhuman beings.

The impact on greenhouse policies today are basically nil as is shown in table 6.5. The control rate and carbon tax are both a shade higher but by much less than the other changes in table 6.5. The reason for this result is that the model is always balancing the needs and opportunities of present and future. Higher levels of economic growth result in much more potential emissions and damaging climate change in the future; but it also leaves the future much wealthier and therefore more able to invest in slow climate change. As a result, looking further out, the high-growth run sets future optimal control and tax rates much higher than in the base case as wealthier future generations commit more of their higher incomes to mitigation efforts, although even with those higher mitigation efforts future generations are still much better off than the present or than they would be without the higher productivity growth. The ethical logic of this result is that the present generation should not be penalized for a productivity windfall to future generations.

Negative-Cost Mitigation and the "Free Lunch"

Many analysts have argued that there are significant gains that can be made at no cost, or even with gains in efficiency; the signal example is the compact florescent light bulb which saves labor, capital, energy, and GHG emissions. The size of the efficiency bonus has been variously estimated between 10 and 40 percent.

While the author is somewhat skeptical of these findings,[9] it will be useful to determine how the existence of sizable efficiency gains will affect the findings of this study. We have therefore taken the optimistic estimate of the low-cost or negative-cost gains from the study by the U.S. National Academy of Sciences (hereafter, NAS),[10] which suggests a costless reduction of 30 percent of current GHG emissions is possible at zero cost; this is consistent with a wide variety of engineering studies.[11] After that reduction, the cost function then takes the shape of the base case. More specifically, this case assumes that the economy can attain a 30 percent reduction in the GHG emissions-output ratio at zero cost.

The results are shown in table 6.5. The first and not surprising finding is that the extent of mitigation is much larger than in the present model, with estimates of emissions reductions on the order of 37 percent (equal to the free 30 percent plus a costly 7 percent) as opposed to the estimates closer to 9 percent here. The carbon tax, on the other hand, is slightly lower at $4.97 and rises less sharply because the need for costly mitigation has been reduced as a result of the existence of so much costless mitigation.

9. See in particular the discussion in Nordhaus 1991a.
10. See NAS 1992.
11. See the many studies referenced in the section on mitigation contained in NAS 1992.

Making: Inefficient Regulation and Wasteful

... model used here presumes that decisions are optimally ...en with respect to timing, stringency of controls, and cost-effectiveness of controls. Some of the alternative policies described above investigate the effect on costs and benefits of alternative approaches—these include waiting a decade to implement control strategies, stabilizing emissions, or stabilizing climate. These are suboptimal in that they substitute intermediate and more easily measured and quantified targets (such as emissions) for ultimate but difficult-to-quantify objectives (such as the economic impacts of climate change).

To be realistic, we might pursue these issues by assuming that policymakers recognize that their instruments are not cost-effective. They might impose waste because controls were applied in such a way as not to equalize the marginal costs of reducing GHGs in different countries or sectors. For example, it seems likely that controls will be more tightly imposed in high-income countries than in poorer countries. Another example is the use of "environmental adders" in regulation of electrical generation in the United States, where companies may be required to impute a cost to GHGs in making their investment decisions, whereas no imputation is required outside the regulated electrical-generation industry in these states. Also, the European carbon-tax proposal is actually a misnomer in that it is levied half on carbon content and half on energy content.

Another potential source of inefficiency arises from the use of the revenues in the case where policy is implemented through taxation. The assumption built into the model is that the funds are recycled back into the economy in a nondistortionary fashion. This could be either too optimistic or too pessimistic. It would be too optimistic if the funds were earmarked for wasteful spending projects—say low-yield public works, infrastructure, or conservation subsidies to inefficient technologies. It would be too pessimistic if the funds were used to reduce other taxes with significant deadweight losses such as labor, capital, or transactions taxes.

To capture the impact of inefficient design of climate-change policy, I modify the base case in two ways. For the first, I assume that the restraints are implemented by policies that cost twice as much as the optimal policy instruments analyzed in the base case; in addition, I assume that the policy is implemented through a tax, where one-half the revenues from the tax are spent in a purely wasteful fashion.

The results shown in table 6.5 indicate that the combination of iı ficient regulation and wasteful expenditure imply that climate pro grams should be abandoned. The optimal carbon tax is lowered by more than a factor of 100 and the optimal control rate is essentially zero. The reason for this result is because the inefficient policy is so wasteful while the adaptation induced by markets will be able to offset a substantial part of the costs of climate change relatively efficiently. This and the next example show that the design of the policy may be just as important as finding the right parameters of the climate and impact functions.

Recycling Carbon Taxes by Reducing Burdensome Taxes

One of the arguments that has been advanced in favor of a high carbon tax is that the revenues can be used to reduce taxes that have large deadweight burdens. For example, at present virtually all federal revenues are levied on "goods" such as capital, leisure (through labor taxes), or consumption. According to standard economic analysis, the taxes will impose deadweight burdens on the economy because there will be wedges between the marginal private value of goods and the marginal social value of goods. The exact value of the marginal deadweight loss of taxes in the United States is controversial, but some have estimated it as high as $.50 per $1.00 of revenue.

If these estimates are correct, it follows that replacing high-marginal-deadweight-loss (MDWL) taxes with low-marginal-deadweight-loss carbon taxes would result in economic efficiencies over and above any economic gains from slowing climate change. For example, if the individual income tax has a 0.5 MDWL (that is, $.50 per $1.00 of revenue), then a carbon tax that was used purely to replace the last dollar of the individual income tax would, in addition to impacts on climate change and costs of mitigation, have a *net* gain of $.50 per dollar of carbon-tax revenue. It follows that the optimal carbon tax including the gains from reduced MDWL on other taxes reduced would be higher than that calculated in the model on the basis of climate change alone (just as the opposite held when the revenues were wastefully spent in the example in the last section).

To test for the implications of revenue recycling, the model was modified to include the possibility of recycling the revenues through reducing high MDWL taxes. More precisely, we assumed that greenhouse policies were implemented wholly through efficient carbon taxes and that the taxes were wholly recycled by reducing taxes with MDWL of 0.3; this coefficient is lower than some that have been estimated but is in the plausible range that might be attained by careful design. In addition, we assume that the rate of MDWL on existing taxes is invariant to the amount of carbon-tax recycling.[12]

The results are shown in table 6.5. The impact on the optimal policy is quite substantial (as was the impact of the wasteful case in the last section). The control rate rises from 8.8 percent to 32 percent and the carbon tax rises from $5.24 per ton to $59 per ton in the first decade. At current levels of GHG emissions from the United States, this represents base emissions of about two billion tons of CO_2 equivalent; with the tax rate and emissions reductions in this example, carbon-tax revenues would equal about $80 billion per year (approximately 5 percent of U.S. federal revenues during the decade of the 1990s). This result is surprising and striking, for it suggests that a combination of concern about future climate changes and the search for more efficient tax bases might lead to a much higher carbon tax than would be justified on grounds of climate change alone. This finding, along with the converse result in the case of inefficient regulation and recycling, emphasizes the critical nature of designing the instruments and use of revenues in a careful manner. The tail of revenue recycling would seem to wag the dog of climate-change policy.

Time Truncation

A final test is for the errors that are induced by optimizing over too short a time period. This issue is of concern because of the very long lags in the economy and in the climate system. Indeed, William Cline has criticized this and an earlier study because these approaches did not take into account the possibility of long-term warming.[13] Cline's criticism is mistaken. In fact, the present model explicitly includes the dynamics of climate change and allows for impacts for quite a long time: in the base run, we have estimated the optimal policy over 40 periods (400 years) with transversality conditions to reflect the (even) longer-term valuation of stock variables. To determine whether four

---

12. A critical assumption for this analysis is that carbon taxes initially have a zero MDWL. Larry Goulder has pointed out that because carbon taxes have significant elements of a consumption tax, the MDWL on carbon taxes may in fact be substantial from the beginning.
13. See Cline 1992a, 306 and passim.

centuries is adequate, a final set of runs estimates the effect on a number of policies of different truncation periods for different policy variables. Table 6.5 shows the impact of extending the length of the run to 60 periods (600 years). In addition, we have investigated the effect on different variables for different horizons and different model periods. An analysis in the appendix to Nordhaus 1992a shows that here is essentially no difference for any variable out through the 21st period (2160–69) from truncating the estimation at 40 rather than 60 periods. The only runs for which the shorter horizon produces some inaccuracies are those with extremely low rates of time preference (less than 0.5 percent per annum). The reason why time truncation is not an issue is that by choosing the correct transversality conditions the solution for the shorter horizon will be identical to that over the infinite horizon.

The Role of Discounting

Analytical Issues

No issue has raised more concern and confusion than the question of the appropriate discounting of the future. The first part of this chapter showed that plausible changes in the pure rate of time preference have a significant impact upon climate-change policy (see tables 6.2 and 6.4). In this section, I review the analytical issues surrounding discounting, present empirical evidence on the cost of and returns on capital, and make a systematic assessment of the impact of alternative assumptions in the DICE model. It must be emphasized that this topic is one that has been extensively studied by economists, and three alternative approaches will be mentioned later in this section.

Beginning with the fundamentals, a *discount rate* is a pure number per unit time that allows us to convert values in the future into values today. The most common form of discount rate is the nominal or money interest rate, which is applied to future dollar values so that they can be converted into present dollar values. When the nominal interest rate is corrected for inflation, we obtain the real interest rate, which represents the rate used to convert future constant-dollar values into today's constant-dollar values.

To understand the economics of real interest rates, economists often use the optimal-growth framework that underlies this study—namely, the Ramsey model. The Ramsey model derives the real interest rate, or the *discount rate on goods,* from a combination of time discounting, the elasticity of marginal utility, and growth in consumption. We begin with the observation that society shows different levels of concern about real incomes of different generations. We call this phenomenon *time discounting*. For example, if, as between equally well-off generations, society is indifferent between an increment of real income today and $(1 + \rho)^{100}$ increments in 100 years, we say that the "pure rate of time preference" is ρ per year. Most economists and political philosophers find it hard to defend a pure rate of time preference above zero on ethical grounds (just as it may be hard to defend the fact that the United States devotes only one-fifth of 1 percent of its national income to overseas development assistance). On the other hand, it would be unrealistic to make decisions based on the premise that there is, in fact, no time preference given that many social decisions are, in fact, tilted in favor of present generations.

A second and more justifiable reason for favoring present consumption, or in the context of this study postponing GHG control costs, comes from the fact that different generations enjoy different levels of consumption. Industrial countries have witnessed more or less continual growth in living standard for more than a century; thus the per capita real consumption in the United States has growth by a factor of four over the twentieth century. Society might well feel that it is appropriate for later, richer generations to pay a larger fraction of GHG control costs, just as high-income people pay a larger fraction of their income in income taxes. We might then discount future costs if average living standards were improving—a phenomenon we call *growth discounting*.

One must take into account both time and growth discounting to understand the phenomenon of *goods discounting*. Goods discounting refers to the real interest rate defined above and concerns the relative valuation of units of goods or consumption at different points in time; the real interest rate combines goods discounting and time discounting.

To put these ideas analytically, we can rely on the Ramsey model of optimal economic growth framework described in chapter 2, ignoring without loss of generality the environmental sector for this exposition. The model is based on two preference parameters: the pure rate of time preference described above and the elasticity of the marginal utility of consumption. The latter is a parameter describing the rate at which the marginal utility of per capita consumption declines with higher consumption. Individuals and society may feel a greater urgency of delivering real consumption to poorer over richer generations. Thus, if c is per capita consumption, $u(c)$ is the social valuation (or "utility") of consumption; then the marginal utility of consumption, or the social valuation of increments of consumption, might decline at higher levels of consumption, implying that $u''(c) < 0$. Say society is indifferent between delivering 1 unit of consumption today and delivering $(1+k/100)$ units for a generation that is 1 percent poorer. In this case, the parameter representing elasticity of the marginal social utility of consumption has value $\alpha = -u''(c)c/u'(c) = k$.

If we follow the approach set out in the Ramsey model developed in chapter 2, we can derive the condition for an optimal path of investment and consumption as

$$\partial\{u'[c(t)]\}/\partial t = u'[c(t)]\ \{\partial Y(t)/\partial K(t) - \delta_K - \rho\}, \tag{6.2}$$

which states that the time rate of change of the marginal utility of consumption equals the marginal utility of consumption times the net marginal product of capital $\{\partial Y(t)/\partial K(t) - \delta_K\}$ minus the pure rate of social time preference (ρ). Assuming riskless competitive markets, the net marginal product of capital will equal the instantaneous real interest rate $r(t)$, so (6.2) reduces to

$$r(t) = \partial\{u'[c(t)]\}/\partial t\ /\ u'[c(t)] + \rho = \alpha g(t) + \rho, \tag{6.3}$$

where $g(t)$ is the growth rate of per capita consumption. In steady state, with stable population and a constant rate of growth of per capita consumption, (6.3) becomes

$$r^* = \alpha g^* + \rho, \tag{6.4}$$

where asterisks represent steady-state values. In equation (6.4), if $\rho = .03, g = .03$, and $\alpha = 1$—parameters that might reflect today's conditions—the real interest rate on goods would be 6 percent. However, if all economic growth ceases and the growth discount evaporates, the real interest rate would fall to 3 percent. *It is crucial to understand that a high real interest rate can be generated either by a high rate of time preference or by a high elasticity of marginal utility in a society where living standards are improving.*

Many discussions of the appropriateness of discounting the future ignore the distinction between goods discounting and utility discounting. We might feel strongly that it is inappropriate to discount the welfare of future generations, which implies that ρ should be low.

This does not necessarily imply, however, that the discount rate to be used in cost-benefit analyses should be low, for the discount rate in cost-benefit analyses generally refers to the discount rate on goods. If society is extremely averse to inequality, implying that α is high, then a growing economy could have a low rate of time discounting and a high rate of growth discounting, resulting in a high discount rate on goods.

The methodology of this study is to anchor the parameters in actual observations wherever possible, and evidence on rates of return are reviewed in the next section. We have constructed the DICE model so that the parameters on the right-hand side of equation (6.3) are constrained to be consistent with observed market returns as represented by the left-hand side of (6.3). The base parameters in the model determine a real interest rate of around 6 percent per annum in the first few periods, with the rate declining slowly in the future as population and economic growth slows. In the next section, we discuss the appropriateness of this approach.

Empirical Evidence on the Return on Capital

In considering the appropriate discount rate to use in long-term models such as the DICE model, there are three different places we can look for empirical evidence. In each case, it is essential that the discount be based on *actual* behavior and returns on assets rather than on a *hypothetical* view of how societies should behave or an idealized philosophy about treatment of future generations. We insist on reliance on actual returns because funds devoted to GHG abatement must come at the expense of consumption or investment in other assets. When society withdraws funds from plant, equipment, or human capital to slow climate change, it will be losing the returns on those investments; to ensure that the climatic investments raise economic welfare, we must make sure that the returns on alternative investments are no higher than those in climatic investments. If investments in equipment or human capital yield 10 percent annually, it would be inefficient to make investments in slowing climate change that yielded only 3 percent.

The issue of the appropriate discount rate is, therefore, fundamentally an empirical matter. We have chosen an approach that is grounded in the Ramsey model of optimal economic growth, but the discount rate that is derived from this approach is consistent with economic evidence on the returns to capital. In this discussion, we will describe three alternative approaches to estimating the rate of return on investments.

1. The first approach is the one that is actually followed in the DICE model: We assume a Cobb-Douglas production function in labor and capital, use estimates of inputs of labor and capital, and derive from these an estimate of the return to capital. Combining the estimates of the return from capital with parameters for the pure rate of time preference and the elasticity of the marginal utility of income, we can then solve the model and estimate the return on investment. Under this approach, the real return on assets averages 6.3 percent during the period 1960–89 (see table 5.6).

2. An alternative approach is to examine the real cost of capital on financial instruments. These returns or measures of the cost of capital indicate the price that investors will use in making investment decisions. In competitive markets, and ignoring taxes for the moment, the return on investments would be equated on the margin to the cost of capital.

Returns on a wide variety of financial and tangible assets have been prepared by Ibbotson and Brinson (1987), and table 6.6 shows the most important asset classes, including returns on equities, bonds, real estate, and farmland for the United States and other countries (all in U.S. dollars, corrected for consumer price inflation). In addition, we show the cost of capital faced by consumers in mortgages, in car loans, and through credit cards.

A number of points emerge from the data on returns to financial assets. First, real returns tend to cluster between 0 and 2 percent per annum for fixed-interest instruments for premium borrowers. Among other equity-type assets, the real cost of capital is generally in the range of 5 to 6 percent. The real cost of capital for less preferred borrowers is markedly higher than for premium borrowers, with consumer borrowing rates ranging from 5 to 11 percent per annum depending upon the source of funds and risky countries paying even higher real interest rates. Note as well, that the estimates of the cost of capital are complicated from an analytical point of view because of their tax treatment. For equity-type assets and bonds, the returns are generally *posttax* returns, and the pretax returns typically will be up to twice as high in areas, such as the corporate sector, where total tax rates exceed 50 per-

Table 6.6
Estimated returns or cost of funds for financial assets

Asset	Period	Real Return
United States		
Equities[a]	1925–92	6.5
Corporate bonds[a]		
Aaa	1926–83	0.5
<Baa	1926–83	2.0
Real Estate[a]	1960–84	5.5
Farmland[a]	1947–84	5.5
Consumer loans[b]		
Mortgages	1975–88	4.8
Credit cards	1975–88	6.8
New car loans	1975–88	11.2
High-income industrial countries[a]		
Equities	1960–84	5.4
Bonds	1960–84	1.6
Real interest rate paid by major debtors[c]	1980–85	16.8
Metals[a]	1960–84	10.7

Notes:
a. Ibbotson and Brinson 1987, updated by author.
b. Federal Reserve Bulletin deflated by increase in deflator on personal consumption from U.S. Bureau of Economic Affairs.
c. Nominal rates adjusted by export price index from UNDP 1992.

cent. For some consumer loans, particularly mortgages, the costs of capital are conceptually *pretax* rates of return, while for others, such as credit-card interest after the 1986 Tax Reform Act, the cost of capital is a posttax rate.

3. The most difficult area to obtain accurate measures is in the actual returns to investments. Table 6.7 displays estimated returns for a number of important assets. The first area is the return to corporate capital, an area which is blessed with relatively reliable data. The real return to corporate capital tends to vary widely over time, space, and because of tax treatment. In the United States over the postwar period, the pretax return on capital (which is the social return on investment) has ranged from 6 to 12 percent per annum. Several studies of the average return on capital are shown in table 6.7, where the pretax returns for the period are estimated to be about 12 percent per annum, with the posttax rate being around 6 percent per annum. Estimates for western Europe and Japan are also widely dispersed but have a central tendency near that of the United States.

Table 6.7
Rates of return on direct investment

Asset class	Period	Rate of Return
All Private Capital, U.S.[a]		
Pretax	1963–85	5.7
Corporate Capital, U.S.[b]		
Posttax		
All corporations	1963–85	5.7
Large firms	1963–85	6.1
Pretax		
Large firms	1963–85	12.3
Human Capital[c]		
United States	1980s	6–12
Developing countries		
Primary education	Various	26
Secondary education	Various	16
Higher education	Various	13
Consumer investments		
10 studies[d]	1976–88	
Mean		68.0
Median		48.5
Energy conservation		
13 studies[d]	1978–88	
Mean		22.6
Median		19.5
Nonresidential capital stock, G-7 countries[e]	1975–90	15.1

Notes:
a. Stockfisch 1982, 269.
b. Brainard, Shapiro, and Shoven 1991.
c. Psacharopoulos 1985.
d. Dubin 1992.
e. UNDP 1992, table 4.7. This measures profit income as percentage of replacement cost of capital. The G-7 countries are the United States, Japan, France, Germany, the United Kingdom, Italy, and Canada.

A second estimate is that for total capital, which is conceptually similar to the results just discussed and includes the noncorporate sector. The estimate of the return to all capital is close to that for the corporate sector for the United States. The pretax return to all nonresidential capital in the G-7 countries was 15 percent for the 1975–90 period.

Another area of great importance is investments in human capital, particularly those in the area of education. There are numerous estimates of the return to human capital; those in developing countries show real returns to investment in the double-digit range while those in high-income countries tend to range between 6 and 12 percent per annum. Two other areas are ones that have a narrower empirical base but are worth mentioning. Estimates of the return to investments in both energy conservation and consumer durables tend to show relatively high returns. Studies in these sectors are based on engineering estimates of the returns to investment, on surveys of firms' hurdle rates of return on energy conservation investments, and on consumer behavior. The estimates shown here are the mean and median of a number of studies surveyed in Dubin 1992; these show returns well above the cost of or returns to capital in the corporate sector and are more than ten times the cost of riskless debt. The estimated returns in these sectors serve to remind us that many firms and households are liquidity constrained and may therefore have extremely high returns on investment.

Taking these different approaches as a whole, it would appear that the first approach (the model results using aggregate data and the Ramsey model) produces a real interest rate, or discount rate on goods, that is reasonably representative of the cost of capital to the economy and of the returns to direct investments. While the return on bonds is lower than the returns employed here, the bond yield represents a special and unrepresentative asset that has risk characteristics quite different from those in either conventional investment or in slowing climate change. To use the lower bond interest rate as a way of rationalizing a low discount rate for climate-change policy is theoretically unjustified and would open the door to accepting a vast array of low-yield public investments that would probably lower real national income and future consumption.

Alternative Approaches: Lind

The issue of discounting has a long history within economics. The classic study in this area is a volume edited by Robert Lind (1982), which presents a number of different points of view and then attempts to synthesize them for purposes of public programs in the energy sector. Because the Lind volume is widely cited, it will be useful to review the principal conclusions. Lind surveys the literature and then lays out the empirical implications of those.

1. In a first-best world, where there are no distortions and where social savings are determined appropriately to balance the interests of the present and the future, all private and social investments should use

the same discount rate, which is the rate of return on private capital and the private real interest rate.[14]

2. When there are distortions due to taxation, unless the risk character-istics of the government investment are superior, government invest-ments should use the posttax return on private assets (the consumption discount rate) as applied to the flow of costs and benefits measured in consumption units. Lind estimated real rate of return to be 4.6 percent per annum.[15]

3. With respect to an adjustment for risk, the issue is the burden of proof. Lind suggests that "unless there is substantial evidence to the contrary, the returns associated with public projects should be as-sumed to be highly correlated with returns to the economy as a whole."[16] They should not, therefore, use the risk-free discount rate unless a substantial case is made that the correlation of the returns with the market returns is close to zero.

4. The novel and unwieldy part of the Lind approach is that each com-ponent of costs and benefits must be translated into a consumption equivalent by use of shadow prices on different spending streams. In the DICE model, which has no distortions, all spending streams have unitary shadow prices, so this translation is straightforward. In reality, if we use the posttax real rate of return, then the streams must be con-verted taking into account their impacts on consumption. According to Lind's theory and empirical assumptions, if costs or benefits reduce consumption, the shadow price on these should be 1.56, while any re-ductions in investment have a shadow price of 3.8. With some work, it can be shown that with these shadow prices, if the costs of greenhouse warming come from investment and the benefits accruing to consump-tion are discounted at 4.6 percent annually, then this is equivalent to a discount rate of 6.3 percent annually in the DICE model.

On the whole, Lind's analytical approach is equivalent to that used here with two exceptions. First, it is difficult to adapt the DICE model to the Lind analysis because the DICE model assumes that there are no distortions. With distortionary taxation, if mitigation costs are more investment-diverting than benefits are investment-enhancing, then the use of posttax returns will understate the appropriate discount rate

---

14. Lind 1982, 27.
15. Lind 1982, 447.
16. Lind 1982, 77.

and the calculated optimal control rate will be too high. The assumption of a 6 percent rate of return is a compromise between the posttax and pretax returns that may minimize the error from distortionary taxation. Second, it is likely that Lind's estimate of the returns to capital (reflected in the assumed 4.6 percent return) are low because they refer only to the corporate sector inside the United States, while (as shown in tables 6.6 and 6.7) there is evidence that outside this sector both costs of and returns to capital may be considerably higher.

Alternative Approaches: Cline

A second related study is that of William Cline. This study argues strenuously for a low discount rate and on that basis espouses a more forceful intervention than is justified on the basis of this study.[17] It will be useful to compare Cline's argument and results with that presented here.

Cline begins with an analytical approach that is similar to that laid out here and in Lind, relying on a utility-based derivation of a discount rate. However, because of his empirical implementation, he arrives at a much lower discount rate. More precisely, he argues for a real discount rate of 1.5 percent per annum applied to consumption. This compares with a rate of return on capital (and discount rate on goods) in the base run of the DICE model that begins around 6 percent per annum and then declines to about 3 percent as growth slows; or to the 4.6 percent per annum discount rate derived in Lind.

Cline bases his approach on two distinct arguments. First, he rejects a positive pure rate of social time preference as ethically indefensible, particularly for very long-term environmental investments. He postulates that "from society's standpoint [a positive rate of pure time preference] is hardly a justifiable basis for making intergenerational comparisons."[18] Based on this postulate, only growth discounting remains as a source of a positive real interest rate. He then reviews a number of studies and concludes that a utility function with an elasticity of the marginal utility of income of 1.5 is the appropriate value.[19] Based on these two arguments, Cline argues that the discount rate on goods should be set at 1.5 percent per annum.

---

17. See Cline 1992a.
18. Cline 1992a, 249.
19. Cline 1992a, 249–255.

While this argument may be compelling to ethicists from a philosophical point of view, it is completely unrealistic from an economic point of view because it ignores the difficulties of imposing a discount rate that does not correspond to market pricing. Should we use Cline's discount rates for all projects? Or only for very long-run projects (like greenhouse warming, hydroelectric projects, and superhighways)? What if "society," as represented by its elected officials, does not agree with Cline? How should we behave if some philosophers or elected officials believe that, at least for the next few decades, a much higher discount rate is appropriate because the yield on investments in poor countries is extremely high? Can we not apply this reasoning to other areas besides the discount rate? What if a philosopher argues that it is unethical and indefensible to pay royalties to rich people or oil companies? Does that imply that we should use $2 per barrel in our cost-benefit calculations for energy policy even though it will cost us ten times that to buy oil? If we consider all the ramifications of this issue, we quickly see that we if we decide to override market prices because of ethical objections, this raises countless paradoxes and contradictions.

The second part of Cline's argument is to identify the discount rate on consumption with the risk-free return on U.S. Treasury securities of approximately 1 percent per annum, which he argues is the "best benchmark estimate for the consumption rate of discount" (Cline 1992, 258). While this definition appears consistent with the analysis just discussed, the usual approach is to identify the consumption discount rate with the posttax return to private investment (see the discussion in the last section as well as Lind, K. Arrow, J. Stiglitz, and others in Lind 1982). The flaw in Cline's argument is that the U.S. Treasury interest rate is a risk-free rate and is well below the real interest rate faced by consumers (see tables 6.6 and 6.7). In addition, Cline does not make any quantitative argument to show that the risk on investments to slow global warming have lower-than-average risk, so the use of the risk-free interest rate is in double trouble.[20] Hence, while Cline's em-

---

20. One concern might be that it is inappropriate to use the rate of return or cost of capital for the private sector because that rate (i.e., the 6 percent per annum proposed here) includes too large a risk premium. This issue raises the conundrum of the equity premium, which holds that the required return on equities is too large to be explained by the observed covariance between equity returns and consumption. One explanation of the high risk premium on equities is that the rate of relative risk aversion is higher than is usually supposed. For example, Grossman and Shiller (1981) find that an elasticity of the marginal utility of consumption (α) of four would be consistent with the covar-

pirical estimate fits neatly into his philosophical stance just discussed, both costs of capital to consumers and firms and private rates of return on assets are generally much higher than the level that Cline chooses.

Hence, from both empirical and theoretical points of view, Cline's argument for the extraordinarily low discount rate is unsupported and unrealistic.

Sensitivity Runs

After reviewing alternative approaches, we conclude that the approach used here, which is to base the DICE model on actual market returns, seems most likely to produce results that are internally consistent and useful for actual policy. In this section, we examine the implications of alternative specifications of discounting. In doing so, we analyze the impact of using alternative rates of time preference (ρ) which constrain the resulting implied market interest rates to be equal to observed rates of return.

The precise runs involve changing other parameters on the right-hand side of (6.3) to compensate for lowering ρ while leaving the real interest rate in the historical period (1960–89) unchanged. The growth rate parameter, $g(t)$, is determined by technology and input growth and cannot be properly changed. However, the elasticity parameter (α) can be adjusted to compensate for changes in ρ while leaving the real return, r(t), unchanged. In effect, we can justify the observed market rates of return either by assuming that society is biased against future generations (seen in high rates of time discounting or high ρ) or by assuming that society has a high aversion to inequality and tilts toward the present generation because it is a poorer generation, which implies high growth discounting or high $\alpha g(t)$. If we want to calibrate the model to the observed existing patterns of returns, however, we cannot lower ρ without a compensatory increase in $\alpha g(t)$.

Putting this point in yet another way, if we arbitrarily decide to lower the rate of time preference in the model, this will lead to substantially higher investment and savings rates because we are in effect

---

iance between consumption and equity returns. It is interesting to note that if we accept the high equity premium and resulting high implicit elasticity of the marginal utility of consumption, then, using Cline's line of reasoning, the growth discount rate would also be much higher than his proposal. For example, if the equity premium is due to an elasticity of the marginal utility of income of 4, then Cline's reasoning would lead to a discount rate on goods of 6 percent per annum.

deciding to set aside more environmental and reproducible capital for the future. As the higher level of savings and investment occurs, the real return on capital and the discount rate on goods will fall. The rub, then, is that assuming a lower discount rate has an observable implication that the savings rate will be higher than in the base case and than is observed in actual economies. If, however, we make the compensatory adjustment in the utility elasticity, the savings rate is unchanged and the sensitivity run will continue to track the actual data in the historical period.

To test the importance of different specifications of the underlying relationship shown in equation (6.3) above, we make two alternative sensitivity runs with low and extremely low rates of time preference. In the low case, we use a rate of time preference of 1 percent per year, while in the extremely low case we use a rate of time preference of 0.1 percent per year.[21] In both cases, we adjust the redistributive parameter to maintain approximately the same real interest rate in the historical period of around 6 percent per annum. These required increasing the redistributive parameter by one point for each 2-percentage-point decline in the pure rate of time preference. Therefore, the values of α are 2 and 2.5 for the two sensitivity runs.

The results of these runs are shown in the last lines of table 6.5. The rise in the redistributive parameter leads to a rough matching of the real interest rate and the savings rate between the new runs and the base run for the early periods. Soon thereafter, however, the savings rate rises and the real interest rate falls as slower economic growth leads to a sharp decline in the growth discount portion of the real interest rate. As a result, the GHG control rates and the carbon taxes are higher in the lower discount rate runs than in the base run, although the increase is less than if the discount rate were changed without the compensating change in the redistributive parameter (compares table 6.4 and 6.5).

In summary, the issue of the discount rate is a complex question involving value judgments about both time and intergenerational equity. A markedly lower utility discount rate cannot be ruled out, but to make it consistent with existing patterns of real interest and savings rates would require a change in the utility function, with a more egalitarian specification than is assumed in the base case. Taking account

---

21. We choose the very low to be essentially zero rather than zero because the latter cannot be properly calculated or approximated in an optimal growth framework.

of both these parameters, a very low discount rate would lead to somewhat more restrictive climate-change policies if economic growth slows in the future, but the change would be much less than would occur if the time discounting issue were to be taken out of the context of the entire growth model. The main challenge to those who propose low discount rates is to reconcile the low discount rates they propose on environmental capital with the observed high returns, and therefore the implicitly high revealed discount rates, on conventional capital goods like plant, equipment, and education.

7   Formal Sensitivity Analysis: Estimation of Uncertainty in Climate Change

Overview of the Approach

The last chapter analyzed the sensitivity of the DICE model to alternative parameters and specifications. In this chapter, we turn to a systematic analysis of the overall uncertainty associated with future projections of the major variables. The plan of the chapter is the following. The first section lays out the methodology of the chapter. The second section then describes the derivation of the probability distributions of the eight major uncertain variables. We then turn to a Monte Carlo study of the uncertainty about future climate change; that section contains both an estimate of the distribution of the overall uncertainty of the major variables (output, GHG emissions and concentrations, and temperatures) and an estimate of the distribution of optimal policies in uncertain states. In the final section, we describe how the very large number of states of the world that are implied by the uncertainty analysis can be reduced to five representative scenarios or states of the world that are used in the next chapter's decision analysis and calculation of the risk premium on greenhouse warming.

To understand the full range of outcomes and policy responses to the threat of global warming, we need to include an assessment of the fact that many of the underlying processes are imperfectly understood. Social scientists have developed a variety of tools to incorporate uncertainty into quantitative modeling, and these can help put bounds on potential future outcomes.[1] Although uncertainties are often critical to determining policies, formal techniques for determining the

---

1. See Morgan and Henrion (1990) for a recent survey of tools for the analysis of uncertainty in quantitative risk and policy analysis.

uncertainty of either future trajectories or impacts have been rarely applied to major policy issues.[2]

The study here follows in the tradition of decision and uncertainty analysis, but adds a new approach that develops a small number of states of the world for use in optimization studies. The approach developed in this and the next chapter rely on recent developments in the embryonic discipline of risk analysis. It develops a new approach to incorporating subjective probabilities into large systems that is called *representative scenario analysis*. This technique allows a very large number of potential outcomes to be aggregated into a manageable number for the purposes of designing optimal control strategies.

An analytical description of the methodology is as follows. We can represent the DICE model with the following set of equations:

$$\mathbf{Y}_t = \mathbf{F}(\mathbf{X}_{t-\tau}; \boldsymbol{\beta}_I, \boldsymbol{\beta}_{II}), \tag{7.1}$$

where $\mathbf{Y}_t$ is the vector of endogenous and policy variables (such as output, GHG concentrations, global mean temperature, and GHG control rate); $\mathbf{X}_{t-\tau}$ is a vector of current and lagged exogenous variables (such as time or exogenous forcings of GHGs) for lags $\tau = 0, 1, \ldots$ In addition, $\boldsymbol{\beta}_I$ is the set of eight important uncertain parameters that will be examined carefully in this chapter; and $\boldsymbol{\beta}_{II}$ is the remaining set of uncertain parameters that were examined in the previous chapter but are omitted from this chapter's uncertainty analysis.

$\mathbf{F}$ is a mapping or vector of implicit functions that represent the discretized Euler equations that are obtained from the optimization of the augmented Ramsey model. The $\mathbf{F}$ mapping cannot be directly calculated; rather, particular points of the mapping can be obtained by making a model run. Indeed, the major difficulty for the uncertainty analysis arises precisely because the mapping in $\mathbf{F}$ cannot be directly observed.

---

2. One notable and controversial example of the systematic application of statistical techniques is the Rasmussen report (Nuclear Regulatory Commission 1975), which estimated the risk of accidents of different levels of severity in commercial nuclear power plants. An exemplary study is one that uses probabilistic assessments for ozone depletion (NAS 1979). A study closely related to this book developed distributions of uncertainties for CO_2 emissions in Nordhaus and Yohe 1983. Some areas of public policy that are crucially related to risk have been notable for the absence of systematic analyses of uncertainties. For example, national primary ambient air quality standards under the Clean Air Act are to be set "to protect the public health," allowing an "adequate margin of safety." This language cries out for a full analysis of uncertainties, yet this has not been undertaken in the quarter century since the original act.

Part I of this study undertook the exercise of deriving the best-guess parameters ($\boldsymbol{\beta}^{50}$, which represents the 50th percentile of the distribution of the parameters) and making runs to obtain estimates of the $\mathbf{Y}_t$ for those best-guess parameters. In the previous chapter, we undertook a sensitivity analysis that took the following form: For each of the model parameters, we constructed a sensitivity run by hazarding a guess as to the subjective 90th percentile of the distribution, $\boldsymbol{\beta}^{90}$. We then calculated an index of sensitivity by calculating the impact on the major target variables of the difference between the best-guess and the alternative value of the parameters as follows:

$$\Delta_i = \mathbf{F}(\mathbf{X}_{t-\tau}; \boldsymbol{\beta}^{50} + \boldsymbol{\delta}_i) - \mathbf{F}(\mathbf{X}_{t-\tau}; \boldsymbol{\beta}^{50}), \tag{7.2}$$

where Δ_i is the effect on the target variables of a change in the ith parameter, $\boldsymbol{\beta}$ is the combined vectors of ($\boldsymbol{\beta}_I, \boldsymbol{\beta}_{II}$), and $\boldsymbol{\delta}_i$ is the difference between the 90th and 50th percentiles of variables (equal to zero except for that of the ith parameter). In the previous chapter, the indexes of sensitivity in (7.2) were ordered and those variables with the largest indexes of sensitivity were separated out for more intensive examination in this chapter; those more important parameters comprise the set $\boldsymbol{\beta}_I$.

The next stage of the analysis, which is performed in the following section, is to undertake a more careful analysis of the subjective probability distribution for each of the elements in the $\boldsymbol{\beta}_I$ set. After that analysis, we undertake a Monte Carlo analysis of the outcomes. For the Monte Carlo stage, each of the eight variables in the $\boldsymbol{\beta}_I$ set of parameters is broken into a discrete distribution with five quintiles; this yields eight quintuples of possible outcomes, or approximately 400,000 combinations of outcomes.

The technique actually used in undertaking the Monte Carlo estimates is a variant of Latin hypercube sampling that is similar to Latin hypercube sampling with replacement. Under this technique, we stratify each of the uncertain variables into five quintiles and take the conditional mean of the uncertain parameter in each stratum. The approach used here differs from conventional Latin hypercube sampling because the sampling is with replacement, and because we use the conditional mean of the variable rather than the midpoint because the variables are not uniformly distributed.[3]

_____

3. The techniques are conveniently described in Morgan and Henrion 1990. We sample with replacement to simplify the calculations and because with such a small sample relative to the population there is little gain in efficiency from sampling without replacement.

The Monte Carlo runs then are calculated by sampling with replacement from the distribution of the eight uncertain variables. This yields a sample, usually from 200 to 500 depending upon the experiment, of realizations as follows:

$$\mathbf{f}[\mathbf{Y}_t(\beta_I)] = \mathbf{f}[\mathbf{Y}_t \mid \mathbf{Y}_t = F(\mathbf{X}_{t-\tau}; \beta_I, \boldsymbol{\beta}_{II})], \tag{7.3}$$

where $\mathbf{f}$ is the joint distribution of the $\mathbf{Y}$ variables and β_I is the *realization* of the sampling from the distribution of the $\boldsymbol{\beta}_I$ variables. The distribution of the outcomes of the sample shown in equation (7.3) will then provide an estimate of the uncertainty about future economic, environmental, and policy variables.

The next step in the analysis requires breaking new ground in risk analysis by generating representative scenarios to use in optimization and policy analyses. In the next chapter, we will analyze the value of information, the risk or insurance premium arising from uncertainty, as well as the impact of constraints on resolving uncertainty. To undertake these tasks, we will need to limit our analysis to a small number of possible scenarios to describe future climate change. The necessary limitation arises because of the curse of dimensionality: the difficulty of solving the DICE model for the optimal policy under uncertainty rises exponentially in the number of states of the world (SOW). Programming the DICE model for five SOW on a PC is moderately straightforward, and solutions on a top-of-the-line PC take thirty minutes as of summer 1993. Clearly, solving for even a few dozen of the 400,000 SOW would require supercomputers.

The task is therefore to collapse the enormous number of SOW into a small number while ensuring that the reduced set of SOW accurately represents the range of outcomes. We therefore need to develop a technique for collapsing the large number of possible outcomes into a manageable number of scenarios that is also representative of the whole range of possible outcomes. For this purpose, we develop a procedure called *generating representative scenarios.*[4]

A brief description of the technique of generating representative scenarios is given here, with a full description reserved for the last section of this chapter. We begin by considering the full panoply of 400,000 SOW that equation (7.3) generates (we call the full set of outcomes the

4. In the language of control theory, this technique relies on Monte Carlo techniques for closed-loop sensitivity measurement and design of optimal control (see Morgan and Henrion 1990, 192–98).

"full population SOW"). We next draw a sample of 500 SOW from which we can determine the characteristics of the trajectories; we call this the "sample SOW." From elementary statistics, we know that the distribution of all variables in the sample SOW is identical to that of the full population SOW.

We need, however, to reduce the number of SOW, and computational limitations suggest a maximum of five SOW for use in the DICE model. We begin by taking the sample SOW and ranking states in terms of the economic impacts of climate change and the induced severity of climate change. More precisely, the segments are constructed by ordering the outcomes according to the stringency of GHG controls in the first period. We then take that ordering and gather the SOW into five groups. The groups are constructed so that the five representative SOW contain 2, 8, 15, 25, and 50 percent of the sample SOW ranked from the most to the least stringent GHG controls. These percentages were chosen to ensure that the extreme outcomes (those with the highest control rates) were well represented, while that half of the sample SOW with only modest GHG control requirements was aggregated into a single aggregate SOW.

Formally, then, we begin with full population SOW ($S_{\text{Full population}} = 5^8$) that are generated by the uncertain variables. We construct sample SOW ($S_{\text{Sample}} = 500$) by sampling from the uncertain variables. We then collapse the sample SOW into five representative scenarios ($S_{\text{Representative}} = 5$) by ordering the sample SOW according to the stringency of GHG controls. This chapter lays out the details of this approach and presents the major results.

Derivation of Distributions for Major Uncertain Variables

Selection of Major Uncertain Variables

The last chapter explored the sensitivity of the DICE model to uncertainties about individual parameters or about specific sectors. We now turn to an assessment of the *overall uncertainty* about economic growth, climate change, and economic policies. To examine the overall uncertainty, we must examine the joint distribution of the uncertain variables. One approach to this would be simply to combine the uncertainties that are examined in the last chapter. This raises a number of analytical and technical objections of which the most important is that estimation of the distributions of the uncertain variables is extremely difficult.[5]

We have instead decided to focus on a subset of the most important uncertain variables. We can thereby devote more attention to the distribution of uncertain parameters in the model, allowing us to select the most important uncertainties for analysis in this chapter. The purpose of the last chapter was to help screen all the variables in the model. The approach here is to develop subjective probability estimates for each of the uncertain variables and then to make projections by taking random draws from the uncertain variables.

As a result of this first and exploratory stage described in the last chapter, we have chosen eight uncertain variables to include in the Monte Carlo stage, in order of their importance for the overall uncertainty:

δ_L: decline of rate of growth of population

δ_A: decline of rate of growth of productivity

ρ: pure rate of social time preference

g_σ: rate of decline in the GHG-output ratio

θ_1:   intercept of the damage function

λ: climate-GHG sensitivity coefficient

b_1:   intercept of the mitigation-cost function

β: rate of atmospheric retention of CO_2

As noted in the last chapter, this list tracks the results of the exploratory stage with two exceptions. First, we use the intercept to represent the uncertainty about the climate-damage and mitigation-cost functions because the intercepts are more easily related to existing studies. In addition, we chose only one parameter to represent the family of parameters associated with population and productivity growth (see the last chapter for a discussion of the choice).

One concern with the current procedure is that it omits a number of important variables and therefore is likely to understate the total uncertainty. To obtain an estimate of the extent to which limiting the analysis to the eight uncertain variables may bias the estimate of the overall uncertainty, we compared the indexes of uncertainty for all variables with the indexes when restricting the estimate to the eight important variables. Examining the total list of uncertain parameters

5. This approach was followed by Nordhaus and Yohe 1983 and Edmonds et al. 1986.

in table 6.2, we can calculate the standard deviation of the sum of all variables (assuming independence). The eight variables included in the above list have a standard deviation of 73 percent of the standard deviation of the full list of variables. If, however, we consider the included variables as proxies of the closely related variables (so that the population decline coefficient is assumed to be a proxy for all the population variables, and so forth), then the eight variables comprise 99 percent of the standard deviation of all uncertain variables.

Put differently, although the analysis that follows may underestimate the uncertainty because it includes an inappropriate specification of the uncertainty about population growth, productivity growth, or of the other eight major classes of variables, the results of the last chapter suggest that omitted classes of variables (such as the initial value of global temperature or GHG concentrations, the depreciation rate on capital, or the elasticity of the marginal utility of consumption) are unlikely to lead to a significant underestimate of the extent of uncertainty about the major target variables.

While the overall uncertainty is only negligibly underestimated by paring down the list of uncertainties to eight variables, some of the uncertainty concerning the environmental variables may be significantly understated. Because several parameters of the climate system are omitted, the standard deviations for these variables are understated significantly—by around 25 percent—by restricting the analysis to the eight variables.

A final problem concerns the potential correlation among the uncertain variables. The simulations that follow are based on the assumption that the variables are statistically independent. For many of the variables, there is little potential for correlation because of the sources of the uncertainty. For example, the uncertainties about the scientific parameters (such as the temperature-CO_2 sensitivity or the carbon cycle) are grounded in sources that are independent of the uncertainties underlying the economic variables. In addition, we have attempted to specify the uncertainties so that they are orthogonal wherever possible. Hence, the uncertainty about the damage function (related to the rate of sea-level rise or the speed of adaptation in agriculture) is grounded in areas quite independent of the uncertainty in mitigation costs (which relates more to supply and demand elasticities in the energy sector). The one area where some correlation may exist is between productivity growth and population growth, although even here the relationship is both complex and controversial. The sole study in this area that has carefully examined the impact of nonindependence (Edmonds et al. 1986) found that the covariance among uncertain variables has a modest effect on the uncertainties. On the other hand, as will shortly be apparent, estimating variances for the uncertain variables is extremely difficult, and the degree of confidence in the covariance estimates must be even lower.

Before launching into the study of uncertainties, it must be reiterated that this is largely uncharted terrain, full of subjectivity, largely devoid of an accepted methodology, with little precise data from which to derive useful estimates, and with no easy way to assess the potential errors of our estimates. Caveat lector.

Derivation of the Uncertain Variables

The derivation of the distributions of the uncertain variables varies considerably because of the nature of the underlying data. The variables fall into three general categories: (1) Variables that have an extensive history but which are evolutionary; this class includes population growth and productivity growth, for which we have historical data for many decades but where the structure is not well enough understood to allow the secure prediction of future values. (2) Next are scientific relationships that are invariant over time but whose values are uncertain because the appropriate experiments cannot be made; this includes important relationships such as the carbon cycle and the temperature-GHG parameters. (3) Finally are the relationships that are both evolutionary and lacking adequate historical data, and which therefore pose the most severe issues for estimating the distribution of uncertain values. This class includes the crucial GHG mitigation-cost function and the climate-damage function.

Techniques for determining the distributions of future uncertain variables sometimes resemble fine arts more than high science at this stage. Studies of the history of uncertainty ranges—whether these be of scientific constants, individual estimates of events, or out-of-sample forecasts—show that forecasters typically display overconfidence in their predictions. This arises either because of the need to sell their work in the marketplace of ideas or because we simply forget how many ways things can go wrong. Even precise questions such as the experimental error in measurement of physical constants seem to be underestimated. A study by Henrion and Fischoff (1986) found that less than half the estimates of the speed of light since 1870 lay within one reported standard error of the 1984 measured value. Similarly, Shlyakhter and Kammen (1992a, b) examined the probability of unexpected events in data on elementary physical particle data and found that about 5 percent of earlier estimates of particle data were more than three estimated standard errors from the mean, whereas for normal variables the number of such large deviations should be about 0.5 percent. Similar results have been found for energy and population forecasts.[6] The present study has uncovered no magic formula for determining the appropriate distribution of future values; rather, past studies would remind us to remain alert to the biases and risk of overconfidence and make adjustments accordingly.

In the uncertainty runs, we have used for each variable a discrete distribution in which the variable takes five alternative values, each having a 20 percent probability. The interpretation is that the value for each cell is the mean of the distribution over the quintile of that variable's distribution.[7] For normal variables, the quintiles represent the 12th, 32nd, 50th, 68th, and 88th percentiles in the distribution. Alternatively, for normally distributed variables, the quintiles can be calculated as the mean plus -1.4, -0.53, 0.0, $+0.53$, and $+1.4$ normal standard errors (these are not centered in the quintile because of the asymmetry of the normal distribution). We sometimes refer to the "quintile range," which is the range between the top and bottom quintiles or between the 10th and 90th percentiles.

GHG-Temperature Sensitivity Coefficient ($T_{2 \times CO_2}$)

The equations used in the DICE model have been derived from a specification used in a small climate model and then calibrated to two larger general circulation models; the equations were also estimated using historical data on global mean temperatures for the last century (see chapter 3 for a discussion of the derivation of the model and parameters). A marked disagreement exists both among the models and

---

6. See Morgan and Henrion 1990, Shlyakhter and Kammen 1992a, and Shlyakhter, Broido, and Kammen 1992.

7. More precisely, assume that a parameter, β, has a cumulative probability distribution $F(\beta)d\beta$. For a uniform distribution, the values of β would simply be the midpoints. More generally, we divide the distribution into quintiles. For the first quintile, the value of β is the mean over the range from $F(\beta) = 0$ to $F(\beta) = 0.2$. Hence, the value for the ith quintile is calculated as $\beta_1 = 5 \int_0^{.2} \beta F'(\beta)d\beta$, $\beta_2 = 5 \int_{.2}^{.4} \beta F'(\beta)d\beta$, etc., where β_i is the value for the ith quintile.

between the models and the historical data, although the statistical estimates using the historical data can be biased if there are slowly moving trend variables that are correlated with the GHG signal.

The first probabilistic assessment of the value of the GHG-temperature sensitivity coefficient $(T_{2 \times CO_2})$ dates back over a decade to the Charney report, which reported:

We estimate that the most probable global warming for a doubling of CO_2 to be near 3°C with a probable error of ± 1.5°C. Our estimate is based primarily on our review of a series of calculations with three-dimensional models of the global atmospheric circulation.[8]

The meaning of the term "probable error" in the Charney report has never been clear; some have interpreted probable error as plus and minus one standard deviation (which is the convention in the natural sciences) or as two standard deviations (which would be a 95 percent confidence interval). This range was endorsed by a National Research Council report[9] and widened to a range of 1 to 5°C for an equilibrium CO_2-equivalent doubling in the 1992 report, although the probabilistic interpretation was removed by 1992.[10] The IPCC report presents a survey in which the GHG-temperature sensitivity coefficient ranges from 1.9 to 5.2°C, but the IPCC concludes that "a value of 2.5°C is considered to be the 'best guess' in the light of current knowledge" and further remarks that, in light of the actual historical record, the coefficient "is unlikely to lie outside the range 1.5 to 4.5°C."[11]

For the analysis undertaken in this study, we proceed under the interpretation that the uncertainty range of 1.5 to 4.5°C should be interpreted as the central estimate minus and plus two standard deviations, which would be a conventional 95 percent confidence interval for normally distributed variables. This would imply a standard deviation of the temperature-sensitivity coefficient of .75°C. To allow for overconfidence, and to reflect the wide range of model results, we allow the quintile extremes to be at the upper and lower values of the conventional range. This increases the standard deviation to 1.06°C, which is in line with the adjustments proposed in Nordhaus and Yohe (1983) and discussed later in this chapter. Under this interpretation, the 1.5 to

8. See National Research Council 1979, 2.
9. National Reseach Council 1983, 276.
10. NAS 1992. According to the chairman of the Effect Panel of the 1992 Report, George Carrier, the 1 to 5°C range was a "plausible range" but one "without a probabilistic interpretation" (personal communication).
11. IPCC 1990, 139.

4.5°C represents the 8th to 92nd percentile range of the distribution of equilibrium temperature-concentration effects.

GHG Atmospheric Retention Rate (β)

The estimates of the uncertainty for the marginal atmospheric retention rate (β) are drawn primarily from the statistical estimates underlying the DICE model and presented in chapter 3. We estimate the model for CO_2 emissions and concentrations using the equation shown in (3.5) as follows:

$$M(t) = [1 - (1/\tau^M)] \, M(t-1) + \beta E(t-1)$$

where $M(t)$ is the deviation of CO_2 concentrations from its preindustrial equilibrium, $E(t)$ is anthropogenic CO_2 emissions, τ^M is the turnover time of deep-ocean CO_2, and β is the marginal atmospheric retention rate. Recall that the time period was from 1860 to 1989. The estimated coefficient was 0.64 with a standard error of 0.015. However, the coefficient was sensitive to the time period of estimation, with a low of 0.55 for the estimate of β using recursive least squares.

An alternative estimate of uncertainty was developed in the study by Nordhaus and Yohe (1983). In that study, the top-bottom range for β of 0.10 was employed based on both the examination of different models and discussions with members of the U.S. National Academy of Sciences' Carbon Dioxide Assessment Committee.

Because of possible saturation effects and other nonlinearities, we assume that the range of estimates from the recursive least squares estimates provides a better estimate of uncertainty than does the sample standard error of β. We therefore take a judgmental standard error of 0.10 for β. This yields a quintile range of 0.14.

Rate of Decline of GHG-Output Ratio (g_σ)

The growth rate in the ratio of uncontrolled GHGs to world output, g_σ, is one of the important but generally overlooked uncertainties. Data prepared for the DICE model showed significant differences in the trend of the CO_2-GNP ratio in different countries and different time periods (see chapter 4). Moreover, different energy models treat this parameter differently.

The trend in advanced industrial countries shows a generally declining trend in the CO_2-GNP ratio for the last six decades, with decline rates ranging from 0.9 to 1.8 percent per year for different subperiods. However, low-income and centrally planned countries show a rising trend in the CO_2-GNP ratio over the postwar period. Another approach is to use surveys of experts as an index of uncertainty. The 1991 International Energy Workshop poll of forecasts showed a two-standard deviation range of 0.6 percent per annum in the growth of the CO_2-GNP ratio for the period 1990–2020. Edmonds et al. (1986) used a closely related parameter—the exogenous end-use energy efficiency—which they estimated to occur at a rate of 1.3 percent per annum with a standard deviation of 0.7 percent per annum.

The variety of results suggest that a quintile range of approximately 2.5 percent per year in g_σ seems consistent with historical data, differences in model results, and the Edmonds et al. study. This assumption gives a one in five chance of no improvement in the CO_2-output ratio in the coming years.

Population Growth (δ_L)

For both population growth and productivity growth, we adopt the uncertainty ranges developed by Nordhaus and Yohe (1983). These ranges were developed for the 1983 National Research Council study on "the CO_2 problem," were carefully reviewed by the committee and the Academy, and have not been superseded in subsequent work. The approach was described as follows:[12]

[A major problem] arose from the need to estimate the uncertainty about key parameters or variables. Our starting assumption was to view the dispersion in results of published studies as a reflection of the underlying uncertainty about the variable studied . . . [S]everal validation exercises revealed that our results were within the statistical realm of reason, i.e., that they fell within reasonable bounds of uncertainty that could be deduced by other means on the basis of historical experience.

This approach suggested viewing the dispersion in the results of different models or scientific studies as a reflection of the underlying uncertainty about the variable under study. The differences in opinion or of study results will usually measure the extent of scientific disagreement at a point in time. There are biases that may tend to either broaden or narrow the range of expert opinion, but this measure is easily replicated and can then be compared with more subjective measures.

For this and the next variable, we use the difference between the high and low values in Nordhaus and Yohe 1983 to provide an esti-

---

12. Nordhaus and Yohe 1983, 90.

Table 7.1
Distribution of major uncertain parameters

Parameter	Expected Value	Standard Deviation	Value of Parameter in Quintile				
			1	2	3	4	5
Population growth decline	0.190	0.106	0.027	0.127	0.195	0.268	0.331
Productivity growth decline	0.112	0.077	0.020	0.051	0.110	0.138	0.243
GHG retention rate	0.640	0.095	0.500	0.587	0.640	0.693	0.780
Climate feedback coefficient	1.624	0.667	0.933	1.120	1.400	1.867	2.800
Climate sensitivity[a]	2.929	1.036	4.394	3.661	2.929	2.196	1.464
Time preference	0.030	0.014	0.010	0.020	0.030	0.040	0.050
GHG-output rate	−0.117	0.076	−0.011	−0.063	−0.117	−0.162	−0.231
Mitigation cost	0.069	0.038	0.027	0.034	0.069	0.080	0.133
Climate damage	0.013	0.011	0.000	0.004	0.013	0.016	0.032

Note:
a. Temperature increase from CO_2 doubling.

mate of the range of values. According to that study, the difference between the high and low (the "high-low range") is very close to what we label the quintile range, which is the difference between the top and bottom quintile in this study. Nordhaus and Yohe estimate the high-low range of the decline rate for population growth to be 2.1 percent per annum over the period 1965–2012. Other periods have slightly different estimates of the high-low range, but this value will be used in what follows.

A study by Edmonds et al. (1986) used a methodology similar to that of Nordhaus and Yohe and prepared estimates of the uncertainty of a number of variables on the basis of both published estimates and interviews with experts. Their estimates of the uncertainty of population growth was quite close to that found in the Nordhaus-Yohe study.

The results of this assumption are shown in table 7.1, which shows the eight parameters that are investigated, the parameter values in the five quintiles of the subjective probability distribution, as well as the mean and standard deviation of each of the values of the variables. Note that we have in each case constrained the expected value to equal the median or best-guess case.

Productivity Growth (δ_A)

The estimates for productivity growth follow the same methodology as those for population growth. The decline rate for productivity growth estimated in Nordhaus and Yohe 1983 was 1.3 percent per annum for the first four decades, as compared to 1.1 percent in the present study (see table 2.1).

The Nordhaus and Yohe survey determined that the high-low range for the decline rate was 1.9 percent per annum for the period 1965–2012. Although this estimate of the range was lower than for other subperiods, this early subperiod had more studies as its basis than did the very long-term estimates. The study by Edmonds et al. (1986) also derived estimates of future productivity growth. Their subjective standard deviations of productivity growth rates were 1.0 percent per annum for developed countries and 1.6 percent per annum for developing countries, as compared to 0.7 percent per annum for Nordhaus and Yohe's long-term estimates for the global economy.

For the current projections, we take the estimate of 2.0 percent per annum as the quintile range of the decline rate for productivity growth. This estimate is slightly higher than the Nordhaus-Yohe estimate to reflect the finding of the Edmonds et al. (1986) study. For the lowest quintile of projections of the deceleration of productivity growth, this implies that the current rate of total factor productivity growth of 1.1 percent per annum will decline very little in the next two centuries, while for the highest quintile of outcomes the current rate of productivity growth is assumed to halve every 30 years.

GHG Mitigation Cost Function

There are numerous estimates, particularly for CO_2, of the cost of reducing GHGs; see the extensive surveys in EPA 1990, Nordhaus 1991a, Dean and Hoeller 1992, Amano 1993, Commission of the European Communities (hereafter, EC) 1992a and 1992b, and the results of EMF-12, presented succinctly in Gaskins and Weyant 1993 as well as the synthesis in NAS 1992. In characterizing the cost function, recall that the final form of the equation used in the model is

$$TC(t) = Q(t) \, b_1 \, \mu(t)^{b_2}, \qquad\qquad (7.4)$$

where $\mu(t)$ is the emissions control rate, $TC(t)$ is the total cost of the reduction, $Q(t)$ is output, and b_1 and b_2 represent the intercept and exponent of the cost function. In the uncertainty analysis, we examine the intercept only because of the difficulty of estimating various values of the exponent.

The range of estimates can be seen by comparing the estimates of the cost function for different models. In the Nordhaus survey (1991a), the high-cost study has a cost about twice the best guess while the low-cost study has a cost of about 40 percent of the best guess. Cline's survey shows a range of 0.8 to 4.2 percent of GNP for a 50 percent reduction rate.[13] For emissions reduction rates up to 50 percent, the OECD survey of four models shows a range from high to low of a factor of about two for the United States and about four for China.[14]

By contrast, the EMF-12 study shows remarkably little divergence among the major eight models on the cost of CO_2 reduction. Examine, for example, the mean percentage reduction in 2010 that would arise from an efficient policy that cost 1 percent of output. The mean estimate of the percentage reduction is 32 percent, while the standard deviation of the percentage reduction is 3.8 percent. (By comparison, the estimated reduction in CO_2 emissions in the DICE model would be 42 percent for a 1 percent reduction in global output. The difference is mainly that the DICE model estimate captures the long-run impact, while the EMF-12 estimate is the cost in the "short run" of 2010.)

Extracting a probability range from the surveys raises the same issues as for the climate models. We can here apply the methodology of Nordhaus and Yohe (1983) by assuming that the estimates of the cost function represent independent draws from the true distribution. For a uniform distribution, the range of the observations is between two and one-half and three times the standard deviation for between four and ten observations, whereas the range between the top and bottom quintiles is 2.8 standard deviations. This suggests that a range from high to low of a factor of four is consistent with the model comparisons. We then adjust this range up to a factor of five to correct for the tendency to underestimate the extent of uncertainty. These assumptions lead to the distribution shown in table 7.1.

Climate-Damage Function
Recall that the equation for the relationship between global-temperature increase and income loss is given by

$$d(t) = Q(t)\theta_1 T(t)^{\theta_2}, \tag{7.5}$$

---

13. Cline 1992a, 184.
14. Hoeller, Dean, and Hayafumi 1992, fig. 2.

where $d(t)$ is the loss of global output, $Q(t)$ is output, θ_1 is the intercept representing the scale of damage, and θ_2 is an exponent that represents the nonlinearity in the damage function. We parameterize the uncertainty about the damage function in terms of the intercept of the function, θ_1, for the same reasons as for the mitigation-cost function in the last section.

Compared with other sectors of the model, there are few studies on which to base estimates of the uncertainty concerning the damages from climate change. An early qualitative discussion is contained in Schelling 1983, and EPA 1989 summarized a number of studies. Nordhaus 1991c put those studies into the context of the national-income accounts and concluded that the best guess of the damage from a CO_2 doubling, including nonmarket elements, was about 1 percent of national income for United States, with a judgmental standard error of 1 percentage point. Cline (1992a) developed a similar estimate for the United States, estimating that a 2.5°C warming would lead to damages of about 1.1 percent of GDP, and used an alternative of 2 percent for sensitivity analyses. A more recent unpublished study by Fankhauser (1993) estimates total impacts of a doubling of CO_2 would lead to a 1.3 percent cost to the United States, a 1.4 percent cost to the OECD, and a 1.5 percent cost to the world. For larger warming, Nordhaus (1991c) estimates the damage function to be quadratic, while Cline assumed an exponent in the damage function of 1.22. Thus for the very long-term warming, Cline's estimate of about 6.1 percent of GDP for a 10°C warming is slightly less than the implicit estimate in Nordhaus 1991c, using the above damage-function parameters, of 10 percent of GDP.

Because the three surveys just mentioned rely primarily on the same set of underlying studies, they do not seem a reliable basis for determining the uncertainty about the impacts of climate change using the Nordhaus-Yohe methodology. To fill in the gap, Nordhaus undertook a survey of experts on the economic impacts of climate change. For this section, we will use the results of the survey, which are shown in table 7.2.

A number of points emerged from the survey that will be helpful in establishing the uncertainty range. To begin with, the median of the experts' estimates of the impact of a 3°C warming in 2090 is approximately 40 percent higher than the estimate used in the DICE model. The experts' median estimate of the impact of a 6°C warming in 2175 is, however, about 10 percent lower than that in the DICE model. We can take the experts' estimates of the 10th and 90th percentiles of im-

Table 7.2
Estimated impact of climate change from survey of experts

Scenario	Loss from Climate Change (percent of world output)			Probability of Catastrophic Loss[a] (percent)
	10th percentile	50th percentile	90th percentile	
A: 3 degrees C in 2090				
Mean	0.7	3.6	8.0	4.8
Median	0.0	1.9	6.0	0.5
B: 6 degrees C in 2175				
Mean	1.5	6.1	13.6	12.1
Median	0.5	4.7	12.0	3.0
C: 6 degrees C in 2090				
Mean	3.3	10.4	21.7	17.5
Median	2.0	5.5	15.0	5.0

Source: Nordhaus 1994.
Note:
a. Catastrophic loss is defined as a sustained loss of global output of 25 percent or more.

pacts to inform the uncertain range. The experts' estimate of the 10th percentile of the impact of a 3°C warming in 2090 is essentially zero, while the median estimate of the 90th percentile of impacts for a 3°C warming in 2090 is 6 percent of global income. Finally, the median estimate of the probability of a catastrophic loss in the survey was very small for a 3°C warming and in the 3–5 percent range for a 6°C warming.

On the whole, the damage function here represents the survey reasonably well, with some tendency to underestimate the impacts relative to the survey for low temperature increases and to overestimate the impacts relative to the survey for the high temperature increases. To construct the quintiles of the damage, we assume that the lowest quintile shows no damage, and that the median equals the mean; this leaves two free parameters. To close the distribution, we place the highest quintiles in such a way as to best approximate the ratio of the 90th percentile to the 50th percentile in the survey. The result is shown in table 7.1.

We have examined a number of alternative ways of estimating the distribution for climate damage, but all modifications of the distribution that stay within the conventions used for constructing the uncertain distributions make little difference to the outcome. Nonetheless, it must be emphasized that the estimates of the climate-damage function are extremely speculative. Although the central estimates of the impact of climate change have been based on observed relations between climate and economic activity, the estimates of the extreme observations are extrapolations well beyond historical experience.

Pure Rate of Social Time Preference (ρ)
The issues involved in choosing the pure rate of social time preference were discussed in detail in the last chapter. Recall that the condition on the real return on capital is given by equation (6.3), which holds that $r(t) = \alpha g(t) + \rho$, where $r(t)$ = real interest rate or the discount rate on goods, α is the elasticity of the marginal social utility of consumption, $g(t)$ is the growth rate of per capita consumption, and ρ is the pure rate of social time preference. I discussed extensively the grounds for selecting the base rate of time preference in the last chapter.

One way of examining the implication of alternative values of the rate of time preference is to examine the implication of changes in time preference on the savings rate. The following shows a comparison of net global savings rates in recent years [15] along with the calculated net savings rate for the DICE model with different rates of time preference:

Actual

| 1970–79 | 9.1 percent |
| 1980–89 | 7.0 percent |

Calculated for 1990–99

$\rho = 0.03$	9.6 percent
$\rho = 0.01$	15.2 percent
$\rho = 0.005$	16.9 percent
$\rho = 0.0001$	18.7 percent

This comparison shows that lowering the rate of time preference has major implications for the global savings rate, which reminds us that this parameter cannot be chosen without consideration to its more general implications.

In addition, the author undertook an informal survey of environmental and resource economists who participated in the 1992 National

15. Actual data are from the data set compiled for this study and discussed in chapter 4.

Bureau of Economic Research (NBER) Summer Workshop to determine their views of the appropriate value of the best guess and uncertainty range for the rate of social time preference.[16] The central
tendency of the best guesses of that group ranged from 1.8 to 3.0 percent per year. For the quintile range, the central tendency of that group
ranged from 3.7 to 5.0 percent per annum.

In the uncertainty runs that follow, we continue to use a rate of time
preference of 3 percent per annum as the central case because that
value calibrates best the data on capital stocks, savings rates, and rates
of return with historical data. For an uncertainty range, we allow for
the possibility that there will be a decline in the rate of time preference
as per capita incomes rise. At the low end, a rate of $\rho = .01$ per annum
is as low as seems plausible given both past trends and the required
near doubling in the net world savings rate implied by the low rate of
time preference. The higher rates of time preference are then determined symmetrically; this range is consistent with the NBER survey.

While allowing for different rates of time preference is straightforward in principle, it raises difficult issues of interpretation and implementation in the DICE model. The appropriate interpretation would
be as a future change in social preferences. We can envision the change
as one in which the world's decision makers weigh the options of present and future and decide to save and invest more because of greater
perceived needs in the future. This decision would require major
changes in the economic policies of a great number of countries; the
changes would require much persuasion and legislation and might
take many years to accomplish (some would say, indeed, that the
trends of the last decade have been in the other direction, with lower
national savings rates in the United States and Japan). An ambitious
assumption would be that the process of changing our attitudes toward thrift would begin sometime in the decade of the 1990s and
would take a generation to accomplish.

A gradual change in taste is complicated to handle computationally,
so to make this change operational in the DICE model we assume that
the change in taste occurs in one period—between the sixth and sev-
enth computational periods (that is, in the year 2020). A simulation
indicates that this assumption produces almost the same result as does
a change in taste that begins in 2000 and is completed in 2040. This

---

16. The detailed numerical results are available from the author.

assumption also allows an analysis of the value of early information through period 6.

Monte Carlo Estimates

Overview

In the present section, we undertake a set of Monte Carlo runs—using the sampling technique described in the first part of the chapter, sampling with replacement—to estimate the uncertainty about future economic growth, climate change, and policy. The theoretical structure was sketched at the beginning of this chapter, and we now lay out the technique in greater detail. The DICE model can be thought of as a mapping from a set of parameters and initial conditions to a set of outcome variables. In the last section, we derived a quintuple of values for each of the eight uncertain variables. In this section, we make a set of 500 runs of the DICE model based on random draws from the 5^8 ($= 390,625$) possible combinations of parameters.

The purpose of the Monte Carlo runs is twofold. First, using this approach, we can obtain an estimate of the degree of uncertainty about future variables such as output and consumption growth, emissions and concentrations growth, temperature increase, and climatic damage. These results will be presented in the next section. Second, on the basis of the Monte Carlo runs, we can aggregate the vast number of possible future states into a small and manageable number of representative scenarios to use in estimating the risk or insurance premiums in the next chapter. This task will be undertaken at the end of this chapter.

Results of the Monte Carlo Runs

We now present the results of the Monte Carlo runs for the DICE model. Recall that we have generated the sample by sampling with replacement for the eight-dimensional distribution of uncertain variables described earlier in this chapter. These runs are presented as probability distributions of the different variables at different points of time. The probabilistic interpretation comes from applying the standard laws of probability to the distributions of the eight uncertain variables assuming statistical independence among the variables.

An interpretative word is in order before we present the results. The distribution of outcomes and policies is one that would occur were policymakers to learn about the structure of the economy and act today on the basis of perfect information about future conditions. These scenarios can be described as "learn, then act." In other words, the values are ones where the policies—both emissions controls as well as investment and consumption decisions—are taken conditional on learning the exact state of the world before taking any policy actions. The outcomes are "superoptimal" in the sense of taking no steps that will later be regretted; they are also clearly unrealistic in assuming that uncertainties will be resolved in the very near future. The reason for taking this superoptimizing approach is twofold. First, from this analysis we may obtain an estimate of the inherent uncertainty about the future (assuming that our findings about the underlying distributions of variables are correct). Second, later in this chapter we will use these results to aggregate states of the world so that a more realistic treatment of learning can be studied in the next chapter.

A summary of the runs is shown in table 7.3, which presents the means, standard deviations, coefficients of variation, and the 10th and 90th percentiles of the major variables for different periods through the year 2100. (The runs are actually made for a 400-year period, but they are so conjectural beyond 2100 that the results are not presented.) The uncertainty of the results grows sharply over time because of the growing uncertainty about future social and economic conditions.

Figures 7.1 through 7.5 show the distributions of the major uncertain variables. Figures 7.1 and 7.2 show the distributions of GHG emissions and concentrations (largely CO_2 in the future). Figure 7.3 shows the estimated distribution of future temperature increases. This figure indicates that the degree of uncertainty is extremely large by the end of the next century, with the 80th percentile range (between the 10th and 90th percentile) ranging from 1.8 to 4.5°C. This range is slightly lower than that provided in the IPCC estimates, although the latter was accorded no probabilistic interpretation.

Figures 7.4 and 7.5 show the estimated distributions of optimal greenhouse policies in terms of the policy variables, the carbon tax, and the GHG control rate. The median estimates from these distributions deviate from the best guess values that were presented in part I of this study—the differences reflecting the interaction of the uncertain variables. The distribution of policies is extremely skewed, with a few

Table 7.3
Distribution of major uncertain variables (from 500 Monte Carlo runs)

	1995	2005	2015	2045	2095
Expected values					
Output	24.6	32.5	42.0	82.4	219.9
GHG emissions	9.1	11.0	13.0	20.4	39.6
GHG concentrations	765	809	862	1073	1655
Temperature increase	0.7	0.9	1.1	1.8	3.1
GHG control rate	0.046	0.060	0.075	0.110	0.153
Carbon tax	11.83	17.24	24.22	49.20	129.43
Standard deviation					
Output	2.3	4.9	9.2	38.5	219.8
GHG emissions	2.0	3.2	4.9	12.8	48.8
GHG concentrations	18.3	30.4	49.2	164.5	759.2
Temperature increase	0.11	0.16	0.22	0.44	1.05
GHG control rate	0.088	0.118	0.153	0.209	0.272
Carbon tax	30.87	48.94	74.22	176.54	594.25
Coefficient of variation					
Output	0.09	0.15	0.22	0.47	1.00
GHG emissions	0.22	0.29	0.38	0.63	1.23
GHG concentrations	0.02	0.04	0.06	0.15	0.46
Temperature increase	0.16	0.18	0.19	0.24	0.33
GHG control rate	1.89	1.97	2.03	1.91	1.77
Carbon tax	2.61	2.84	3.06	3.59	4.59
10th percentile					
Output	21.8	26.7	31.6	42.9	55.5
GHG emissions	6.7	7.4	7.8	8.4	6.4
GHG concentrations	740	768	799	889	988
Temperature increase	0.55	0.67	0.80	1.22	1.85
GHG control rate	0.010	0.010	0.010	0.010	0.010
Carbon tax	0.00	0.00	0.00	0.00	0.00
50th percentile					
Output	24.1	31.3	39.7	73.0	138.3
GHG emissions	8.9	10.5	12.1	16.9	24.1
GHG concentrations	765	809	858	1049	1425
Temperature increase	0.8	1.0	1.2	1.8	3.0
GHG control rate	0.014	0.017	0.019	0.026	0.037
Carbon tax	4.51	5.56	6.99	11.64	18.62
90th percentile					
Output	27.7	39.2	54.7	136.7	432.2
GHG emissions	11.8	15.3	19.5	36.2	82.4
GHG concentrations	789	849	929	1288	2554
Temperature increase	0.86	1.12	1.40	2.41	4.52
GHG control rate	0.116	0.159	0.211	0.338	0.525
Carbon tax	25.77	36.93	51.33	97.77	207.09

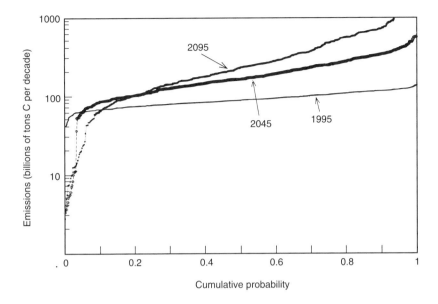

Figure 7.1
Distribution of greenhouse-gas emissions
(500 Monte Carlo runs)

extremely large values that reflect the small probability of extremely large outcomes. Whereas the median value of the carbon tax is $4.45 per ton carbon in the first control period, the expected value is $11.83 per ton, and the 95th percentile is $42 per ton. The probability of an extremely high optimal carbon tax (one being over $100 per ton carbon) is estimated to be 2 percent in 1995, 10 percent in 2045, and slightly under 20 percent in 2095. The extent of skewness of the distribution suggests that there may be a large risk premium attached to greenhouse warming—a question that is investigated in the next chapter.

In addition, whereas the median control rate for 1995 is 1.4 percent, the expected value is 4.6 percent, and the 95th percentile of control rates for 1995 is 19 percent. Another way of expressing the point is to note that the probability that the optimal control rate is greater than 20 percent is around 5 percent for 1995, 12 percent for 2045, and about 20 percent for 2095.

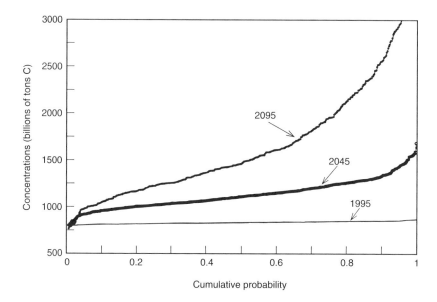

Figure 7.2
Distribution of greenhouse-gas concentrations
(500 Monte Carlo runs)

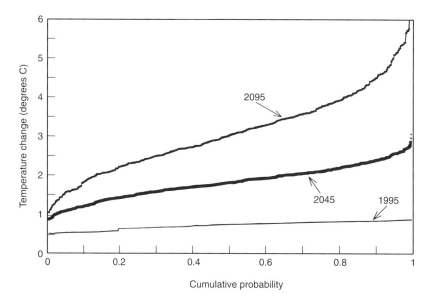

Figure 7.3
Distribution of temperature change
(500 Monte Carlo runs)

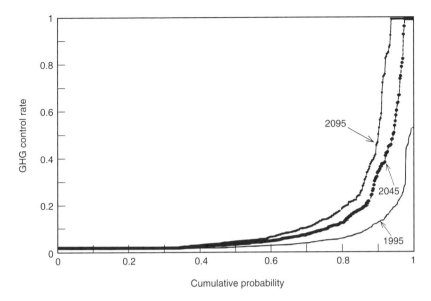

Figure 7.4
Distribution of GHG control rates
(500 Monte Carlo runs)

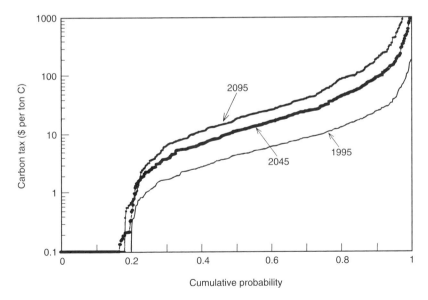

Figure 7.5
Distribution of carbon taxes
(500 Monte Carlo runs)

In summary, by applying the techniques of subjective probability theory and Monte Carlo sampling to the DICE model, we have in this chapter derived distributions of the major outcome variables—both the economic and climate variables as well as the policy variables. Because of the long time horizon and the intrinsic uncertainty about many features of both the scientific basis and future social and economic trends, the uncertainties about future greenhouse warming as well as the policy implications are vast. In this and the next chapter, we turn to an investigation of the implication of the uncertainties for economic policy.

Derivation of the Representative Scenarios

In this final section, we describe how we aggregate the large number of potential scenarios into five *representative scenarios.* To reiterate the purpose of this step, it will be recalled that we will derive five states of the world for our optimization and decision analysis in the next chapter. This small number is the maximum that we can easily handle with a full analysis of decision making under uncertainty in the DICE model; it is computationally infeasible to incorporate the full Monte Carlo results, and we must therefore reduce to a very small number the number of states of the world that are considered here. However, in constructing the representative scenarios, it is essential that the scenarios be designed so that they have the same properties as the underlying population of states of the world (SOW). Using these representative scenarios, we can calculate the value of information and a "risk premium" to account for the uncertainty about future climate and impacts as well as to incorporate risk aversion; because the scenarios are representative in the sense of having the same probability distribution as the underlying population of scenarios, we can be confident that the measures of the value of uncertainty and the calculated risk premia for the limited number of states of the world are (except for sampling error and nonlinearity in the mapping from the parameters to the outcomes) identical for the full population.

From a theoretical perspective, the technique for aggregating the large number of SOW into a small number of representative SOW is shown in figure 7.6. On the horizontal axis we show a single uncertain variable, represented in terms of the fractile of the distribution. On the vertical axis we show the outcome variable (say the stringency of the GHG restraints). The wavy line is the complicated mapping in equa-

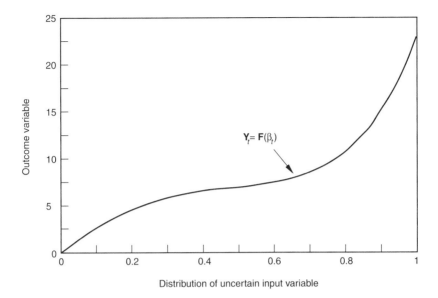

Figure 7.6
Hypothetical distribution of uncertain and outcome variables

tion (7.1) that maps the parameters into the outcomes; for example, the line represents a simplified version of $Y_t = F(X_{t-\tau}; \boldsymbol{\beta_I}, \boldsymbol{\beta_{II}})$, where Y_t is on the vertical axis and $\boldsymbol{\beta_I}$ on the horizontal axis.

To obtain the representative scenarios, we need to rank the states of the world by some common characteristic. In figure 7.6, because there is only one input and output variable, it would be natural to group the uncertainties by quintile. Then, SOW1 would aggregate together all input variables that lie within the interval for β of [0, 0.2] along with the associated outcomes. Because the **F** mapping is monotonic increasing in the uncertain variable, this grouping would mean that the first SOW would also contain the quintile of *outcomes* with the lowest score.

Unfortunately, there are a number of serious complications that arise in aggregating the 400,000 potential full population SOW (or a sample of 500 "sample SOW" from that 400,000) into the five representative scenarios or states of the world. Three complications arise in the problem at hand. First, there are multiple uncertain variables, so that there is no obvious grouping of uncertain variables into "low" and "high" values; in terms of figure 7.6, this means that the horizontal axis is actually an eight-dimensional space. Second, there are multiple outcomes of interest, such as the GHG control rate, the carbon tax, world

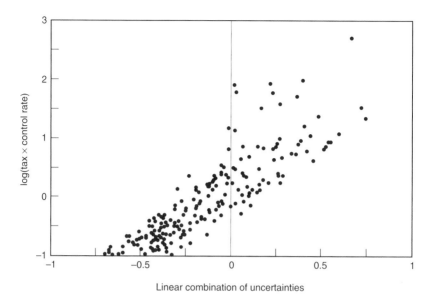

Figure 7.7
Outcome and uncertain variables in DICE model Monte Carlo runs

output, and global temperature, and all of these variables over time; in terms of figure 7.6, this is seen as a high dimensionality in the outcome space of the vertical axis. And third, the **F** mapping appears to be highly nonlinear, so that the uncertainty analysis is primarily concerned with the extremes of the distribution rather than the central tendency or best guess examined in the first part of this study.

Figure 7.7 illustrates the difficulty of constructing the representative states of the world. For this purpose, we have defined the outcome variable on the vertical axis in terms of current climate-change policy as represented by the logarithm of the product of the current optimal carbon tax times the GHG reduction rate. With that outcome variable, we estimated the best linear statistical relationship between the eight uncertain variables and the outcome. We have placed the best linear combination of uncertain variables on the horizontal axis of figure 7.7. The scatter plot shows that there is no simple mapping (or what is known as a "response surface") from uncertain variables to the outcomes. In addition, figure 7.7 shows how skewed the distribution of outcomes is, and that there are a few very large outlying values.

The solution to the three difficulties is as follows. First, we choose to aggregate the uncertain input variables on the basis of the outcomes rather than on the basis of a ranking of the inputs. The reason for this choice is that the input variables have no intrinsic interest; rather, we are concerned about grouping them so as to obtain useful representative scenarios for the purpose of handling the uncertainties of climate change.

To handle the second issue—the high dimensionality of the outcomes—we focus on the implications of uncertainty for current climate-change policy. To do this, we construct a linear index representing the overall degree of cost associated with a particular scenario (this index is called the "severity index"). The severity index is defined as the product of the carbon tax times the GHG control rate. This index reflects the severity of climate-change policy in terms of the two major control variables. It appears that alternative specifications of the severity index do not change the outcome in a significant manner.

The third question—the skewness of the distribution of outcomes—is handled by a stratification of the states of the world that overrepresents the low-probability, high-consequence events. To construct the representative SOW, we group the outcomes into ones we might call calamitous (SOW1, $p = .02$), extremely unfavorable (SOW2, $p = .08$), unfavorable (SOW3, $p = .15$), disadvantageous (SOW4, $p = .25$), and favorable (SOW5, $p = .50$). By overrepresenting the costly outcomes, we can ensure that policies take into account the implications of low-probability, high-consequence events.

Using these assumptions, we next determine the parameter values for the five sets of runs that are grouped into the five SOW. The technique here is to map *backwards* from the groupings of the SOW to the values of the uncertain parameters. In effect, we take the top 2 percent of the 500 sample SOW (that is, the top 2 percent of outcomes or 10 points shown in figure 7.7) and map backward to the values of uncertain variables to get the parameters for SOW1. If there were only one uncertain variable, we would simply average the values of the variable on the horizontal axis in figure 7.7 that would correspond to the top 2 percent of the outcomes to obtain SOW1. We then take the next 40 points to obtain the next 8 percent of outcomes for SOW2. And so forth.

The actual problem has more dimensions than are displayed in figure 7.7 but follows the same principles. We then order the 500 Monte Carlo runs by rank according to the severity index and group the runs into the top 10 runs (SOW1), the next 40 runs (SOW2), and so forth. We then map backward from each of the 500 runs to the underlying

Table 7.4
Distribution of major parameters in five representative SOW

		Time Preference	Population Growth	Productivity Growth	GHG-Output Ratio	Climate Damage	Mitigation Cost	GHG Retention Rate	T-Sensitivity $T(2 \times CO_2)$
Best guess:		0.030	0.195	0.110	−0.117	0.013	0.069	0.640	2.908
Average parameter value in:									
SOW1	0.02	0.012	0.027	0.074	−0.117	0.017	0.067	0.677	3.808
SOW2	0.08	0.014	0.124	0.099	−0.128	0.024	0.068	0.665	3.222
SOW3	0.15	0.023	0.167	0.123	−0.110	0.022	0.064	0.653	3.310
SOW4	0.25	0.030	0.193	0.115	−0.117	0.018	0.072	0.652	2.999
SOW5	0.5	0.033	0.204	0.106	−0.124	0.006	0.067	0.635	2.656
Mean		0.029	0.186	0.110	−0.120	0.013	0.068	0.645	2.908
Deviation[a]		0.043	0.047	0.003	0.028	0.025	0.007	0.008	0.000
Results of Monte Carlo sample:									
Mean[b]		0.029	0.186	0.110	−0.120	0.013	0.068	0.645	2.908
Stan. dev.[b]		0.001	0.005	0.003	0.003	0.000	0.002	0.004	0.046
t-stat[c]		−2.093	−1.879	−0.097	−0.983	−0.669	−0.266	1.205	0.013

Notes:
a. Absolute value of difference of mean of SOW from true mean divided by true mean.
b. Mean and standard deviation of the sample of 500 Monte Carlo runs.
c. Difference between mean of sample of 500 runs and population mean divided by sample standard deviation.

set of the eight uncertain parameters that generated that run. Finally, we average the values of the eight uncertain parameters for the 10 runs in SOW1 to obtain the parameters for SOW1; we average the values of the eight uncertain parameters for the forty runs in SOW2 to obtain the parameters for SOW2; and so forth. Formally, we compute the conditional average of each uncertain parameter value for the runs in each state of the world. These generate the parameter values to use in the uncertainty and decision analysis in the next chapter. The results of this step are shown in table 7.4.

To generate the five representative scenarios, we then make a DICE-model run with five SOW; in these runs, the parameters have the same distribution as the underlying population (except for sampling error). In addition, to the extent that the mappings from the parameters to the outcomes are linear in the regions represented by the individual SOW, the representative scenarios and the outcome variables will also have the same distribution of outcomes as the full population of SOW. An examination of both the distributions of the outcomes and the moments of the representative scenarios as compared to the sample SOW indicates that the stratification of the SOW has succeeded in preserving the central tendency and the dispersion of the larger sample.

To summarize, we have introduced a new technique for generating representative scenarios for use in uncertainty analysis. This technique allows us to analyze a wide range of uncertainties and at the same time to aggregate the uncertainties into a small number that will in the next chapter be embedded into an optimization model to determine the optimal policies and the value of information under conditions of uncertainty.

8

Decision Analysis and the Value of Information

Introduction

Overview

We have seen that vast uncertainties are posed by the threat of global warming—uncertainties about future emissions paths, about the GHG-climate linkage, about the timing of climate change, about the impacts of climate upon flora and fauna and human societies, about the costs of slowing climate change, and even about the speed with which we can reduce the uncertainties. How should we proceed in the face of uncertainty? The last two chapters have developed a methodology for analyzing the implications of uncertainty for policies concerning greenhouse warming. This chapter takes the final step of examining the range of possible outcomes to determine how risk and uncertainty would affect the optimal strategy for curbing greenhouse warming.

For many problems, it is reasonable to take a "certainty-equivalent" or best-guess approach, acting as if the uncertainties were unimportant. Such an approach is appropriate as long as the risks are symmetrical, the stakes are small, and there is no learning. In fact, none of these conditions is likely to be satisfied for the greenhouse effect. We showed in the last chapter that the risks are highly asymmetrical and skewed, with a high probability of a small loss and a small probability of a very large loss; in addition, for the extreme cases, the stakes are likely to be large, particularly for poor countries and regions; and finally, many of the uncertainties are ones that can be resolved by further study or at the least by the passage of time.

This chapter attempts to investigate these issues systematically. We begin by reviewing three of the ways in which societies can cope with uncertainties: insurance, consumption smoothing, and precautionary investments. We then proceed to examine the implication of uncertainty for the optimal policy. Does uncertainty imply that we should take more stringent GHG controls, or that the carbon tax should be higher? It further examines the implications of learning: How does the gradual revelation of information affect our investment strategies? Should we move aggressively to reduce our uncertainties, with our first investments being in knowledge? Or is it possible that the strategies are robust to the timing of resolution of uncertainties? By using the results of the last two chapters on the distribution of uncertainties, we can hope to obtain answers to these questions.

We then turn to the question of the value of better information or earlier resolution of the uncertainties. Some uncertainties can be reduced by careful study while others will be resolved by the mere passage of time—for example, uncertainties about the growth of population between now and 2020 can be reduced by demographic research; but in any case the uncertainty will be resolved by actual events by the time 2020 arrives. Early knowledge about economic and geophysical aspects of greenhouse warming can be useful in allowing us to better adapt our strategies to the future. If we know for sure that sea-level rise will be minimal for a century, we can postpone expensive investments to protect our coastlines. By examining the value of resolving uncertainties at different points in time we can obtain estimates of the value of information; these results can also help point efforts toward those fields where research can have the largest payoffs.

The Risk Premium on Global Warming

One of the major concerns, if not *the* major concern, lies in the uncertain and imponderable impacts of climate change. In light of this concern, it might be worthwhile to pay a substantial risk premium to avoid or reduce the probabilities of running aground on the poorly charted shoals of sea-level rise, desertification, unforeseen pests, or other hazards. Many have called for paying an insurance premium in the face of uncertainties, and this approach was emphasized in a path-breaking study, *Buying Greenhouse Insurance.*[1]

This chapter addresses the implications of uncertainty for policy, focusing particularly on the steps that might be taken to cope with the uncertainties of future climate change. Should society undertake more

---

1. See Manne and Richels 1992.

or less GHG reductions because the future is uncertain? To what extent can we insure against uncertainty, as individuals, as nations, or as a globe? Does the fact that we will eventually learn about the scale and consequences of global warming tilt policies in one direction—toward present abatement or future adaptation? We begin by analyzing the implications of risk in the context of global warming and considering how we might insure against uncertain future events. For concreteness, we label as *mitigation of uncertainty* actions that are designed to reduce the harms that flow from uncertainty, while the economic costs of these actions are labeled a *risk premium.*

To begin with the fundamentals, we should recall that an important goal of economic and social institutions is to reduce the impact of random or capricious events on individuals and society. Broadly speaking, things like insurance, capital markets, tribes and families, spare tires, government transfer policies, and unemployed resources serve as buffers to reduce the vulnerability of individuals to uncertain events. Three specific kinds of activities can mitigate the effects on economic welfare of uncertainty about climate change: traditional insurance, consumption smoothing, and precautionary investments.

1. The first approach is *traditional insurance.* Strictly speaking, insurance is a mechanism by which, in return for an insurance premium, an insurer reimburses an insured party for a loss. Insurance relies upon the existence of a large number of diversifiable risks; upon the law of large numbers, which allows spreading of individual risks among a large number of people; and upon the existence of risk aversion, which implies that risk pooling raises average utility of consumption. In more precise terms, an *insurance premium* is the amount that society or individuals pay to replace the uncertain distribution of outcomes with the expected value of outcomes.

Once we recall the nature of traditional insurance, it becomes clear that the central risks posed by global warming do not fall into the traditional insurance framework. The traditional principles of insurance apply when individual risks can be pooled by the law of large number across different individuals; the nature of the global warming problem is precisely that it *is* global, so there is a major component of undiversifiable and therefore uninsurable risk.

At the same time, insurance may form an important part of an appropriate policy to cope with greenhouse warming. While there might not be large aggregate impacts of global warming, individual people, regions, and nations may well be seriously affected. Some homes may be washed into the sea while others are thereby afforded fine vistas; some low-lying areas may be inundated, diverting trade in favor of landlocked regions; some nations may find their grain belts turn into deserts while others see their terms of trade and incomes rise as a consequence. It is exactly in this circumstance of diversifiable private risk—ones that average out in the aggregate—that traditional insurance can reduce the private distress and social frictions that may attend climate change.

2. A second way in which society can cope with uncertainty is the intertemporal version of traditional insurance—this is *consumption smoothing over time*. Say that there is a small probability of a large, one-time disastrous loss of income from climate change—perhaps the possibility of a mammoth storm surge, glacial disintegration, or shift in ocean currents that might reduce the income of a generation substantially after which incomes would recover back to the trend line. Society can indeed insure against this event by accumulating some extra capital in normal times and then maintaining consumption by running down the capital right after the disaster.

The DICE model is well designed to examine the appropriate degree of consumption smoothing in the face of different kinds of income loss. Indeed, the optimization is expressly designed to determine the optimal distribution of consumption losses over different generations that would be induced by a particular specification and a given utility function. In this study, we have examined the response to smooth and continuous impacts of climate change, but it can be easily modified to examine sharp and one-time changes as well.

3. A third way to cope with uncertainty is through *precautionary investments*; these are expenditures in abatement, adaptation, or information that are undertaken because the future is uncertain and serve to increase the expected utility of consumption. Just as we provide fire protection for those states of the world in which no fires occur, so we might make investments in abatement (by curbing energy use or planting trees), in adaptation (by raising dikes or through research in high-CO_2 crops), or in improving our knowledge (through climate or social science research) even though global warming might not occur and the oceans might not rise.

The most obvious form of precautionary investment comes when society decides to increase the rate of GHG reduction; this has the effect of reducing the probability of extreme outcomes and being better positioned to take severe cuts in GHGs if the dice roll unfavorably. This form of precautionary investment is specifically examined in the

Table 8.1
Alternative policies to mitigate uncertainty

Category	Source of Uncertainty	Policy
1. Traditional insurance	1. Diversifiable (individual) risk	1.a) Private insurance (weather, flood, crop) b) Social insurance (against terms-of-trade or income losses)
2. Consumption smoothing over time	2. Risk of large or catastrophic loss	2. Investment ("for a rainy day")
3. Precautionary investments	3. Uncertain scope of damage or abatement costs	3.a) Precautionary abatement (higher carbon tax) b) Precautionary adaptation (retreat from coastline) c) Investment in knowledge (geophysical and social-science research)

DICE model, and an example is shown later in this chapter in figure 8.3 and table 8.2. These examples show that the mean value of GHG reductions is indeed higher because decision makers do not know the future evolution of the climate.

Research is another example of precautionary investment. Research serves to reduce the uncertainties about future abatement costs and climate-change damage, and thereby increases the expected utility of consumption. Research provides better information and early resolution of uncertainties; better information is valuable because it allows us to fine tune our policies to the actual threats that we face. Later in this chapter, we will see that society will benefit enormously from reducing uncertainties about future climate change. Given the high value of reducing uncertainties, society may well decide to invest in precautionary investments in scientific research.[2]

In conclusion, coping with uncertainty is a rich subject for analysis and policy. As is suggested in table 8.1, which summarizes this discussion, a wide variety of techniques is available to reduce the impact of

---

2. Another form of uncertainty or risk premium arises because of *nonlinearities* of the payoff with respect to the parameters. We will see below (see especially the difference between the results on perfect information and certainty equivalent in table 8.2) that increasing uncertainty (in the sense of a mean-preserving spread) harms real incomes by reducing the expected value of utility. Let us call this source of concern the "nonlinearity premium." It is defined as the difference between the median outcome and the outcome

uncertainty—ones ranging from private and social insurance to pre-cautionary investments in scientific research.

Optimal Policy under Uncertainty

Decision Analysis and the Resolution of Uncertainty

In this section we apply the analysis of the first half of this chapter to investigate the empirical implications of uncertainty for climate-change policies. We begin with the impact of uncertainty in a situation where the uncertainties will be immediately resolved. We then move on to the more realistic situation where we must act under conditions of uncertainty, recognizing that the uncertainties will be resolved over time.

The different situations are analyzed using the tools of "decision theory," and the different approaches are shown in figure 8.1. In this case, the only uncertainty is whether climate damages from green-house warming are high or low; there are therefore two states of the world. In situations of uncertainty, we must determine the sequence of actions and learning, always considering "what will you know and when will you know it." If we are fortunate, we can determine the state of the world and then act. This situation is shown in figure 8.1a and is called "learn then act." One approach would be that we might first learn whether the damages from greenhouse warming are high or low; then we would adapt our strategies to that knowledge, with high or low carbon taxes attached to the high or low damages, respectively. In terms of the conventions of decision theory, a circle represents a point at which uncertainties are resolved, while a box represents a decision.

A more realistic case arises where we must act *before* nature reveals which state of the world we are in; this case is shown in figure 8.1b. We must decide on a climate-change policy before we know whether damages are high or low. In this case, policy follows a middle of the road approach of a medium carbon tax in 1990, and only a decade later do we learn whether that was too high (if damages prove to be low)

---

at the median of the parameter values. The difference arises because of the underlying nonlinearity of the economic or geophysical processes. The unfortunate reality of nonlin-earity and the penalty from uncertainty, however, has no operational significance. There is no way we can pay a premium to some Higher Entity that will either insure us against the nonlinearities or remove them.

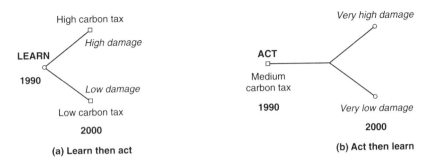

Figure 8.1
Decision tree for preventive steps
A fundamental issue in decision theory is "what you know and when do you know it." In (a), information is available before the decision must be made, so the decision maker can act differently depending on the state of the world. In (b), the decision maker is ignorant as to the state of the world, so no state-dependent policies can be taken—that is, decisions are taken and then the state of the world is revealed. Decisions are more efficient in (a) because people only take raincoats on rainy days.

or too low (if damages prove to be high). Clearly, we would prefer to have the information early, for then we would not have mistakenly set the carbon tax too high or too low. The difference between society's real incomes in case (a) and those in case (b) is the *value of early information.*

Figure 8.2 shows the further elaboration of sequential decisions and resolution of uncertainties, which we might call "act, learn, act, learn, act, . . . " For this example, assume that there are two sets of uncertainties—a high and a low mitigation cost and a high and a low climate-damage function, for a total of four SOW. In this case, it is assumed that carbon taxes can be set in years 1995, 2005, 2015, . . . , while certain information is revealed in 2000 and 2010. In 1995, a first and tentative carbon tax is set, but there is very poor information about both mitigation costs and climate-change damages; policies therefore find a middle-of-the-road approach of a medium carbon tax. Next, in the year 2000 it is learned whether mitigation costs will be high or low, although the damage function is still uncertain. On the basis of that information, the carbon tax is set either high or low. Then in 2010 the final uncertainty is resolved, and we know both the damage function and the mitigation-cost function. At our next decision point, 2015, we then fine tune the carbon tax to the exact state of the world. Here again, we might calculate society's real incomes for the sequence shown in figure 8.2 and compare this with the case where, say, information is

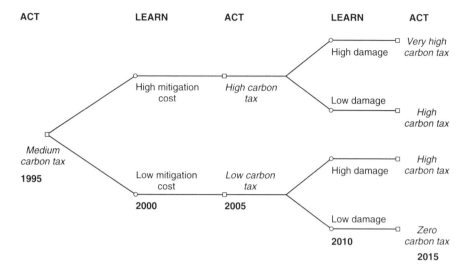

Figure 8.2
Sequential decision making
This figure shows how decisions are revised as new information becomes available. There is no useful information in first period, so carbon tax is set at middle-of-the-road value. In 2000, information becomes available as to mitigation costs, which allows the decision maker to choose between high and low tax. As further information becomes available on damages in 2010, decision can be further refined. Note that the number and efficiency of policies increase as information improves.

revealed a decade earlier. The difference between the real incomes would be the value of early information.

In the calculations that follow, we have implemented the ideas shown in figures 8.1 and 8.2. We first calculate the optimal policies under different assumptions about the resolution of uncertainties; from the different results, we can determine the optimal policy and the value of perfect information or early information.

Optimal Policy with Perfect Information

The first and unrealistic case involves optimal policy with perfect information. This involves the ability to set different policies in the different states of the world and represents the example shown in figure 8.1a's depiction of "learn, then act." In this case, one state of the world might be high damage while another might be low damage. Upon learning the state of the world, policymakers could then set the appropriate policies. This experiment shows the pure impact of uncertainty on policies.

Table 8.2
Value of GHG control rate and carbon tax rate under uncertainty

	1995	2005	2015	2045
GHG CONTROL RATE				
(fraction of uncontrolled rate)				
Expected Value of Parameters (CE)	0.088	0.096	0.104	0.122
Median of 500 Random Runs (PI)	0.015	na	na	0.025
Expected Value of 500 Random Runs (PI)	0.046	na	na	0.110
Expected Value of 5 SOW Runs (PI)	0.103	0.119	0.135	0.171
Expected Value of for Early Information in 5 SOW Runs				
Perfect Information 1990	0.103	0.119	0.135	0.171
Perfect Information 2000	0.127	0.119	0.135	0.171
Perfect Information 2010	0.128	0.156	0.136	0.171
Perfect Information 2020	0.128	0.157	0.193	0.171
CARBON TAX (1989 prices)				
Expected Value of Parameters (CE)	$ 5.24	$ 6.73	$ 8.34	$13.40
Median of 500 Random Runs (PI)	4.51	na	na	11.64
Expected Value of 500 Random Runs (PI)	11.82	na	na	49.20
Expected Value of 5 SOW Runs (PI)	11.98	18.00	26.48	52.84
Expected Value of for Early Information in 5 SOW Runs				
Perfect Information 1990	11.98	18.00	26.48	52.84
Perfect Information 2000	12.03	18.04	26.54	52.94
Perfect Information 2010	12.06	18.17	26.66	53.07
Perfect Information 2020	12.11	18.26	27.02	53.37

Symbol: "na" = not available.

The results of this experiment are shown in table 8.2, which compares the results of optimal policy with perfect information (PI) with the certainty-equivalent (CE) case. Recall that we have constructed the uncertain cases as mean-preserving spreads; that is, the means of the certainty-equivalent and uncertain cases are the same and the only difference is the spread of outcomes in the latter case.

Table 8.2 shows both the results of the full Monte Carlo experiment (with 500 random runs) and the results of compressing the results into the five macro SOW. The first important result can be seen by comparing the certainty equivalent case with the expected value of policies. As can be seen, the expected value of the emissions control rate for GHGs is considerably lower for the PI case than for the CE case; on the other hand, the carbon tax rate is almost doubled in the PI case relative to the CE case. The reason for these results lies in the nonlinearity of the impacts and control functions. Basically, the impacts are highly skewed, so that the median result has lower controls and carbon taxes than does the expected value.

A second result concerns the relationship between the five SOW runs and the Monte Carlo results. It can be seen from table 8.2 that the results of the five macro SOW runs are quite close to those of the full 500 runs for the carbon taxes, while the expected value of the control rate is considerably higher for the five SOW runs. The latter result arises because of the effect of aggregation of parameters is to eliminate many cells that produce low control rates. On the other hand, the more important carbon tax results indicate that the process of compressing the results for purposes of undertaking the study of the impact of constraining behavior in the different SOW has represented the underlying distribution of uncertainty reasonably well.

Optimal Policy with Learning

The more realistic case arises where we must "act, then learn," the case depicted in figure 8.2. In this case, we must undertake policies before we know which particular state of the world we are in; upon learning the true state, we will reappraise our policies and almost certainly find that we have been too ambitious or too relaxed in our policies. To model policy with learning, we break time into three phases: (1) the first period is one in which we are assumed to act to maximize the expected value of the outcome based on knowledge of the true probability distribution of the economic and geophysical parameters; (2) next, at some future date, we learn about the true state of the world—that is, nature takes a draw from the distribution of parameters, and we learn the true value of the economic and geophysical parameters; and, finally, (3) for all subsequent periods, we act with *perfect information* about the state of the world and the actual value of the parameters. The extreme case where phase 1 vanishes becomes equivalent to the PI case examined in the last section.

The technique for modeling the constraints of ignorance is as follows. Assume that the information about the true SOW becomes available at the end of period θ. This implies that for periods $1, \ldots, \theta$ the decisions cannot be state dependent; in other words, the level of GHG controls must be the same for all SOW. We can write these constraints as follows. Using the notation of the last chapter, we can write the DICE model succinctly as

$$Y_t(s) = F[X_{t-\tau}(s); \beta(s)], \tag{8.1}$$

where F is the mapping representing the Euler equations from the maximization; Y_t is the vector of endogenous and policy variables (such as output, GHG concentrations, and GHG control rate); $X_{t-\tau}$ is a vector of exogenous variables; β is the set of uncertain parameters; and s is the state of the world. For the first θ periods, decisions must be made in ignorance of the true SOW; hence, policymakers operate under the constraint

$$\mu_t(s) = \mu_t \qquad t \leq \theta, \text{ for all states of the world } s, \tag{8.2}$$

where μ is the GHG control rate. Equation (8.2) states that the GHG control rates must be the same in all SOW for the first θ periods because policymakers cannot distinguish between SOW. After period θ, however, μ becomes state dependent as policymakers learn about the true state of the world.

To implement the constraints of the three phases of ignorance, learning, and perfect information, we rely on the DICE model constructed with the five macro SOW described in the last chapter. In practice, the equalities in (8.2) are added as different constraints to the model represented in (8.1) across the five macro SOW in the DICE model. Figure 8.3 shows the results for one case, that in which the true state of the world is revealed after the fifth period or in 2010. This figure shows the optimal state-dependent carbon taxes on a logarithmic scale. For the first five periods, the optimal state-dependent carbon taxes are all the same because policymakers cannot distinguish between the SOW. After the true state of the world is revealed, then policymakers can set the optimal state-dependent carbon tax. The optimal non-state-dependent carbon taxes for this case are $12 per ton carbon for 1995 and $18 for 2005. When the true state of the world is revealed in 2010, policymakers then set highly differentiated carbon taxes. For the most likely SOW5 (with $p=.50$), the state-dependent tax for 2015 is $4. For SOW4 ($p=.25$), the tax is $14. For the most unfavorable SOW1 ($p=.02$), the carbon tax is an astronomical $425 per ton of carbon.

We have made four alternative assumptions about the resolution of uncertainty, where the resolutions are in 1990 (perfect information), 2000, 2010, and 2020. Table 8.3 shows some of the details of the runs. Reading across the first row, we see the state of the world number, the probability that the state of the world will occur, the first-period carbon tax for the four cases, and the first-period control rate for the cases.

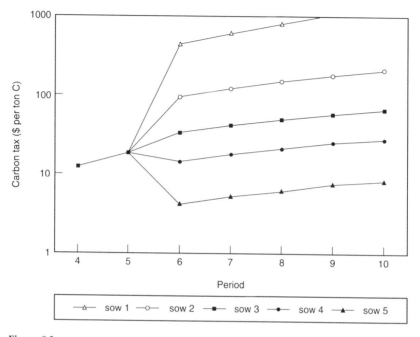

Figure 8.3
State-dependent carbon taxes
(1989 U.S. dollars per ton C in each state of world)

Note that before the uncertainties have been resolved, the control rates are equal in all states of the world.[3] In addition, figure 8.4 shows the expected value of the GHG control rate for the four assumptions about the resolution of uncertainty.

Returning to table 8.2, we can compare the results of the four alternative assumptions about the resolution of uncertainty as the last block of four rows in both halves of the table. These blocks show the implications of the need to act under conditions of uncertainty about the true state of the world. The first set of results concerns the impact of ignorance on the GHG control rate. As can be seen, the presence of uncertainty (or late resolution of uncertainties) is to increase the GHG control rate. For example, with perfect information, the expected value of the control rate is 8.8 percent; however, if policymakers must act before knowing about the extent, damages, and costs of slowing cli-

---

3. An alternative approach would be to have constrained the carbon taxes to be equalized across SOW. This approach is not feasible because carbon taxes are not primal control variables.

Table 8.3
Impact of uncertainty on greenhouse gas control rates

Data for First Period (1990–99)

		CARBON TAX Resolution Time				CONTROL RATE Resolution Time			
SOW	Prob	Perfect	Early	Middle	Late	Perfect	Early	Middle	Late
1	0.02	146.51	148.69	150.39	152.93	0.462	0.127	0.128	0.157
2	0.08	39.79	39.89	39.96	40.03	0.230	0.127	0.128	0.157
3	0.15	17.05	17.05	17.09	17.09	0.156	0.127	0.128	0.157
4	0.25	8.05	8.04	8.02	8.02	0.098	0.127	0.128	0.157
5	0.50	2.59	2.58	2.58	2.57	0.055	0.127	0.128	0.157
Average		11.9795	12.0254	12.0649	12.1204	0.1030	0.1270	0.1280	0.1570

Data for Second Period (2000–09)

		CARBON TAX Resolution Time				CONTROL RATE Resolution Time			
SOW	Prob	Perfect	Early	Middle	Late	Perfect	Early	Middle	Late
1	0.02	250.00	252.19	258.09	262.30	0.584	0.587	0.156	0.157
2	0.08	62.38	62.39	62.59	62.59	0.278	0.278	0.156	0.157
3	0.15	24.33	24.33	24.33	24.39	0.182	0.182	0.156	0.157
4	0.25	10.81	10.81	10.80	10.80	0.110	0.110	0.156	0.157
5	0.50	3.32	3.30	3.30	3.30	0.061	0.061	0.156	0.157
Average		18.0030	18.0383	18.1716	18.2647	0.1192	0.1193	0.1560	0.1570

Data for Third Period (2010–19)

		CARBON TAX Resolution Time				CONTROL RATE Resolution Time			
SOW	Prob	Perfect	Early	Middle	Late	Perfect	Early	Middle	Late
1	0.02	417.25	420.22	425.60	442.661	0.722	0.725	0.730	0.193
2	0.08	94.78	94.96	94.99	95.1939	0.329	0.329	0.329	0.193
3	0.15	33.45	33.45	33.54	33.5462	0.207	0.207	0.207	0.193
4	0.25	13.96	13.96	13.96	13.9554	0.122	0.122	0.122	0.193
5	0.50	4.10	4.07	4.07	4.06541	0.066	0.066	0.066	0.193
Average		26.4841	26.5433	26.6668	27.0222	0.1353	0.1354	0.1355	0.1930

Notes: For definitions of variables, see text. Resolution times are perfect for perfect information, early for resolution in 2000, middle for resolution in 2010, and late for resolution in 2020.

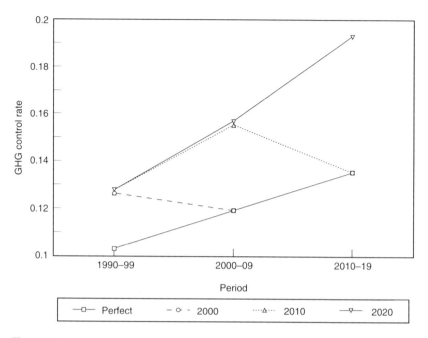

Figure 8.4
Expected value of GHG control rate
(Alternative resolution times)

mate change, this will lead to a higher average GHG control rate—12.7 percent or one-third again as high as the perfect information control rate. This result arises from the shape of the marginal cost curve, in which the sharp diminishing returns to GHG controls implies that it will be economical to undertake somewhat greater controls today if there is a likelihood that the controls may be stepped up in the future.

The other surprising result in the top half of table 8.2 is the implication of the timing of the resolution of information on future control rates. It turns out that the optimal GHG control rates for the period *after* the revelation of the true state of the world are virtually independent of the timing of the resolution of information. Examine as an example the last column of the top of table 8.2. This shows that up to the three significant digits, the control rate in 2045 is independent of whether uncertainties are resolved in 1990 or 2020. This result comes from low dependence of the stock of GHGs upon the control rates in the early periods; that is, because the expected value of the stock of GHGs is almost unaffected by the timing of the resolution of uncertainties, the expected value of the GHG control rates in the future is also

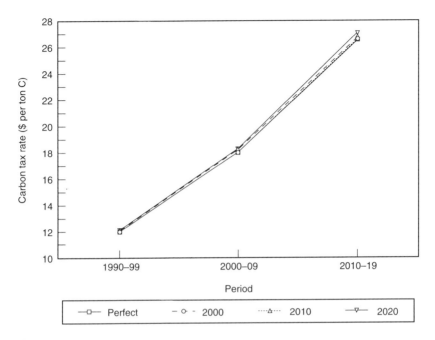

Figure 8.5
Expected value of carbon tax rates
(Alternative resolution times)

virtually independent of the timing of the resolution of uncertainty. All these results depend, of course, on the assumptions that the distribution of uncertainties has been correctly estimated and that the policies are optimally chosen.

The bottom half of table 8.2 shows the results for the carbon-tax rate. The carbon-tax rate can be interpreted as the social cost of emissions calculated at the optimal GHG control rate. The first surprise that emerges from examining the Monte Carlo runs is that the expected value of the carbon tax in the perfect-information case is much higher than in the certainty-equivalent case—$11.82 for the PI case as compared to $5.24 for the CE run or a 125 percent increase. This result arises because of the skewness in the distribution, with a small probability of very large impacts and a high probability of small losses.

The results for the timing of the resolution of the uncertainties contain a second major surprise: the carbon tax in these cases is virtually independent of the timing of the resolution of the uncertainty. This point is shown emphatically in figure 8.5, which displays the expected value of the carbon tax in the first three periods for the four assumptions about uncertainty resolution. The figure shows that the optimal carbon tax is very close to the expected value of the carbon tax in the case of perfect information. *In all cases of the resolution of uncertainty, the optimal carbon tax is within 2 percent of the expected value of the carbon tax in the case of perfect information.* The reason for the invariance of the carbon tax for different times of the resolution of the uncertainties lies in the nature of the damage function. Climate damages are a function of the *stock* of GHGs, while mitigation costs are a function of the *flow* of GHG emissions. While early resolution of uncertainty will reduce the expected value of the costs of the optimal program, it does not affect the expected value of the carbon tax.

A final point concerns the impact of the resolution of uncertainties on the expected carbon tax in the more distant future. The last column of the bottom half of table 8.2 shows that the future carbon tax is almost invariant to the timing of the resolution of uncertainty. The reason for this is parallel to the reasoning for the invariance of the control rate to uncertainty resolution.

The results of the timing of the resolution of uncertainty have an important implication for greenhouse policies. Table 8.2 shows that the optimal carbon tax is much less sensitive to the structure of information than is the optimal GHG control rate. The expected value of the optimal carbon tax is virtually invariant across the different informational assumptions, while the expected value of the optimal GHG control rate varies by a factor of almost three. This result suggests that a carbon tax may be a more efficient instrument in light of the enormous uncertainties that societies face in determining their greenhouse policies. The superiority of pricelike policies over quantity restrictions may be a general result of the structure of costs and damages that characterize the greenhouse effect.[4]

---

4. Weitzman (1974) has shown that the comparative advantage of prices over quantities as regulatory devices depends upon the relative curvature of the benefit and cost functions. If the benefit function is relatively more curved (in the sense of the size of the second derivative of the damage function being positive), then quantity-type regulations are more efficient. But if the cost function is more curved (in the sense of the second derivative of the cost function being positive), then price-type regulations are more efficient. In both cases, the functions depend upon the flow of emissions. The greenhouse effect is characterized by highly nonlinear costs with respect to the emissions controls but linearity of damages with respect to emissions. The latter relationship occurs because damages are a function of the stock of the pollutant, and the stock has virtually a linear dependence on the flow of emissions. These relationships imply that pricelike strategies are a more efficient way of coping with the uncertainties about the greenhouse effect than are quantitative restrictions. This result may extend to the treatment of uncertainty with stock pollutants more generally.

Table 7.3
Distribution of major uncertain variables (from 500 Monte Carlo runs)

	1995	2005	2015	2045	2095
Expected values					
Output	24.6	32.5	42.0	82.4	219.9
GHG emissions	9.1	11.0	13.0	20.4	39.6
GHG concentrations	765	809	862	1073	1655
Temperature increase	0.7	0.9	1.1	1.8	3.1
GHG control rate	0.046	0.060	0.075	0.110	0.153
Carbon tax	11.83	17.24	24.22	49.20	129.43
Standard deviation					
Output	2.3	4.9	9.2	38.5	219.8
GHG emissions	2.0	3.2	4.9	12.8	48.8
GHG concentrations	18.3	30.4	49.2	164.5	759.2
Temperature increase	0.11	0.16	0.22	0.44	1.05
GHG control rate	0.088	0.118	0.153	0.209	0.272
Carbon tax	30.87	48.94	74.22	176.54	594.25
Coefficient of variation					
Output	0.09	0.15	0.22	0.47	1.00
GHG emissions	0.22	0.29	0.38	0.63	1.23
GHG concentrations	0.02	0.04	0.06	0.15	0.46
Temperature increase	0.16	0.18	0.19	0.24	0.33
GHG control rate	1.89	1.97	2.03	1.91	1.77
Carbon tax	2.61	2.84	3.06	3.59	4.59
10th percentile					
Output	21.8	26.7	31.6	42.9	55.5
GHG emissions	6.7	7.4	7.8	8.4	6.4
GHG concentrations	740	768	799	889	988
Temperature increase	0.55	0.67	0.80	1.22	1.85
GHG control rate	0.010	0.010	0.010	0.010	0.010
Carbon tax	0.00	0.00	0.00	0.00	0.00
50th percentile					
Output	24.1	31.3	39.7	73.0	138.3
GHG emissions	8.9	10.5	12.1	16.9	24.1
GHG concentrations	765	809	858	1049	1425
Temperature increase	0.8	1.0	1.2	1.8	3.0
GHG control rate	0.014	0.017	0.019	0.026	0.037
Carbon tax	4.51	5.56	6.99	11.64	18.62
90th percentile					
Output	27.7	39.2	54.7	136.7	432.2
GHG emissions	11.8	15.3	19.5	36.2	82.4
GHG concentrations	789	849	929	1288	2554
Temperature increase	0.86	1.12	1.40	2.41	4.52
GHG control rate	0.116	0.159	0.211	0.338	0.525
Carbon tax	25.77	36.93	51.33	97.77	207.09

An interpretative word is in order before we present the results. The distribution of outcomes and policies is one that would occur were policymakers to learn about the structure of the economy and act today on the basis of perfect information about future conditions. These scenarios can be described as "learn, then act." In other words, the values are ones where the policies—both emissions controls as well as investment and consumption decisions—are taken conditional on learning the exact state of the world before taking any policy actions. The outcomes are "superoptimal" in the sense of taking no steps that will later be regretted; they are also clearly unrealistic in assuming that uncertainties will be resolved in the very near future. The reason for taking this superoptimizing approach is twofold. First, from this analysis we may obtain an estimate of the inherent uncertainty about the future (assuming that our findings about the underlying distributions of variables are correct). Second, later in this chapter we will use these results to aggregate states of the world so that a more realistic treatment of learning can be studied in the next chapter.

A summary of the runs is shown in table 7.3, which presents the means, standard deviations, coefficients of variation, and the 10th and 90th percentiles of the major variables for different periods through the year 2100. (The runs are actually made for a 400-year period, but they are so conjectural beyond 2100 that the results are not presented.) The uncertainty of the results grows sharply over time because of the growing uncertainty about future social and economic conditions.

Figures 7.1 through 7.5 show the distributions of the major uncertain variables. Figures 7.1 and 7.2 show the distributions of GHG emissions and concentrations (largely CO_2 in the future). Figure 7.3 shows the estimated distribution of future temperature increases. This figure indicates that the degree of uncertainty is extremely large by the end of the next century, with the 80th percentile range (between the 10th and 90th percentile) ranging from 1.8 to 4.5°C. This range is slightly lower than that provided in the IPCC estimates, although the latter was accorded no probabilistic interpretation.

Figures 7.4 and 7.5 show the estimated distributions of optimal greenhouse policies in terms of the policy variables, the carbon tax, and the GHG control rate. The median estimates from these distributions deviate from the best guess values that were presented in part I of this study—the differences reflecting the interaction of the uncertain variables. The distribution of policies is extremely skewed, with a few

The Value of Early Information

Society can invest resources to obtain better information about the future climate. Investments include those in the natural sciences (to improve monitoring, climate modeling, or to develop crops that will be adaptable to the new and changing climate), in the social sciences (to develop a better understanding of population trends, economic growth, as well as the impacts of climate change), and in other areas. How much would such investments in better information pay off if they were to reduce the uncertainty about the future?

One way to understand this issue is to estimate the value of the early resolution of uncertainties. To take a simple case, assume that if we do not step up our scientific studies, the uncertainties will be resolved in 2020, in part through the advance of normal science and in part because history will have revealed its hand. How much would the economy benefit if research allowed early information, so that the true state of the world would be known in 2010, 2000, or even in 1990?

The answer to this question in the DICE model in shown in the first column of table 8.4. Moving perfect information from 2020 to 2010 would gain over $700 billion of discounted consumption; an additional decade's gain would improve discounted consumption by almost $350 billion; and moving from 2000 to 1990 would gain $120 billion. Clearly, the incremental gains become larger as our ignorance extends further, the reason being that the damage from climate change or from our efforts to slow climate change become much greater as we progress further into the next century.

In terms of overall macroeconomic policy, we might inquire as to the impact on consumption of the uncertainties studied here. The last columns of table 8.4 show the calculated difference between the expected value of consumption in the fifth period (2000–10) for the assumption about uncertainty shown in the first column as compared to the value of consumption using late information. *The surprising result is that greater uncertainty in the sense of later resolution of uncertainty leads to higher consumption rather than lower consumption (although the extent of the change is relatively modest).* For example, perfect information lowers consumption by $11 billion in the fifth period, or about 0.03 percent of that period's consumption. This counterintuitive result—greater uncertainty leading to higher consumption—is one that has been found to hold when the elasticity of the marginal utility of consumption or

Table 8.4
Value of early arrival of information and effect on expected value of consumption (billions of 1989 dollars)

Scenario	Value of Information at Different Times[a] (billions of 1989 dollars)	Impact of Resolution on Consumption, 2005[b]	
		(billions of 1989 dollars)	(percent of 2005 consumption)
Perfect Information	1176.3	−10.7	−0.0325
2000 Information	1056.1	−9.9	−0.0300
2010 Information	719.6	0.0	0.0000
2020 Information	0.0	0.0	0.0000

Notes:
a. Discounted value of program in 1989 prices and in terms of 1990 consumption. Value of information is relative to perfect information being obtained in the year 2020.
b. This shows the difference between the expected value of consumption in the case shown as compared to the expected value with late information, that is, uncertainties resolved in 2020.

risk aversion is relatively high (i.e., with α near unity).[5] Perhaps the ultimate surprise is that the great uncertainty about greenhouse warming does not have an appreciable effect on the optimal savings rate today.

Final Words

It will be useful to summarize briefly some of the results of our analysis of the implications of uncertainty. First, it appears that, with current knowledge about the scope and consequences of global warming, uncertainty does tend to raise the stakes in future climate change. By moving from a situation where we act in light of the best-guess case to one in which we maximize the expected value of utility, the optimal policy tends to increase both the optimal carbon tax and the optimal control rate. Roughly speaking, the optimal carbon tax doubles when uncertainty is taken into account, and the optimal control rate increases by slightly less than half. The increased stringency of controls results from the interaction of different uncertain variables, whereby extreme events may cause significant economic costs.

---

5. Levhari and Srinivasan (1969) show in the simplest Ramsey model that current consumption rises, is unaffected, and falls if the elasticity of the marginal utility of consumption (α) is greater than, equal to, or less than one.

A second issue involves the impact of the timing of the resolution of uncertainties on climate-change policy. Estimates presented in table 8.4 show that early information has considerable value to society, with a resolution of uncertainties adding more than $100 billion if resolution is moved forward by a decade. This result suggests the high premium that should be placed on careful and well-designed research into the sources and consequences of climate change.

A third issue concerns two surprises that accompany these results on the timing of the uncertainties. The first is that even though early information has great value, consumption actually rises in the presence of late resolution of uncertainty. Even more surprising is the finding that the optimal carbon tax is virtually invariant to the timing of the arrival of information; this result reflects a more general conclusion about the optimality of taxes as opposed to quantitative controls for global environmental problems that reflect stock externalities.

A fourth issue that requires emphasis is the unpleasant fact of inertia in climate change. Scientific estimates suggest that the stock of greenhouse gases in the atmosphere will lead to significant climate change *even if we take stringent steps to reduce emissions.* For example, we examined above a policy that caps emissions at 80 percent of 1990 levels, producing emissions reductions of 70 percent of the baseline late in the next century, and costs that total $11 trillion in discounted consumption. Even so, global temperatures rise by 2.2°C by 2100 with this stringent set of controls as opposed to 3.1°C in the optimal policy or 3.3°C in the uncontrolled run. These calculations show how, even with major technological breakthroughs and stringent controls, the momentum of past GHG emissions appears to be leading us to an inevitable rendezvous with massive climate change. Mitigate we might; adapt we must.

After so many words and equations, how should we conclude? Depending on one's perspective, it is easy to become either optimistic or pessimistic about our ability to understand and cope with threats to our global commons. On the one hand, it is true that we are moving into uncharted waters, depleting many resources while altering others in an irreversible manner, and gambling with our universe in more ways than we know. Humans seem just as quarrelsome as they were at the dawn of recorded history, and they have devised weapons that are awesomely effective at avenging their quarrels. At the same time, our powers of observation and analysis are also orders of magnitude more powerful. The combination of monitoring, measuring, analyzing, and computing is growing even faster than our ability to emit wastes and cut trees. What will win this race between our tendency to quarrel and pollute and our power to reason and compute? Answers to these questions must await the roll of the dice called history.

Appendix:
Computer Program
for the DICE Model

This appendix contains the computer program used to generate the code for the standard DICE model runs used in this book. It is known as "ICE.1.2.3." The elaborations of the model to make sensitivity runs are either minor modifications, incorporate uncertainty via multiple states of the world, or iterated versions of the model below for the Monte Carlo runs.

The easiest way to run the DICE model is to use the GAMS software. This is available as an inexpensive student version, but to obtain the full results, the 386 or work-station version is needed. The GAMS package is available (but not inexpensive) from The Scientific Press, 507 Seaport Court, Redwood City, California 94063. Documentation is available in Brooke, Kendrick, and Meeraus (1988).

The code is made freely available to users and is not proprietary. The author would be grateful if users acknowledge the source of the code and send any publications or working papers resulting from its use to him at the Department of Economics, Yale University, New Haven, CT 06520, USA.

The following is the computer code. Note that any line beginning with an asterisk (*) is documentation.

```
*ICE.1.2.3

* This is an optimal growth model to calculate the optimal control
* rate and timing for the abatement of CO₂ and other greenhouse
* gases.
* This is the revised version of the model as of August 1993
* to use for the basic calculations and documentation.

* This version contains the data
* corrections through August 1993.
```

* It includes calibrations using Z. Yang's world output, population,
* and capital data, as well as transversality condition from 60-period
* run.

SETS
T	Time periods	/1*40/
TFIRST(T)	First period	
TLAST(T)	Last period	

SCALARS
BET	Elasticity of marginal utility	/0/
R	Rate of social time preference per year	/.03/
GL0	Growth rate of population per decade	/.223/
DLAB	Decline rate of population growth per decade	/.195/
DELTAM	Removal rate carbon per decade	/.0833/
GA0	Initial growth rate for technology per decade	/.15/
DELA	Decline rate of technology per decade	/.11/
SIG0	CO2-equiv-GWP ratio	/.519/
GSIGMA	Growth of sigma per decade	/-.1168/
DK	Depreciation rate on capital per year	/.10/
GAMA	Capital elasticity in output	/.25/
M0	CO2-equiv concentrations 1965 billion tons carbon	/677/
TL0	Lower stratum temperature (C) 1965	/.10/
T0	Atmospheric temperature (C) 1965	/.2/
ATRET	Marginal atmospheric retention rate	/.64/
Q0	1965 gross world output trillions 1989 US dollars	/8.519/
LL0	1965 world population millions	/3369/
K0	1965 value capital billions 1989 US dollars	/16.03/
C1	Coefficient for upper level	/.226/

LAM	Climate feedback factor	/1.41/
C3	Coefficient trans upper to lower stratum	/.440/
C4	Coeff of transfer for lower level	/.02/
A0	Initial level of total factor productivity	/.00963/
A1	Damage coeff for CO2 doubling (fraction GWP)	/.0133/
B1	Intercept control cost function	/.0686/
B2	Exponent of control cost function	/2.887/
PHIK	Transversality coefficient capital	/140/
PHIM	Transversality coefficient carbon ($ per ton)	/-9/
PHITE	Transversality coefficient temperature (billion $ per degree C)	/-7000/

PARAMETERS

L(T)	Level of population and labor
AL(T)	Level of total factor productivity (TFP)
SIGMA(T)	Emissions-output ratio
RR(T)	Discount factor
GA(T)	Growth rate of TFP from 0 to T
FORCOTH(T)	Exogenous forcings from other greenhouse gases
GL(T)	Growth rate of labor 0 to T
GSIG(T)	Cumulative improvement of energy efficiency
DUM(T)	Dummy variable 0 except 1 in last period;

TFIRST(T) = YES$(ORD(T) EQ 1);

TLAST(T) = YES$(ORD(T) EQ CARD(T));

DISPLAY TFIRST, TLAST;

GL(T) = (GL0/DLAB)*(1-exp(-DLAB*(ord(t)-1)));

L(T) = LL0*exp(GL(t));

GA(T) = (GA0/DELA)*(1-exp(-DELA*(ord(t)-1)));

AL(T) = a0*exp(GA(t));

GSIG(T) = (GSIGMA/DELA)*(1-exp(-DELA*(ord(t)-1)));

SIGMA(T) = SIG0*exp(GSIG(t));

DUM(T) = 1$(ord(T)eq card(T));

RR(T) = (1+R)**(10*(1-ord(t)));

FORCOTH(T) = 1.42;

FORCOTH(T)$(ord(t) lt 15) = .2604+.125*ord(T)−.0034*ord(t)**2;

VARIABLES

MIU(T)	Emission control rate GHGs
FORC(T)	Radiative forcing, W per m2
TE(T)	Temperature, atmosphere C
TL(T)	Temperature, lower ocean C
M(T)	CO2-equiv concentration billion t
E(T)	CO2-equiv emissions billion t
C(T)	Consumption trillion US dollars
K(T)	Capital stock trillion US dollars
CPC(T)	Per capita consumption thousands US dollars
PCY(t)	Per capita income thousands US dollars
I(T)	Investment trillion US dollars
S(T)	Savings rate as fraction of GWP
RI(T)	Interest rate per annum
TRANS(T)	Transversality variable last period
Y(T)	Output

UTILITY;

POSITIVE VARIABLES MIU, E, TE, M, Y, C, K, I;

EQUATIONS UTIL	Objective function
YY(T)	Output

CC(T)	Consumption
KK(T)	Capital balance
KK0(T)	Initial condition of K
KC(T)	Terminal condition of K
CPCE(t)	Per capita consumption
PCYE(T)	Per capita income equation
EE(T)	Emissions process
SEQ(T)	Savings rate equation
RIEQ(T)	Interest rate equation
FORCE(T)	Radiative forcing equation
MM(T)	CO2 distribution equation
MM0(T)	Initial condition for M
TTE(T)	Temperature-climate equation for atmosphere
TTE0(T)	Initial condition for atmospheric temp
TLE(T)	Temperature-climate equation for lower oceans
TRANSE(t)	Transversality condition
TLE0(T)	Initial condition for lower ocean;

KK(T).. K(T + 1) = L = (1-DK)**10 *K(T) + 10*I(T);

KK0(TFIRST).. K(TFIRST) = E = K0;

KC(TLAST).. R*K(TLAST) = L = I(TLAST);

EE(T).. E(T) = G = 10*SIGMA(T)*(1-MIU(T))*AL(T)*L(T)**(1-GAMA)
*K(T)**GAMA;

FORCE(T).. FORC(T) = E = 4.1*(log(M(T)/590)/log(2))
+ FORCOTH(T);

MM0(TFIRST).. M(TFIRST) = E = M0;

MM(T + 1).. M(T + 1) = E = 590 + ATRET*E(T) + (1 - DELTAM)
*(M(T)-590);

TTE0(TFIRST).. TE(TFIRST) = E = T0;

TTE(T + 1).. TE(T + 1) = E = TE(t) + C1*(FORC(t)-LAM*TE(t)
-C3*(TE(t)-TL(t)));

TLE0(TFIRST).. TL(TFIRST) = E = TL0;
TLE(T + 1).. TL(T + 1) = E = TL(T) + C4*(TE(T)-TL(T));

YY(T).. Y(T) = E = AL(T)*L(T)**(1-GAMA)*K(T)**GAMA
(1-B1(MIU(T)**B2))/(1 + (A1/9)*SQR(TE(T)));
SEQ(T).. S(T) = e = I(T)/(.001 + Y(T));
RIEQ(T).. RI(T) = E = GAMA*Y(T)/K(T)- (1-(1-DK)**10)/10;

CC(T).. C(T) = E = Y(T)-I(T);
CPCE(T).. CPC(T) = e = C(T)*1000/L(T);
PCYE(T).. PCY(T) = e = Y(T)*1000/L(T);

TRANSE(TLAST).. TRANS(TLAST) = E = RR(TLAST)
*(PHIK*K(TLAST) + PHIM*M(TLAST) + PHITE*TE(TLAST));

UTIL.. UTILITY = E =
SUM(T, 10 *RR(T)*L(T)*LOG(C(T)/L(T))/.55 + TRANS(T)*DUM(T));

*Upper and lower bounds for economic reasons or stability
MIU.up(T) = 0.99;
MIU.lo(T) = 0.01;
K.lo(T) = 1;
TE.up(t) = 20;
M.lo(T) = 600;
C.LO(T) = 2;

*Upper and lower bounds for historical constraints

MIU.fx('1')=0.;
MIU.fx('2')=0.;
MIU.fx('3')=0.;

*Solution options

option iterlim = 99900;
option reslim = 99999;

```
option solprint = off;
option limrow = 0;
option limcol = 0;
model CO2 /all/;
solve CO2 maximizing UTILITY using nlp;
display Y.l, C.l, S.l, K.l, MIU.l, E.l, M.l, TE.l, FORC.l, RI.l,
    CC.m, EE.m, KK.m, MM.m, TTE.m, CPC.l, TL.l, PCY.l, i.l;
display SIGMA, RR, L, AL, DUM, FORCOTH;
```

References

Amano, Akihiro. 1993. Economic costs of reducing CO_2 emissions: A study of modeling experience in Japan. In *Costs, impacts, and benefits of CO_2 mitigation*, CP-93-2, ed. Y. Kaya et al. Laxenburg, Austria: International Institute for Systems Analysis.

Ausubel, Jesse H. 1993. Mitigation and adaptations for climate change: Answers and questions. In *Costs, impacts, and benefits of CO_2 mitigation*, CP-93-2, ed. Y. Kaya et al. Laxenburg, Austria: International Institute for Systems Analysis.

Boden, Thomas A., Paul Kanciruk, and Michael P. Farrell, eds. 1990. *Trends '90: A compendium of data on global change.* Carbon Dioxide Information Analysis Center, ORNL/CDIAC-36. Oak Ridge, TN: Oak Ridge National Laboratory.

Bodlund, Birgit, Evan Miller, Tomas Karlsson, and Thomas B. Johansson. 1989. The Challenge of Choice: Technology Options for the Swedish Electricity Sector. In *Electricity: Efficient end-use and new generation technologies, and their planning implications,* Thomas B. Johansson, Birgit Bodlund, and Robert H. Williams. Lund, Sweden: Lund University Press.

Brainard, William C., Matthew Shapiro, and John Shoven. 1991. Fundamental value and market value. In *Money, macroeconomics, and economic politics: Essays in honor of James Tobin, ed.* William C. Brainard, William D. Nordhaus, and Harold W. Watts, 277–307. Cambridge, MA: MIT Press.

Broecker, W. S., and T. H. Peng. 1982. Tracers in the sea. In *Eldigio press.* Palisades, NY: Lamont-Doherty Geological Observatory.

Brooke, Anthony, David Kendrick, and Alexander Meeraus. 1988. *GAMS: A user's guide.* Redwood City, CA: The Scientific Press.

Cline, William. 1991. The economics of the greenhouse effect. *The Economic Journal* 101 (July): 920–37.

———. 1992a. *The economics of global warming.* Washington, DC: Institute of International Economics.

———. 1992b. Discounting. Paper presented at the International Workshop on Costs, Impacts, and Possible Benefits of CO_2 Mitigation, IIASA, Laxenburg, Austria, September.

Dansgaard, W., et al. 1993. Evidence for general instability of past climate from a 250-kyr ice-core record. *Nature,* 15 July, 218–20.

Dean, Andrew, and Peter Hoeller. 1992. Costs of reducing CO_2 emissions: Evidence from six global models, OCDE/GD(92)140. Organisation for Economic Co-operation and Development, Paris. Mimeo.

Dubin, Jeffrey A. 1992. Market barriers to conservation: Are implicit discount rates too high? In *The economics of energy conservation,* ed. Matthew G. Nagler. Proceedings of a POWER Conference, Berkeley, CA.

EC (Commission of the European Communities). 1992a. *The climate challenge: Economic aspects of the community's strategy for limiting CO_2 emissions,* 51, ECSC-EEC-EAEC, Brussels, May.

EC (Commission of the European Communities). 1992b. *The economics of limiting CO_2 emissions,* Special Edition no. 1, ECSC-EEC-EAEC, Brussels.

Edmonds, J. A., and J. M. Reilly. 1983. Global energy and CO_2 to the year 2050. *The Energy Journal* 4:21–47.

Edmonds, J. A., J. M. Reilly, R. H. Gardner, and A. Brenkert. 1986. *Uncertainty in future energy use and fossil fuel CO_2 emissions 1975 to 2075,* Department of Energy, DOE/NBB-0081, December.

EPA (U.S. Environmental Protection Agency). 1989. *The potential effects of global climate change on the United States: Report to Congress,* EPA-230-05-89-050, December.

Fankhauser, Samuel. 1993. The economic costs of global warming: Some monetary estimates. In *Costs, impacts, and benefits of CO_2 mitigation,* CP-93-2, ed. Y. Kaya et al. Laxenburg, Austria: International Institute for Systems Analysis.

Gaskins, Darius W., and John P. Weyant. 1993. EMF-12: Modeling comparisons of the costs of reducing CO_2 emissions. *American Economic Review* (May): 318–23.

Gordon, Robert, Tjalling Koopmans, William Nordhaus, and Brian Skinner. 1988. *Toward a new iron age?* Cambridge, MA: Harvard University Press.

GRIP (Greenland Ice-Core Project). 1993. Climate instability during the last interglacial period recorded in the GRIP ice core. *Nature,* 15 July, 203–8.

Grossman, Sanford J., and Robert J. Shiller. 1981. The determinants of the variability of stock market prices. *American Economic Review* 71 (May): 222–27.

Hammitt, James K., Robert J. Lempert, and Michael E. Schlesinger. 1992. A sequential-decision strategy for abating climate change. *Nature* 357, 28 May, 315–18.

Henrion, M., and B. Fischoff. 1986. Assessing uncertainty in physical constants. *American Journal of Physics,* 54, no. 9 (September): 791–98.

Hoeller, Peter, Andrew Dean, and Masahiro Hayafumi. 1992. New issues, new results: The OECD's second survey of the macroeconomic costs of reducing CO_2 emissions, OCDE/GD(92)141. Organisation for Economic Co-operation and Development, Paris. Mimeo.

Ibbotson, Roger G., and Gary P. Brinson. 1987. *Investment markets.* New York: McGraw-Hill.

IPCC (Intergovernmental Panel on Climate Change). 1990. *Climate change: The IPCC scientific assessment,* ed. J. T. Houghton, G. J. Jenkins, and J. J. Ephraums. New York: Cambridge University Press.

Jones, P. D., T. M. L. Wigley, and P. B. Wright. 1990. *Global and hemispheric annual temperature variations between 1861 and 1988,* Carbon Dioxide Information Center, NDP-022/R1. Oak Ridge, TN: Oak Ridge National Laboratory.

Jorgenson, Dale W., and Peter J. Wilcoxen. 1990. The cost of controlling U. S. carbon dioxide emissions. Paper presented at the Workshop on Economic/Energy/Environmental Modeling for Climate Policy Analysis, Washington, DC, October.

Jorgenson, Dale W., and Peter J. Wilcoxen. 1991. Reducing U.S. carbon dioxide emissions: The cost of different goals. In *Energy, Growth, and the Environment,* ed. John R. Moroney, 125–28. Greenwich, CT: JAI Press.

Kasting, James F., and James C. G. Walker. 1992. The geochemical carbon cycle and the uptake of fossil fuel CO_2. In *AIP conference proceedings 247, global warming: Physics and facts,* ed. B. G. Levi, D. Hafemeister, and R. Scribner, 175–200. New York: American Institute of Physics.

Kolstad, Charles D. 1993. Looking vs. leaping: The timing of CO_2 control in the face of uncertainty and learning. In *Costs, impacts, and benefits of CO_2 mitigation,* CP-93-2, ed. Y. Kaya et al. Laxenburg, Austria: International Institute for Systems Analysis.

Koopmans, Tjalling. 1967. Objectives, constraints, and outcomes in optimal growth models. *Econometrica* 35:1–15.

Kram, T., and P. A. Okken. 1989. Two 'low CO_2' energy scenarios for the Netherlands. Paper prepared for IEA/OECD Expert Seminar on Energy Technologies for Reducing Emissions of Greenhouse Gases, Paris, April.

Levhari, D., and T. N. Srinivasan. 1969. Optimal savings under uncertainty. *Review of Economic Studies* 36 (April): 153–63.

Lind, Robert C., ed. 1982. *Discounting for time and risk in energy policy,* 257–71. Washington, DC: Resources for the Future.

Lindzen, Richard. 1992. Global warming, *Regulation* (summer).

Luce, R. Duncan, and Howard Raiffa. 1958. *Games and decisions: Introduction and critical surveys.* New York: Wiley.

Machta, Lester. 1972. The role of the oceans and biosphere in the carbon dioxide cycle. *Nobel Symposium* 20:121–45.

Maier-Reimer, E., and K. Hasselmann. 1987. Transport and storage of carbon dioxide in the ocean, and an organic ocean-circulation carbon cycle model. *Climate Dynamics* 2:63–90.

Manabe, S., and R. J. Stouffer. 1988. Two stable equilibria of a coupled ocean-atmosphere model. *Journal of Climate* 1:841–66.

Manabe, S., and R. J. Stouffer. 1993. Century-scale effects of increased atmospheric CO_2 on the ocean-atmospheric system. *Nature* 364, 15 July, 215–18.

Manabe, S., R. J. Stouffer, M. J. Spelman, and K. Bryan. 1991. Transient response of a coupled ocean-atmospheric model to gradual changes of atmospheric CO_2, part I: Annual mean response. *Journal of Climate* 4:785–818.

Manne, Alan S., and Richard G. Richels. 1990a. CO_2 emission limits: An economic cost analysis for the USA. *The Energy Journal* 11, no. 2 (April): 51–74.

———. 1990b. Estimating the energy conservation parameter. November. Mimeo.

———. 1992. *Buying greenhouse insurance: The economic costs of CO_2 emission limits.* Cambridge, MA: MIT Press.

Mendelsohn, Robert, William Nordhaus, and Dai Gee Shaw. 1993. The impact of climate on agriculture: A Ricardian approach. In *Costs, impacts, and benefits of CO_2 mitigation,* CP-93-2, ed. Y. Kaya et al. Laxenburg, Austria: International Institute for Systems Analysis.

———, with R. Mendelsohn and Dai Gee Shaw. 1994. The impact of global warming on agriculture: A Ricardian approach. *American Economic Review* (September).

Morgan, M. G., and M. Henrion. 1990. *Uncertainty: A guide to dealing with uncertainty in quantitative risk and policy analysis.* New York: Cambridge University Press.

NAS (National Academy of Sciences). 1979. *Stratospheric ozone depletion by halocarbons: Chemistry and transport.* Report of a committee of the National Research Council, Washington, DC.

———. 1992. *Policy implications of greenhouse warming: Mitigation, adaptation, and the science base,* Committee on Science, Engineering, and Public Policy. Washington, DC: National Academy Press.

National Research Council. 1978. *International perspectives on the study of climate and society.* Washington, DC: National Academy Press.

———. 1979. *Carbon dioxide and climate: A scientific assessment.* Washington, DC: National Academy Press.

———. 1983. *Changing climate.* Washington, DC: National Academy Press.

Nordhaus, William D. 1979. *The efficient use of energy resources.* New Haven, CT: Yale University Press.

———. 1991a. A survey of the costs of reduction of greenhouse gases. *The Energy Journal* 12, no. 1:37–65.

———. 1991b. A Sketch of the economics of the greenhouse effect. *The American Economic Review* 81, no. 2 (May): 146–50.

———. 1991c. To slow or not to slow: The economics of the greenhouse effect. *The Economic Journal* 101 (July): 920–37.

———. 1991d. Economic policies and the greenhouse effect." In *Economics of climate change,* ed. Rudiger Dornbusch and James Poterba. Cambridge, MA: MIT Press.

———. 1992a. Explaining the "DICE": Background paper on a dynamic integrated model of climate change and the economy. Yale University, New Haven, CT, January. Mimeo.

———. 1992b. How much should we invest to preserving our current climate? In *Economic process and environmental concerns,* ed. Herbert Giersch, 255–99. Berlin: Springer-Verlag.

———. 1993. Economic growth on a planet under siege. In *Economic growth in the world economy,* ed. Horst Siebert, 223–42. Tübingen, Germany: J. C. Mohr.

———. 1994. Expert opinion on climatic change. *American Scientist* 82, no. 1 (January–February): 45–51.

Nordhaus, William D., and Gary Yohe. 1983. Future carbon dioxide emissions from fossil fuels. In *Changing climate,* National Research Council. Washington, DC: National Academy Press.

Nuclear Regulatory Commission. 1975. *Reactor safety study: An assessment of accident risks in U.S. commercial nuclear power plants,* NUREG-75/014 WASH-1400, Washington, DC.

Parikh, Jhodi. 1992. Emissions limitations: The view from the South. *Nature* 360 (December): 507–8.

Peck, Stephen C., and Thomas J. Teisberg. 1992. CETA: A model for carbon emissions trajectory assessment. *The Energy Journal* 13, no. 1:55–77.

Psacharopoulos, George. 1985. Returns to education: A further international update and implications. *Journal of Human Resources* 20 (fall): 583–604.

Ramsey, Frank P. 1928. A mathematical theory of saving. *The Economic Journal* (December): 543–59.

Ravelle, Roger R., and Paul E. Waggoner. 1983. Effects of a carbon dioxide–induced climatic change on water supplied in the western United States. In *Changing climate,* National Research Council, 419–32. Washington, DC: National Academy Press.

Reilly, John, and Neil Hohmann. 1993. Climate change and agriculture: The role of internation trade. *American Economic Review* 83, no. 2 (May): 306–23.

Samuelson, Paul A. 1949. The market mechanism and maximization, I, II, and III. Rand Corporation, Santa Monica, CA. Mimeo.

Savage, L. J. 1954. *The foundations of statistics.* New York: Wiley.

Schelling, Thomas C. 1983. Climatic change: Implications for welfare and policy. In *Climate change,* National Research Council, 449–82. Washington, DC: National Academy Press.

Schlesinger, Michael E., and Xingjian Jiang. 1990. Simple model representation of atmosphere-ocean GCMs and estimation of the timescale of CO_2-induced climate change." *Journal of Climate* 3:1297–1315.

Schmalensee, Richard. 1993. Comparing greenhouse gases for policy purposes. *The Energy Journal* 14, no. 1:245–55.

Schneider, Stephen H., and Starley L. Thompson. 1981. Atmospheric CO_2 and climate: Importance of the transient response. *Journal of Geophysical Research* 86, no. C4 (20 April): 3135–47.

Shlyakhter, Alexander I., Clair L. Broido, and Daniel M. Kammen. 1992. Quantifying the credibility of energy projections from trends in past data: The U.S. energy sector. Department of Physics, Harvard University, October 16. Mimeo.

Shlyakhter, Alexander I., and Daniel M. Kammen. 1992a. Quantifying the range of uncertainty in future development from trends in physical constants and predictions of global change. Global Environmental Policy Project, Working Paper 92-06, Harvard University, October 16.

Shlyakhter, Alexander I., and Daniel M. Kammen. 1992b. Sea-level rise or fall. *Nature* 357, 7 May, 25.

Siegenthaler, U., and H. Oeschger. 1987. Biospheric CO_2 emissions during the past 200 years reconstructed by deconvolution of ice core data. *Tellus* 39B:140–59.

Solow, Robert M. 1970. *Growth theory: An exposition.* New York: Oxford University Press.

Stockfisch, J. A. 1982. Measuring the social rate of return on private investment. In *Discounting for time and risk in energy policy,* ed. Robert C. Lind, 257–71. Washington, DC: Resources for the Future.

Stouffer, R. J., S. Manabe, and K. Bryan. 1989. Interhemispheric asymmetry in climate response to a gradual increase of atmospheric CO_2. *Nature* 342, 7 December, 660–62.

UNDP (United National Development Programme). 1992. *Human development report, 1992.* New York: Oxford University Press.

Wang, W.-C., M. P. Dudek, X.-Z. Liang, and J. T. Kiehl. 1991. Inadequacy of effective CO_2 as a proxy in simulating the greenhouse effect of other radiatively active gases. *Nature* 350:573–77.

Weitzman, Martin. 1974. Prices v. quantities. *Review of Economic Studies* 41:477–91.

Whalley, John, and Randall Wigle. 1991. The international incidence of carbon taxes. In *Global warming: Economic policy response,* ed. Rudiger Dornbusch and James M. Poterba, 233–63. Cambridge, MA: MIT Press.

Yang, Zili. 1993. Essays on the international aspects of resource and environmental economics. Ph.D. diss. Yale University, New Haven, CT.

Index